EXPLORING THE ROLE OF MORPHOLOGY
IN THE EVOLUTION OF SPANISH

Volume 179

Joel Rini

Exploring the Role of Morphology in the Evolution of Spanish

EXPLORING THE ROLE OF MORPHOLOGY IN THE EVOLUTION OF SPANISH

JOEL RINI
University of Virginia

JOHN BENJAMINS PUBLISHING COMPANY
AMSTERDAM/PHILADELPHIA

∞ TM The paper used in this publication meets the minimum requirements of American National Standard for Information Sciences — Permanence of Paper for Printed Library Materials, ANSI Z39.48-1984.

Library of Congress Cataloging-in-Publication Data

Rini, Joel.
   Exploring the role of morphology in the evolution of Spanish / Joel Rini.
       p.   cm. -- (Amsterdam studies in the theory and history of linguistic science. Series IV, Current issues in linguistic theory, ISSN 0304-0763 ; v. 179)
   Includes bibliographical references and indexes.
       1. Spanish language--Grammar, Historical. 2. Spanish language--Morphology. I. Title. II. Series.
PC4101.R56   1999
465--DC21   99-31510
ISBN 90 272 3685 2 (Eur.) / 1 55619 956 2 (US) (Hb; alk. paper)   CIP

John Benjamins Publishing Co. • P.O.Box 75577 • 1070 AN Amsterdam • The Netherlands
John Benjamins North America • P.O.Box 27519 • Philadelphia PA 19118-0519 • USA

To Ernst Pulgram,

Scholar, teacher, and co-founder of the program in Romance Linguistics at the University of Michigan, Ann Arbor.

Table of Contents

Acknowledgments

I would like to thank the Office of the Vice Provost for Research of the University of Virginia for a Sesquicentennial Associateship during Spring Semester 1997, during which time the core of this project was completed. I would also like to thank Professor E. F. Konrad Koerner, editor of this series, for his most professional handling of my manuscript. Finally, I would like to express my sincerest thanks to my colleagues, Javier Herrero, Donald Shaw, and the late Tibor Wlassics, as well as to my wife, Pam, and children, Chris and Marcus, all of whom gave me, throughout the entire period in which this book was produced, the kind of support and encouragement that cannot be described in words.

Preface

The purpose of this book is to explore how morphological change has been perceived as having operated in the evolution of Spanish and, with the ever-present potential for morphological influence in mind, to reexamine certain problematic developments of Spanish historical grammar. Some of the questions that will be raised here are the following: How have scholars traditionally dealt with general concepts of morphological change such as leveling and analogy? Have the less systematic types of morphological change such as backformation, blending, contamination, and morphemicization been thoroughly explored, or accurately invoked, as possible explanations to difficult problems of diachronic morphology and etymology? Have some changes in the history of Spanish been hastily attributed to processes of sound change when they were in fact the result of some morphological process? Moreover, can one find in the evolution of Spanish cases of apparent sound change that were actuated by morphological conditions? And finally, can morphological factors be found to have played a role, hitherto unbeknownst to practitioners of Spanish historical grammar, in what on the surface appear to be incontrovertibly syntactic in nature?

Our discipline has no doubt progressed greatly during the 20th century, particularly since the last revision of Menéndez Pidal's monumental *Manual de gramática histórica española* in 1941. Years of analysis and reanalysis of individual problems of Spanish historical grammar have culminated in recent years in new syntheses of the history of Spanish. I refer specifically to Lloyd's paramount *From Latin to Spanish* (1987). I might also mention here the publication of Penny's *A History of the Spanish Language* (1991), and Alvar and Pottier's *Morfología histórica del español* (1983). There is no doubt that these works, in conjunction with one another, will serve serious students and scholars of Spanish historical grammar for many years to come.

But despite their thorough treatment of the history of Spanish, a comparison of Lloyd (1987) and Penny (1991), for example, immediately reveals that many aspects of Spanish historical grammar, despite having received intense examination by the most adept scholars of our discipline, are still debatable. Taking just one verbal paradigm as an example, one notes that the infinitive *ser* 'to be' is attributed to SEDERE by Lloyd (1987: 299), but to *ESSERE by Penny (1991: 191); the origin of *eres* is still not totally clear in Lloyd's opinion (1987: 299), though Penny (1991: 162) seems confident that it continues the Latin future indicative ERIS; on the other hand, the question of the provenance of the -*y* of *soy* (and *doy, voy, estoy*) seems to be somewhat resolved as far as Lloyd (1987: 357–58) is concerned, while Penny (1991: 162) thinks not. These and many other unsolved mysteries of Spanish historical grammar remain to be explained. Scholars will no doubt continue to analyze and reanalyze the enigmatic developments of Spanish until, once again, someone provides us with a new synthesis, perhaps not until sometime well into the 21st century. It is my belief that one of the subfields of Spanish historical linguistics that is in need of further attention, despite the publication of the aforementioned works, is that of historical morphology. Hence, the present modest contribution.

This book owes its existence, to some degree, to my *Doktorgrossvater*, the late Yakov Malkiel. It was through one of Malkiel's most successful students, Steven N. Dworkin, my *Doktorvater*, that I received the "bug" to pursue the study of Spanish historical grammar. I was then lucky enough to take three courses with Ernst Pulgram before he retired in 1985, during which time my love for Romance Linguistics intensified. These two former teachers of mine were not only responsible for my academic initiation into the field of Spanish and Romance Linguistics, but also continue to influence and inspire me through their exemplary scholarship.

Some Notes About the Present Book

The present book is intended for two different audiences. On the one hand, it is intended for students and specialists of Spanish historical grammar, and on the other, for students and specialists of general historical linguistics. Writing a book for two different audiences is not an easy task, and is an enterprise that runs several risks. First, by going into great detail on a given problem for the sake of the specialist of Spanish historical grammar, I run the risk of losing the interest of the specialist of general historical linguistics. Second, by glossing basic vocabulary items for the sake of the specialist of general historical linguistics whose knowledge of Spanish may be minimal, I run the risk of insulting my colleagues of Spanish historical grammar. Third, by glossing these basic Spanish vocabulary items, I may insult the specialist of general historical linguistics whose knowledge of Spanish is quite good. Fourth, by setting out to resolve some long-standing issues of Spanish historical grammar whose solutions may be discovered only by adducing an abundance of new textual evidence, I may be accused of being "too philological" and "not theoretical enough" by my colleagues in general historical linguistics. That my fear of such an accusation is not irrational is supported by the title of a conference paper on some aspect of pragmatics that I once saw in a program for a conference on general historical linguistics: "First she called me a *philologist*, then I insulted *her*." Fifth, by attempting to solve some problems through "thought experiments" based on general historical linguistic theory when there is insufficient textual evidence, I may be accused of being "philologically irresponsible" by my colleagues in Spanish historical grammar who feel that somehow I could have looked further to get the hard evidence. Despite these risks, I offer this book to both audiences in the hope that each will glean something of value from it. And although this may seem an idealistic thought, perhaps each camp may find something beneficial in the methods and procedures of the other.

What has allowed me to make some advancement in the problems of

Spanish historical grammar that follow in this book is the recent publication of two CD-ROM programs that offer an immense corpus of data for Old Spanish which may not be totally familiar to all readers (whether their specialty is Spanish historical grammar or general historical linguistics). These two programs are: (1) ADMYTE (= *Archivo digital de manuscritos y textos españoles*); and (2) *The Electronic Texts and Concordances of the Prose Works of Alfonso X, el Sabio* (Kasten et al. 1997). ADMYTE consists of two volumes, 0 and 1. ADMYTE vol. 0 contains the following manuscripts and texts (the titles of which are reproduced exactly as given in the CD-ROM: *Cancionero Castellano Catalán de París*, *Poema de Mío Cid*, *Santa María Egipciaca*, *Fueros de Castilla*, *Tratado de Cetrería*, *Libro de los Halcones*, *Libro de Apolonio*, *Fueros de Aragón*, *Biblia latina*, *Poridat de la* [sic] *Poridades*, *Poema de Fernán Gonzalez* [sic], *Tres Reyes de Oriente*, *Libro de los Animales de Caza*, *Fuero Juzgo*, *Castigos y Documentos para bien vivir* (parts I, II, and III), *Libro del Consejo de los Consejeros*, *Gran comquista del Ultramar*, *Sumas de la Historia Troyana*, *Crónica de Alfonso X*, *Leyes de Estilo* (parts I and II), *Crónica de Veinte Reyes*, *Fuero General de Navarra*, *Libro de la Montería*, *Crónica Troyana*, *Proverbios Morales*, *Viaje de Juan de Mandavilla*, *Historia Troyana*, *Libro de la Caza de las Aves*, *Cuento de Tristán de Leonis*, *Libro de Marco Polo*, *Libro del Tesoro*, *Anales de los Reyes de Castilla*, *Cancionero Castellano Misceláneo*, *Suma de las Crónicas de España*, *Cirugía Rimada*, *Menor Daño de Medicina*, *De la Rethórica*, *De los Oficios*, *Cancionero de Baena*, *Cancionero Castellano de París*, *Libro de las Doñas*, *Invencionario*, *Espejo de Medicina*, *Cancionero de Salvá*, *Tratado de la Música*, *Cancionero de París*, *Arte Cisoria*, *Esopete Historiado* (parts I and II), *Breve Confesionario*, *Lux Bella*, *Imitatio Christi*, *Tratado de Amores de Arnalte y Lucenda*, *Meditaciones Vitae Christi*, *De las Mujeres Ilustres en Romance*, *Glosa sobre Lux bella*, *Morales de Ovidio*, *Pierres y Magalona*, *Strategemata*, *Historia de las Amazonas*.

ADMYTE vol. 1 contains: *Introductiones latinae*, *Crónica de España*, *Ordenanzas reales*, *Visión delectable*, *Cuadernos de las leyes nuevas de la hermandad*, *Escritura de cómo y por qué razón no se debe dividir, partir, ni enajenar los reinos y señoríos de España*, *Compilación de las batallas campales*, *Letra sobre los matrimonios y casamientos entre los reyes de Castilla y de León de España con los reyes y casa de Francia hechos*, *Doctrina de los caballeros*, *Valerio de las historias eclesiásticas y de España*, *Universal Vocabulario en latín y romance*, *Siete Partidas*, *Nobiliario vero*, *Gramática castellana*, *Dictionarium latino-hispanicum*, *Ordenanzas de la ciudad de Sevilla*, *Ordenanzas sobre los escribanos de la ciudad de Sevilla, Fasciculus medicinae.Compendio de la salud humana, Tratado de la fisonomía en breve suma contenida, De propietatibus rerum.Propiedades de las cosas, De epidemia et peste.Tratado de la peste, Ordenanzas sobre los abogados, Lilium medicinae.Lilio de medicina, Prognostica.Las pronósticas, Tratado de los niños con el regimiento del alma, De ingeniis curandorum morborum.Tratado de las tablas de los diez ingenios de curar enfermedades agudas, Bocados de oro, De regimine acutorum morborum.Regimiento de las agudas, Dictionarium Hispano-Latinum, Sumario de la medicina, Cura de la piedra y dolor de la ijada y cólica renal, Tratado de Roma, Peregrinatio in Terram Sanctam.Viaje siquier peregrinación de la tierra sancta, Llibre del arte de menescalia.Libro de albeitería, Vocabulario eclesiástico, Leyes hechas por la brevedad y orden de los pleitos* (parts I and II), *Crónica de Aragón, Ordenanzas sobre los paños, Capítulos de gobernadores, asistentes y corregidores, Claros varones de Castilla, Letras, Regimiento contra la peste, Bías contra Fortuna, Crónica popular del Cid, Tabla de la diversidad de los días y horas, Ceremonial de principes, Tratado de las armas.Tratado de los rieptos y desafíos, Libro de Marco Polo, Egloga de Plácida y Victoriano, Nunc dimittis, Es amor en quien se esfuerza, Egloga de Fileno, Zambardo y Cardonio, Libro de las maravillas del mundo y del viaje de la Tierra Santa, Testamento de amores, Todos servid al amor, A su amiga porque se le escondía en viéndola, Villancico nuevo sobre el perdón de Santa María Magdalena, Coplas hechas sobre el casamiento de la hija del Rey de España, Coplas del memento homo, Coplas hechas sobre la Pasión.*

The CD-ROM program of the Alfonsine corpus includes the following texts: *Canones de Albateni, Libros de ajedrez, dados y tablas, Libros del saber de astronomia, Libro de las cruzes, Estoria de España* (parts I and II), *General estoria* (parts I, II, IV, V, and VI), *Judizios de las estrellas, Lapidario de Alfonso X, Libro de las leyes, Moamyn — Libro de las animalias, Picatrix de Alfonso X, Libro del cuadrante señero, Libro de las formas y de las imagenes, Tablas de Zarquiel.*Although these two CD-ROM programs have proven to be indispensable, I have not used these two sources exclusively. I have supplemented ADMYTE and the Alfonsine corpus with various microfiches and printed editions of other sources of Old Spanish whenever I deemed it necessary. I believe that the use of ADMYTE and the Alfonsine corpus (together with supporting materials), either to refute or to support a given theory of historical development, is one of the strengths of this book. As in any investigation, the evidence is open to interpretation. Whether or not the reader agrees with my interpretations is less important than having set the data before him.

Finally, I would like to make perfectly clear which topics of this book have been previously published (albeit in a less developed form), and which have not, so that I am not wrongly accused in any future review of this book of having put together a collection of what we call in the Hispanic tradition "refritos". My desire to spell out this information here is due to an unfortunate experience with my first book (Rini 1992). One reviewer of that book mentioned twice in a one-page review that "all three chapters" had been previously published (see Penny 1994). Although Chapters 2 and 3 were indeed revised and expanded versions of work that had been previously published, to this day I have no idea where Chapter 1 of that book had appeared in print! Those sections of chapters of the present book which constitute reworkings of previously published material are: (a) The section entitled "The /ée/ > /éi/: Sound Change or Backformation?" of Chapter 3, which appeared as Rini (1998a); and (b) The section entitled "The -y of Spanish *hay*" of Chapter 5, which appeared as Rini (1998b). I also remind the reader of these facts with a footnote at each of these two points in the book. I have incorporated these topics into the present book because they demonstrate very well some of the important points that I wish to make about the role of morphology in the evolution of Spanish. All other topics are discussed here in this book for the first time.

Joel Rini, February 1999

CHAPTER 1

Concepts of Morphological Change

Past and Present

20th-Century Perceptions of Morphological Change in the Evolution of Spanish

One of Menéndez Pidal's legacies to modern Spanish philologists was a pretty good, though certainly not perfect, understanding of morphological change in the evolution of Spanish. In the last revised edition of his *Manual de gramática histórica española* (1941), Menéndez Pidal not only discussed the general concept of analogical change, but also made, at times, sophisticated distinctions between different, though related, diachronic morphological processes. One example of such a distinction can be found in his discussion of the "Influencia de una palabra sobre otra" (1941: 185–88), where he makes the important distinction between the notions of *contamination* and *blending*. With regard to the former, he explains that, despite the arbitrary symbolic character of language:

> hay muchos casos en que el hablante no se limita a usar de la palabra como de signo indiferente fijado y animado por la tradición, sino que la *contamina* con alguna otra representación psíquica concurrente, que viene a alterar la articulación de la palabra [emphasis added]" (1941: 186).

According to Menéndez Pidal, this type of morphological change may result when two words of similar or related meaning occur frequently in a series or together in discourse. With regard to the notion of blending, he writes (1941: 187):

> Hay también *cruce de dos voces* aunque no pertenezcan a una serie. Dos palabras de significado muy parecido o igual y de sonido semejante, funden o cruzan sus sonidos, pues al tratar de expresar la idea pueden acudir juntamente al pensamiento ambas voces, y como se distinguen poco por el sonido, el

> hablante puede confundirlas en la enunciación, mezclando sonidos de ambas
> bajo un mismo acento, o sea haciendo de las dos una misma palabra.

For Menéndez Pidal, then, the processes of contamination and blending differ from one another as regard the conduit that leads the two words to their morphological interaction. In contamination the connection is syntactic, while in blending, it is phonetic. However, Menéndez Pidal recognized that both processes presuppose a semantic relatedness between the words involved in the morphological change.

Menéndez Pidal also identified the semantic relatedness of forms within the same verbal paradigm as the link through which such forms could influence each other's shape: "las múltiples formas que reviste un mismo tema en la conjugación, *estando unidas estrechamente entre sí por la unidad esencial de significado*, no pueden dejar de influir unas sobre otras más a menudo que dos palabras extrañas en su origen" (1941: 269). It is precisely this semantic connection, i.e., the basic meaning of the verb contained in the lexical morpheme (or in some cases, in the lexical allomorphs), shared by all inflected forms of a verbal paradigm, that led Menéndez Pidal to the logical conclusion that "la fuerza de la analogía es mucho más activa en la conjugación que en nunguna otra parte del dominio gramatical" (1941: 269). Menéndez Pidal has described here what is now commonly called *leveling* or *paradigmatic leveling* (or more specifically, *intraparadigmatic* leveling, to be discussed in more detail below). Thus it appears that Menéndez Pidal made no theoretical distinction between contamination and blending on the one hand, and leveling on the other. This view can still be found among historical linguists. Compare the following statement, which likens contamination to paradigmatic leveling:

> One special class of changes appears to be related to leveling in a certain
> sense, but its domain is neither the morphological nor grammatical paradigm.
> It often happens that the phonetic shape of a word or morpheme is changed in
> such a way that it becomes more like some other word or morpheme in a
> situation where both words and morphemes belong to a class defined by some
> close semantic relationship. We might consider this type of change a form of
> leveling within a semantic paradigm. The traditional term for such changes is
> *contamination*. (Jeffers 1982: 57).

In addition to contamination and blending, Menéndez Pidal discussed morphological change in terms of general "analogical influence", stating that:

> la **influencia analógica** tiene su principal campo de acción en la morfología, pues actúa principalmente para asimilar categorías de palabras que desempeñan igual función gramatical, por ejemplo, *igualando* la terminación de los singulares, de los femeninos o las diversas formas del verbo [bold original, italics added] (1941: 204).

His use of the term "igualando", however, might best translate as "leveling" (i.e., putting on equal or level ground, making equal or level). The singular suffix to which Menéndez Pidal refers involves the originally singular OSp. *pechos*, *tiempos*, *peños*, *cuerpos* (< Lat. sing. nom. & ac. PECTUS, TEMPUS, PIGNUS, CORPUS). As Menéndez Pidal correctly states regarding these Old Spanish singulars: "Pero naturalmente, esta -*s* no podía sonar sino a plural, y hubo de formarse un singular antietimológico: *empeño*, *pecho*, *tiempo*, *cuerpo*..." (1941: 215). In effect, Menéndez Pidal identified and described an example of the backformation process (also to be discussed in more detail below). His examples of "leveling" of the feminine suffix include Lat. fem. SOCRUS 'mother-in-law', NURUS 'daughter-in-law' > Old and ModSp. *suegra*, *nuera*, a change which might be better described in modern terms as a case of analogical change (also to be discussed in more detail below). Thus, despite his accurate application of the term *leveling* in the case of the verb, the use of the same term, together with the term "influencia analógica", to describe the other processes referred to in this passage (i.e., backformation and analogical change) reveals, perhaps, a less-refined understanding at this point in our tradition of the various diachronic morphological processes. However, in this same statement we see that Menéndez Pidal has added another dimension to our understanding of morphological change. Not only can semantic similarity (combined with syntactic or phonetic phenomena) serve as the basis for morphological change, but so too can the same grammatical function of different forms, which may otherwise be semantically unrelated and/or phonetically dissimilar.

García de Diego took up the discussion of morphological change in his *Gramática histórica española* (1951). He believed that the role of analogy was of paramount importance to the understanding of the evolution of any language, and that the study of analogical change should make up an even greater part of the historical analysis of a given language than should the study of phonetic change:

> El estudio de la analogía en cada lengua debiera ser más extenso que el de la fonética, porque es más complicado; y es tan importante como aquél, porque una parte considerable del idioma es producto de la analogía. Sobre todo la

masa ingente de la flexión verbal está afectada por ella, al punto de que no se halla un solo verbo fonético y etimológicamente regular (1951:134).

He then divided his discussion into three sections: "Analogía fonética" (1951: 135–41), "Analogía morfológica" (1951: 142–53); and "Analogía sintáctica" (1951: 154–55). He defined "analogía fonética" as an "error de equivalencia acústica" or "equivalencia acústica errónea" and gave examples such as the following: (1) The substitution of the Old Spanish diphthongs /oi/, /ui/, and /uo/ by the more frequent /we/ (e.g., Early OSp. *moira, cuida, cuomo* > OSp. *muera, cueda, cuemo*); (2) The monophthongization of initial atonic /je/ > /e/ (where /j/ continues Lat. /g/), e.g., OSp. *yelar, ienero, iermano* > *helar, enero, (h)ermano*, due to the association with the alternation between tonic /jé/ ~ atonic /e/ (as in *tierra* ~ *terreno*); (3) Confusion of consonants such as /b/ and /g/ (e.g., *juega, aguja* > non-standard *jueva, abuja*), /b/ and /m/ (e.g., *boñiga, albondiga* > non-standard *moñiga, almóndiga*), /n/, /l/ and /r/ (e.g., Lat. ANIMA > *anma > alma*, Lat. SANGUINE > *sangne > sangre*), /l/ and /r/ (e.g., *palma, alma, mujer, pastor* > non-standard *parma, arma, mujel, pastol*). While there may be some justification in invoking the term "phonetic analogy" in some of these cases — in particular, in cases (1) and (2) above — most of García de Diego's examples in the remainder of this section can be explained in purely phonetic terms such as assimilation (e.g., *albóndiga* > *almóndiga*), dissimilation (e.g., *anma > alma*, *sangne > sangre*), etc. Therefore, I do not feel that García de Diego made any real advance in our understanding of analogy by presenting us with what he called "analogía fonética".

Conversely, in his section on "analogía morfológica", in the first subcategory, called "analogía formal", García de Diego's first statement adds to what had been previously thought: "La sola semejanza formal de dos voces sin afinidad de significado basta frecuentemente para la confusión" (1951: 142). And although some of his examples are questionable, let suffice his example of *betónica* 'medicinal plant', falsely associated with and consequently contaminated by *bretón* 'Breton' to yield *bretónica*. Thus in addition to semantic similarity or similarity of grammatical function as previously outlined by Menéndez Pidal, we can add formal or structural resemblance (without a semantic or functional connection) to the list of ways in which two forms may be attracted to one another for morphological interaction.

The other subcategories of his section on "Analogía morfológica" include "Hiperurbanismo" (i.e., hypercorrection), "Analogía de prefijos", "Analogía de sufijos", "Analogía sinonímica", "Analogía antonímica", "Analogía entre verbos", "Analogía entre voces del mismo tema", "Analogía autonímica" (i.e., intra-paradigmatic leveling), and "Analogía de las series". The only categories here that further the discussion initiated by Menéndez Pidal are "Hiperurbanismo", and the distinction made between "Analogía sinonímica", "Analogía antonímica", "Analogía entre voces del mismo tema", all three of which had been seen as one and the same by Menéndez Pidal in his discussion of contamination of words which frequently appear in a series or together in discourse (1941: 186–87). While these appear to be useful distinctions — "Analogía antonímica", it should be noted, was also recognized by Yakov Malkiel in the same year (1951), though termed "lexical polarization" — his description of hypercorrection leaves little to be desired: "Se produce como reacción del hablante culto. En los procesos de evolución fonética del vulgo los eruditos pueden sentir la forma etimológica y hacer una falsa corrección por confusión con casos fonéticos semejantes." To his credit, "Analogía autonímica" included examples of leveling, not only in verbal paradigms, but in pronominal and nominal paradigms as well. Finally, his section on "Analogía sintáctica" offers some good examples of syntactic blends, but is irrelevant to our discussion of morphological change in the evolution of Spanish.

In 1983 Alvar and Pottier published their *Morfología histórica del español*, but despite the fairly recent vintage of this 533-page volume dedicated solely to the historical morphology of Spanish, one finds very little that is new in the way of the perception of morphological change. They discuss *morfología indepen-diente* (i.e., those lexical items whose form is the result of regular phonetic development) and *morfología dependiente* (i.e., those lexical items whose form is the result of some influence beyond the realm of diachronic phonetics and phonology). In their discussion of *morfología dependiente* (1983: 20–22, 25–29), Alvar and Pottier identify the "íntima conexión dentro de una serie" and the "idéntico significado de la raíz" (1983: 20–21) as causes of morphological change and thus provide examples of serial contamination and leveling (of both segmen-tal and prosodic features). Although their examples are good and interesting, their terminology is less precise than one might expect from a volume whose jacket boasts "la precisión en las definiciones". For example, both the evolution of the days of the week and the contamination of *nuera* by *suegra* are considered to be examples of serial contamination when the latter is not really a series; the evolution of Lat. POTUIT, TENUIT, HABUIT, TRAXIT to *pudo, tuvo, hubo, trujo* is included in the discussion of leveling (which will be shown in Chapter 2 to be incorrect); and their use of the term *analogía* is quite unrestricted, as it is applied to the change of Lat. NURUS > *NURA, the contamination of this form by *SOCRA (yielding *nuera*), the contamination of Lat. CINQUE by QUATTUOR yielding *cinco*, etc. In effect, throughout the book, no real attempt to distinguish between contamination, leveling, and analogy is ever made.

The best and most up-to-date discussion of the various types of morphological change appears, without question, in Paul Lloyd's *From Latin to Spanish* (1987). Lloyd brought into the tradition of Spanish historical grammar real advancements through his vast reading and incorporation of material from general historical linguistics. For example, he was the first of our tradition, to the best of my knowledge, to present the concept of "analogy" in the form of a proportion, giving the following example from the history of Spanish (1987: 58):

$$\frac{aver}{ove} \quad : \quad \frac{tener}{X \text{ (where } X = tove)}$$

Before Lloyd, as was seen above, analogy had only been discussed as regards the history of Spanish in terms of contamination, blending, leveling, and hypercorrection. Lloyd's presentation of analogy underscores the importance of the functional relationship of elements involved in morphological change. Lloyd (1987: 60) points out, for example, that by analogy with *drive : drove* (as well as *thrive : throve, strive : strove, ride : rode, write : wrote*) many speakers have produced *dive : X = dove* (which exists alongside regular *dived*) because of the functional relationship of non-past : past. No such relationship exists between, for example, *ear : hear*, so speakers are not likely to create *eye : X = *heye*. Hock (1991: 172) has similarly stated that such analogical creation will simply not occur on the basis of phonetic similarity alone, as he demonstrates with his example of *ring : rang :: king : *kang*). Lloyd (1987: 60) adds that frequency of occurrence of a given pattern, however small in number the members of that set may be, is also a factor which must be taken into account in analogical change: "In the case of *dive*, for example, the creation of *dove* may not be due to the large number of verbs meeting the structural requirements of the proportion but to the frequency of usage of the verbs showing the /ay/ : /ow/ relation. Thus frequency of occurrence of one pattern may serve to offset to some extent the larger number of items in another pattern." Other important points that Lloyd (1987: 58–60) makes regarding analogy are: (a) Several patterns may serve as a model for the analogical formation of a word, and there is no way of predicting which pattern will exert the strongest influence on any particular speaker or group of speakers; (b) Speakers may actually be conscious of the model they are following; (c) Many analogical changes of the proportional type are probably made by speakers all the time but are not adopted by the speech community at large and thus go unnoticed; and (d) There is a great degree of indeterminacy in analogical formations as regards both the models that speakers are likely to follow, as well as the strength of a particular model.

Lloyd was also the first in the Hispanic tradition to discuss the process of reanalysis (albeit briefly) as a preliminary step in analogical change: "Purely chance resemblance of words may provoke reanalysis" (1987: 63). He gave as his example the case of OSp. *ascuchar* 'to listen' (< Lat. AUSCULTARE) and *asconder* 'to hide' (< Lat. ABSCONDERE), whose common first element *as-* led these two otherwise dissimilar lexical items down the same developmental path: since a great number of words contained word-initial *es-* before /k/ (e.g., *escuela* 'school', *escala* 'ladder', *escaño* 'bench', *escoba* 'broom', *escribir* 'to write', etc.), OSp. *ascuchar* and *asconder* were brought into line with these by restructuring to ModSp. *escuchar* and *esconder*.[1]

Lloyd's treatment of morphological change also includes phenomena already found in earlier discussions, such as leveling, contamination, etc. However, he did make some modifications. For example, in his discussion of leveling, he introduced the idea of what has since been called *extra-paradigmatic leveling* (1987: 62), though he did not use this or any other term to describe it. He simply exemplified this phenomenon with the paradigm of Lat. PĒNSARE, whose long stem vowel should have led to non-diphthongized forms such as **penso*, **pensas*, etc. (< Lat. PĒNSO, PĒNSAS, etc.). The large number of Latin verbs with short stem vowel /e/, however, provided the model upon which Sp. *pienso*, *piensas*, etc. was based. Thus, verbs like SENTIRE 'to feel', whose forms with tonic open /ẹ/ evolved through regular phonetic evolution to lexical morphemes with /jé/, e.g., *siento*, *sientes*, etc., in effect leveled *extra-paradigmatically* the forms **penso*, **pensas*, etc. to *pienso*, *piensas*, etc.

Lloyd (1987: 63–66) then classified the "different sorts of analogies" as follows:

(1)   A word with a similar meaning or belonging to the same category as another word may adopt a phonetic feature from that word.

---

1. Menéndez Pidal (1941: 68) had suggested that confusion from the prefix *es-* (< Lat. EX-) probably influenced these two words, in which case we would identify the change of OSp. *ascuchar* and *asconder* > ModSp. *escuchar* and *esconder* as a case of pure *reanalysis*, rather than reanalysis followed by analogical change.

(2)   A word with the opposite meaning of another word may adopt a phonetic feature from that word, especially if both have partial formal similarity.

(3)   A word with the same function but different phonetic form of another word may become more similar in form to that word.

(4)   Morphemes with the same form but different functions may lose one function.

In class (1), Lloyd is clearly referring to the phenomenon of contamination, though he does not use this or any other term. He gives examples of contamination of words occurring in a series (e.g., days of the week) and of words belonging to the same semantic category (e.g., *suegra* 'mother-in-law' and *nuera* 'daughter-in-law'). Also included here is the process of paradigmatic leveling. Lloyd's class (2) is clearly the phenomenon of "lexical polarization". In class (3) he offers an example of proportional analogy (e.g., *tener : tove :: seer : X = sove*), while in class (4) one finds an example of reanalysis (e.g., Lat. plural FOLIA 'leaves' > *hoja* 'leaf'), as well as an example of reanalysis followed by backformation (e.g., Lat. sing. TEMPUS > OSp. *el tiempos*, reanalyzed as plural *(los) tiempos*, resulting in backformed *el tiempo*).

Lloyd concludes his discussion with examples of *popular* or *folk etymology* (1987: 66). As stated above, Lloyd's treatment of morphological change and analogy is by far the best and most complete. One notes, however, the lack of any discussion of *blending*.

In a slightly more recent historical grammar of Spanish, *A History of the Spanish Language* (1991), Penny devotes a brief section to a discussion of morphological change (1991: 99–101). But despite the more recent vintage of this historical grammar, Penny's contribution to our understanding of morphological change is minimal. His discussion centers around the interaction of "phonological change" and "analogical adjustment" (i.e., leveling). Penny (1991: 100–101):

> Morphological change, then, may be viewed as (in part) the result of competitive struggle between phonological change (which normally operates without regard to the meaning or function of the words it affects and leads to disruption of paradigms) and analogical adjustment (which maintains or restores phonological similarity between forms which have a related function).

Though not inaccurate, Penny's view of morphological change is limited to the paradigm. Moreover, his definition of analogy is over-simplified and outright dismisses other factors (1991: 100): "Analogy is the process whereby forms which are related in grammatical function come to have a similar form. (Analogy also operates in the case of semantically related words, but this type of analogy does not concern us here.)." Penny thus excludes concepts such as contamination, blending, and moreover, the important concept that Lloyd had finally introduced to Hispanists, namely, analogy (i.e., in the proportional sense). Penny does describe folk or popular etymology, however, in his chapter on semantic change (1991: 265). The only real contribution Penny makes toward a general model of morphological change based on examples from the history of Spanish is his distinction between "intra-paradigmatic analogy" and "extra-paradigmatic analogy" (1991: 160, 181). The former refers to leveling within a given paradigm, while the latter refers to leveling between paradigms (as exemplified, though not so termed, by Lloyd 1987: 62).

A Not-too-untraditional Model of Morphological Change

One observation that can be made regarding all of the foregoing treatments of morphological change is the loose definition and use of the term "analogy". It has been used in reference to every kind of morphological change — from contamination and blending, to proportional analogy, to popular etymology, to paradigmatic leveling (witness Penny's use of "paradigmatic analogy" 1991: 160, 181), etc., etc. In fact, this very non-restricted use of the term "analogy" has resulted in an almost interchangeable use of the terms "morphological change" and "analogy". For example, Lloyd's section on morphological change is entitled "Morphological Change: Analogy" (1987: 55). This is not only the case among Hispanists, however, as one finds similar equating of these terms in excellent manuals of general historical linguistics, such as Hock's truly superb *Principals of Historical Linguistics*, in which his chapters on morphological change are entitled "Analogy: General Discussion and Typology", "Analogy: Tendencies of Analogical Change", and "Analogy and Generative Grammar" (1991: 167–279). Although there is no doubt that there is a connection between morphological change and analogy, they are not one and the same thing. That is, while analogy is indeed a type of morphological change, not all morphological changes are necessarily examples of analogy. The equating of these terms (and the phenomena to which these terms are attached) holds two dangerous consequences for future research in historical morphology: (1) Our understanding of, and distinction between the various types of morphological changes that have already been identified may become blurred; and (2) Our view as to what kinds of diachronic processes may be considered morphological changes becomes limited, and even closed. I would therefore like to present, at this point, a slightly revised view of morphological change as I currently understand it, and as it will be presented in the studies that follow in this book. By no means do I wish to imply, however, that what follows is the only way to conceptualize morphological change. Nor is the following conceptualization intended to be a "new theory" of morphological change.

Morphological Change

I shall use this term to refer to any change in the phonetic structure of any part of a word (where "word" = either a lexical morpheme + one or more derivational morphemes, e.g., lexical morpheme *chic-* [young] + -*a* [female] + -*s* [plural] → *chicas* 'girls', or an invariable lexeme, e.g., *me* 'me, to me') that cannot be accounted for in purely diachronic phonetic terms such as assimilation, dissimilation, sonorization, syncope, etc. In **morphological change**, words that are semantically, syntactically, or already structurally (i.e., morphologically) similar become more similar to each other in form. Unlike sound change, which, with certain qualifications, can be described as fairly "regular" (though some sound changes are clearly "more regular" than others), morphological change, by comparison, may be considered quite irregular or sporadic. Nevertheless, as in the case of sound change, some types of morphological change have been traditionally considered more regular or more systematic than others (e.g., proportional analogy and leveling).[2] Those types of morphological change that have had the greatest impact on the evolution of Spanish are listed and defined below.[3]

---

2. Hock (1991: 167): "[T]wo processes, **leveling** and **four-part analogy**, tend to be considerably more regular or systematic than most of the other [morphological] changes." Anttila (1989: 104): "In the survey of the various types of analogical changes, two ways of classifying them were occasionally referred to: leveling and extension [= proportional, or four-part analogy]."

3. Other types of morphological change that will not be defined in this section or explored in this book (most of which may be considered "minor" or less systematic and less frequent types of morphological change), regardless of whether or not they have been found to occur in the evolution of Spanish, include **hypercorrection**, **ellipsis**, **recutting**, and **clipping**. For these types of morphological change I refer the reader to Hock (1991: 189–206).

Analogy and Analogical Change

The first definition of *analogy* in *Webster's New World Dictionary of the American Language* (1956: 53) is "similarity in some respects between things otherwise unlike; partial resemblance." Another is "the inference that certain admitted resemblances imply probable further similarity" (Webster's 1956: 53). It is understandable how taking definitions of *analogy* like these two, applying them to the study of linguistics, and adding to them a diachronic perspective could produce a definition of analogical change such as "the process by which words that are similar in some way (though dissimilar in other respects) become more similar to one another." And it is further understandable how such a definition and understanding of analogy and analogical change could apply to morphological processes like contamination, paradigmatic leveling, folk etymology, etc. This is no doubt what has happened to the term *analogy* in historical linguistics. Emphasis has been put on the notions of a starting point of "resemblance, similarity" and a product of "further resemblance, similarity", and thus the terms *analogy* and *analogical change* have long been used by many historical linguists to describe a broad range of morphological changes that lead to closer resemblance between forms, or more regularity between forms and in paradigms. In *A Dictionary of Linguistics and Phonetics*, Crystal (1985: 16) defines the word *analogy* as follows:

> A term used in historical and comparative linguistics, and language acquisition, referring to a process of regularisation which affects the exceptional forms in the grammar of a language. The influence of the regular pattern of plural formation in English, for example, can be heard in the treatment of irregular forms in the early utterances of children, e.g. *mens, mans, mouses*: the children are producing these forms 'on analogy with' the regular pattern. Dialects also often illustrate analogical processes at work, which the standard language has so far resisted, e.g. *goed/seed/knowed* for *went/saw/knew*, etc., and this process is, of course, common in the errors of foreign learners of the language. Processes of 'analogical creation' are one of the main tendencies in the history of languages, as when verbs which had an irregular past tense form in Old English came to be produced with the regular *-ed* ending, e.g. *help* becoming *helped*.

But while regularization is a result of the analogical process, the term 'regularization' does not really describe the process of analogy. However, Crystal should not be faulted here, for he is simply reporting how the term *analogy* has come to be used in linguistics (though his example of *mens* would be better described as a *blend* between etymological *men* and analogical *mans*). Webster's (1956: 53) defines *analogy*, as it pertains to linguistics, as follows: "the process by which new or less familiar words, constructions, or pronunciations conform with the pattern of older or more familiar (and often unrelated) ones: as, *energize* is formed from *energy* by analogy with *apologize* from *apology*." And more recently, one finds the following definition of *analogy*: "correspondence between the members of pairs or sets of linguistic forms that serves as a basis for the creation of another form" Webster's (1984: 82). The key words here, which seem to have been forgotten by some, are "pairs or sets ... that serve as a basis." A definition like this one brings us back to the original meaning of *analogy* as found in Greek *analogia*, meaning 'proportion' < *analogos* 'in due ratio'; *ana-* 'according to' + *logos*, 'ratio' (Webster's 1984: 82). The Romans thus equated correctly Gk. *analogia* with their Lat. PROPORTIO 'proportion, ratio'. In its strictest sense, then, the terms analogy and **analogical change** refer to the processes of the extension of some element to an existing form, or the creation of a totally new form that can be traced back to elements which can be presented in the form of a proportion. This type of morpholgical change necessarily involves two base forms and one derived form, as shown in the hypothetical model in (1):

(1)   <u>Base form 1</u> :   <u>Base form 2</u>
        Derived form :   X = New form

The two base forms are connected, as in any morphological change as defined above, by a semantic, syntactic, or structural (i.e., morphological) similarity. Based on base form 1 and its derived form, and through the connection (semantic, syntactic, or morphological) between base form 1 and base form 2, a new form is produced. The creation of Eng. *cows*, for example, which replaced earlier *kine*, may be formulized as in (2):

(2)   <u>Base form 1</u> <u>dog</u>   :   <u>Base form 2</u> <u>cow</u>
        Derived form dog-s   :   X = cow-s

This kind of morphological change, which can be presented in the form of a proportion or ratio, has been called "proportional analogy" or "four-part analogy". However, there may actually be more than two base forms involved, as in the case of those speakers (particularly children) who will generate the plural of Eng. *ox* as *oxes*, rather than *oxen* as shown in (3), perhaps because of the semantic connection with *cow* ~ *cows*, together with the formal similarity to plural formations such as *box* ~ *boxes*:

(3)   Base forms: <u>cow</u> : <u>(box)</u> : <u>ox</u>
        Derived forms: cow-s : (box-es) : X = ox-es

Because there may often be more than four parts involved in this type of morphological change, some historical linguists prefer the term "analogical extension".

In cases where we do not simply have a newly remodeled form replacing an older form, but rather, the creation of an entirely new word (or *neologism*), some historical linguists prefer the term "analogical creation". This process is preceded by a process of reanalysis or reinterpretation of some segment of the form derived from base form 1. For example, in the word *hamburger*, the segment *ham-* has been reinterpreted to mean 'meat patty', while the segment *-burger* has come to mean 'sandwich'. Speakers have therefore created analogically the following neologisms in (4):

(4)   <u>ham</u>   :   <u>cheese</u>   : <u>steak</u>   :   <u>fish</u>
        hamburger: X = cheeseburger: X = steakburger: X = fishburger

Other examples of analogical creation from American English involve the words *alcoholic* and *Watergate*. In the case of the former, the segment *-oholic* has acquired the meaning 'someone addicted to something', while in the latter, the segment *-gate* has been reinterpreted as meaning 'a scandal involving a high-ranking politician (usually the President)'. Accordingly, speakers of American English have produced the following analogical creations shown in (5):

(5)
<u>alcohol</u> : <u>work</u>   :   <u>chocolate</u>   : <u>sex</u>
alcoholic : X = workoholic :   X = chocoholic : X = sexoholic
<u>water</u>   : <u>Iran-Contra (scandal)</u>   :   <u>zipper (re., Monica Lewinsky)</u>
Watergate : X = Iran-Contragate : X = Zippergate

One notes here that the term "analogical creation" has often been used by historical linguists when what is actually meant is "analogical extension", in spite of the very important way in which these two types of analogical change differ from one another (i.e., the former involves a previous step of reinterpretation, the latter does not).

In this book, for the sake of clarity, I shall return to the basic, original meaning of the Greek word *analogia* and use the terms **analogy** and **analogical change** to refer only to the foregoing types of morphological changes which have been called "proportional analogy", "four-part analogy", "analogical extension", and "analogical creation". In the present view, then, the terms *analogical change* and *morphological change* are not interchangeable. Rather, analogical change is but one type of morphological change. Moreover, there will be no need to use the terms "proportional analogy" or "four-part analogy" since analogical change in the present view necessarily involves at least four parts presented in the form of a proportion. The term analogical change will also imply an "analogical extension", so there will not be any need for this term either. Only if there is truly a case of a neologism created by analogical change, then the term "analogical creation" will be used.

Leveling

Leveling differs greatly from analogical change in that it does not involve two different base forms (and their respective derived forms) connected by some semantic, syntactic, or morphological similarity. Rather, it occurs in a well-defined parameter called a "paradigm", i.e., the set of inflected forms of a given word. These inflected forms, by their very nature, are already connected by semantic, syntactic, and in most cases, morphological similarity. For example, in a verbal paradigm, the syntactic connection lies in the fact that all members of the paradigm carry out the same function (i.e., expressing the action), the lexical morpheme or root connects all members of the paradigm semantically (i.e., the basic meaning of the lexical morpheme is the same in all persons of the verb), and usually, there is some structural similarity between these roots (though one can easily provide lots of exceptions to this general tendency). Leveling, therefore, unlike analogical change, need not, indeed cannot, be presented in the form of a proportion, since there are not two different base forms. It would thus be wrong to say, for example, that EOSp. *veno* 'he came' > Old and ModSp. *vino* "by analogy with" EOSp. *vine* 'I came', since such a statement would imply a distorted proportion such as that shown in (6), where the infinitive is repeated as the base form (by definition of "analogy", an impossibility):

(6)   *venir*   :   **venir* (cannot repeat base form 1)
       vine   :   X = (*vino*?)

In paradigms, then, membership alone is sufficient to cause one form to become more like another form. Therefore, rather than attempting to present leveling in the form of a proportion, perhaps the leveling process would be better described as the spreading within a given paradigm, by means of a type of domino effect, of a particular linguistic feature from one form to another. Or, perhaps the particular linguistic feature that levels the other members of the paradigm can be envisaged as a type of cancer which is originally found in one or more of the forms and then spreads systematically to either some or all of the remaining forms.

The leveling process may lead to either the partial or complete elimination of morphophonemic alternations, particularly if these alternations do not seem to signal important differences in meaning. Thus one may speak of either @**partial leveling** or @**complete leveling**. The history of Spanish attests to both of these types of leveling, as exemplified in (7a & b). In (7a), leveling of /e/ > /i/ occurs in the preterite only, while in (7b), leveling of /l/ > /ʎ/ has spread to all tenses and forms of the verb:

(7)   a.   Early Old Spanish   Modern Spanish
          infinitive   *venir*   *venir*
          pret.   *vine*   *venimos*   *vine*   *vinimos*
                                veniste   *venistes* >   *viniste*   *vinisteis*
                                veno   *vinieron*   *vino*   *vinieron*

        b.   Old Spanish   Modern Spanish
          infinitive   *levar*   >   *llevar*
                                        ⟋
          pres.ind.   *llevo* → *levamos*   *llevo*   *llevamos*
                                llevas   *levades* >   *llevas*   *llevades*
                                lleva   *llevan*   *lleva*   *llevan*
                                ↓
          pret.   *levé*   *levamos*   *llevé*   *llevamos*
                                levaste   *levastes* >   *llevaste*   *llevasteis*
                                levó   *levaron*   *llevó*   *llevaron*
                                ↓
          imp.ind.   *levaba*   *levábamos*   *llevaba*   *llevábamos*
                                levabas   *levábades* >   *llevabas*   *llevabais*
                                levaba   *levaban*   *llevaba*   *llevaban*
                                ↓
          past.part.   *levado*, etc.   >   *llevado*, etc.

Thus the primary consequence of the leveling process is the restoration of uniformity or symmetry to paradigms which have previously experienced the disruption of an earlier symmetry. It is phonological change that initially brings about irregularity or asymmetry in grammatical systems. One can therefore

observe in the history of any language the constant interaction between phonological change and leveling.[4] A closer look at the story behind example in (7a)
above demonstrates quite well this diachronic struggle.

The paradigm of the perfect indicative of Latin VENIRE 'to come' exhibited complete symmetry in the root morpheme, where all six forms contained the
front mid-vowel /e/, as shown in Stage One of (8). However, the raising of /e/ >
/i/ occurred in two of these forms because of two different, though related,
phonological processes: (1) In the first singular, assimilation to the high word-
final vowel [-i] (known as metaphony); and (2) assimilation to the word-medial
semiconsonant [j] (which arose through diphthongization of open /é/). The other
four forms, which contained neither [-i] nor [j], underwent no change, thus
resulting in an asymmetrical Early Old Spanish paradigm with root allomorphs
in /vin-/ and /ven-/ as shown below in bold print in Stage Two of (8). Eventually, the /i/ spread to the remaining forms, leveling the paradigm to the state
shown in Stage Three of (8) thus restoring the once lost symmetry, though now
with the high front vowel /i/:

(8)   The Past Tense of Latin VENIRE, Old and ModSp. *venir*

Stage One	Stage Two	Stage Three
VENIRE	*venir*	*venir*
VENI	*vine*	*vine*
VENISTI	*veniste*	*viniste*
VENIT	*veno*	*vino*
VENIMUS	*venimos*	*vinimos*
VENISTIS	*venistes*	*vinisteis*
VENERUNT	*vinieron*	*vinieron*[5]

---

4. Anttila (1989) and McMahon (1994) make similar statements, though with regard to morphological change in general, as conveyed by their broad use of the term "analogy". Anttila (1989: 94):
"Typical for language change is the constant tug of war between sound change and analogy.
Sturtevant phrased this as a paradox: sound change is regular and causes irregularity; analogy is
irregular and causes regularity. That is, the mainly regular sound change can pull regular paradigms
apart; analogy is generally irregular, in that it does not occur in every case where it could, but when
it does, the result is greater regularity in morphology." McMahon (1994: 70): "Analogy is therefore
seen as a kind of housekeeping device, which resignedly picks up at least some of the mess made by
the more impetuous sound change as it hurtles blindly through the grammar."

5. Whether it was the /i/ of first singular *vine* or third plural *vinieron*, or both, that leveled the other
forms is a question which requires further investigation, as does the question of why partial and not
complete leveling occurred here. See Chapter 2 of this book for details.

Most cases of leveling involve segmental features (i.e., vowels and consonants), as demonstrated in the examples above. However, one can find leveling of prosodic features as well. The history of Spanish provides us with an example of such leveling. In the Latin imperfect indicative, for example, the phonological stress fell on the stems of all but the first and second persons plural, which bore the stress on the suffix. Leveling shifted the stress of the first and second plurals from the suffix to the stem as demonstrated in (9), where the tonic vowel appears in bold) such that in Spanish the stress falls uniformly on the stem:

(9)   Lat. AMARE 'to love'   Sp. *amar*
        /amábam/   /amába/
        /amábas/   /amábas/
        /amábat/   /amába/
        ↓
        /amabámus/   >   /amábamos/
        /amabátis/   >   /amábais/
        ↑
        /amábant/   /amában/

It is not exactly clear why this leveling occurred in the imperfect, since many Spanish verbal paradigms in other tenses and moods do not show such uniformity in their stress patterns (cf. pres.ind. /ámo/ ~ /amámos/; pres.subj. /áme/ ~ /amémos/).

Although leveling has most often been observed in the verbal paradigm, it is not restricted to this grammatical context. Leveling can also be found in pronominal and nominal paradigms. Take, for example, the case of the third person singular and plural reflexive pronouns in some varieties of American English, which appear as *his self* and *their selves* instead of *himself* and *themselves*.[6] What has clearly occurred here is leveling from the first and second person forms, as well as the feminine of the third person singular, which are composed of forms identical to the possessive adjective, i.e., *my-*, *your-*, *our-*, *her-*, plus the suffix *-self/selves*. The standard third person forms *himself* and *themselves*, on the other hand, are composed of forms identical to the object pronouns, i.e., *him-*, *them-*, plus the suffix *-self/selves*. Consequently, leveling has eliminated this asymmetrical pattern by pushing out the stems *him-* and

---

6. I must credit my seven-year-old son, Marcus, for bringing to my attention these examples, which he reported (with disapproval) as being rather common among some of his first-grade classmates.

them- with forms identical to the possessive adjective, thus equalizing the basic components of these structures throughout the paradigm as shown in (10):

(10)   <u>Standard American English</u>   <u>Non-standard Am.Eng.</u>

my+self	our+selves		my+self	our+selves
your+self	your+selves		your+self	your+selves
↓				
him+self	them+selves	>	his+self	their+selves
↑				
her+self (→)	them+selves	>	her+self	their+selves

The root of the feminine *herself*, which functions as both a possessive adjective and an object pronoun (e.g., *I see her*, *I have her book*), may have played a key role in this leveling process.

Similarly one observes leveling in the pronominal paradigm from Latin to Old Spanish as exemplified in (11a & b). Taking the second person as an example, one notes that while various forms have remained in the singular, (i.e., *tú*, *ti*, *te*), in the plural, leveling resulted in one form (i.e., *vos*). Leveling (indicated by →) stemmed from both singular and plural forms:

(11)   a.   <u>Earlier Latin</u>   <u>Later Latin</u>

		sing.	plur.	sing.	plur.
	nom.	TU	UOS	TU	UOS
	gen.	TUI	UESTRI	(forms discontinued)	
	dat.	TIBI	UOBIS	AD TIBI	AD UOBIS
	ac.	TE	UOS	TE	UOS
			→		
	ab.	TE	UOBIS >	TE	UOS

b.   <u>Later Latin</u>   <u>Old Spanish</u>

		sing.	plur.	sing.	plur.
	nom.	TU	UOS	*tú*	*vos* (tonic)
			↓		
	dat.	AD TIBI	AD UOBIS >	*a ti*	*a vos* (tonic)
			↑		
	ac.	TE	UOS	*te*	*vos* (atonic)
	ab.	TE	UOS		

First, the fact that the accusative and ablative forms were identical in the singular resulted in leveling of accusative and ablative plurals, originally two distinct forms, to one form, as shown in (11a). Later, further leveling of the dative occurred from the nominative, accusative, and ablative forms as shown in (11b).[7]

Leveling in the nominal paradigm can be found in the case of the Classical Latin imparisyllabic nouns (e.g., nom. sing. BOS 'ox', gen. sing. BOVIS, etc.), whose nominative singular forms were found in non-literary Latin (Penny 1991: 105) to have been expanded one syllable via leveling of the other forms of the paradigm, as shown in (12):

(12)		Earlier Latin			Later Latin	
		singular	plural		singular	plural
	nom.	**BOS**	BOVES	>	**BOVIS**	BOVES
		↑				
	gen.	BOVIS	BOVUM		BOVIS	BOVUM
	dat.	BOVI	BOVIBUS		BOVI	BOVIBUS
	ac.	BOVEM	BOVES		BOVEM	BOVES
	ab.	BOVE	BOVIBUS		BOVE	BOVIBUS

Finally, some historical linguists have suggested that in addition to *intra-* and *extra-paradigmatic leveling*, leveling can occur in the context of a given grammatical category. Jeffers (1982: 57), for example, writes:

> [S]tandardization in the marking of some grammatical category may develop across morphological paradigm classes. In such cases the paradigmatic context in which leveling takes place is the grammatical category (such as accusative singulars of nouns) ... In Ancient Greek a final *-n* < **-m* occurs in all accusative singular forms, except in consonant stems (*tamian* 'treasurer', *polin* 'city', *lukon* 'wolf' — but *patera* 'father', *Hellada* 'Greece' ... In Modern Greek the accusative singular ending *-n* has been generalized to all nouns; Modern Greek has *pateran* and *Elladan*. Allomorphy in the form of the accusative singular morpheme has been "leveled out."

Although on the surface the foregoing quote seems to make sense, there are a couple of problems with Jeffers' statement. The first problem is a theoretical one. In the present book, the parameter for leveling has been identified as the paradigm, and the paradigm has been defined as a set of inflected forms of a

---

7. For further discussion of this development, see Rini (1992: 8–15).

given word. A grammatical category such as the accusative singular cannot constitute, therefore, a "paradigmatic context", and so, in the strictest sense of the word, *leveling* (which is by nature *paradigmatic*) cannot occur across the same grammatical category, since this would mean the involvement of more than one lexical morpheme (plus its prefixes and suffixes). The second problem with Jeffers' view is that it can lead to oversimplified and therefore erroneous presentations of the process of morphological change. I shall demonstrate what I mean with the morphological change of OSp. *la señor* > Old and ModSp. *la señora*.

In Old Spanish, one finds a number of feminine nouns ending in a consonant or /-e/ which in modern Spanish exhibit final /-a/, e.g., OSp. *la señor, la pastor, la pariente, la ladrón, la infante, la español* > ModSp. *la señora, la pastora, la parienta, la ladrona, la infanta, la española*. The Old Spanish forms exhibited either a consonant or /-e/ because they are the direct descendents of Latin nouns which ended in /-e/, which was apocopated except when the result would have been a consonant sequence (i.e., Lat. SENIOREM > [senjór(e)] > *señor*; but Lat. PARENTEM > [parjént(e)] > *pariente*). The plural forms of these nouns ended in /-es/, such that one finds, for example, OSp. *la señor ~ las señores*. It would be easy to state that the acquisition of, or change to /-a/ in each case resulted from "leveling across the grammatical category of feminine nouns", since most feminine nouns already ended in /-a/ (particularly those which descended from the Latin first declension, e.g., Lat. AMICAM > Sp. *la amiga*, Lat. ROSAM > Sp. *la rosa*, Lat. TERRA(M) > Sp. *la tierra*, etc.) This statement, however, would be an oversimplification of the evolution at hand, and consequently would not explain why many other feminine nouns did not undergo the alleged leveling (e.g., *la mujer* not **la mujera, *la madre* not **la madra).[8] One might find it even more puzzling that some Spanish nouns originating from a grammatical category even more specific than "feminine nouns" have acquired /-a/ while others have not. I refer to the comparative adjectives (used as substantives) of Lat. SENEX, MAGNUS, PARVUS, BONUS, and MALUS, whose accusative singular forms were SENIOREM, MAIOREM, MENOREM, MELIOREM, and PEIOREM respectively. These forms, through regular phonetic development (i.e., loss of final /-m/ followed by apocope of final /-e/), yielded *señor, mayor, menor*, and *peor*, which functioned in Old Spanish as they did in Latin as either masculine or feminine, thus: *el señor ~ la señor, el mayor ~ la*

---

8. Double asterisks here and throughout this book indicate denial of existence, particularly in Old Spanish, following Wright (1992).

mayor, el menor ~ la menor, el mejor ~ la mejor, el peor ~ la peor. Curiously, only the first of these has acquired the "feminine" suffix *-a*. If one invokes "leveling across the grammatical category of feminine nouns" to explain *la señor* > *la señora*, then one is left without an explanation for why we do not likewise find in modern Spanish **la mayora*, **la menora*, **la mejora*, **la peora*. If, however, one invokes analogy as it has been defined here, then we may begin to get a clearer picture of what actually happened. What sets OSp. *la señor* apart from the other substantival comparative adjectives is that it came to be used as a title. Other titles had already exhibited a distinction between masculine and feminine by means of a "feminine" suffix, e.g., Lat. DOMINU(M) > [dómno] > [dónn(o)] > *don* vs. Lat. DOMINA(M) > [dómna] > [dónna] > *doña* (cf. as well, OSp. *conde ~ condessa, duque ~ duquessa,* etc.). Therefore, OSp. *la señor* soon became *la señora* most likely by analogy with the existing set *don ~ doña* as shown in (13), the connection being the semantic category of "title":

(13)   *el don*   :   *el señor*
        la doña   :   X = *la señora* (ousting *la señor*)

This application of the analogical model accounts as well for the change of *la infante* (also a title) to *la infanta*. As for the other words that underwent this change (i.e., *la pastor, la pariente, la ladrón, la español* > ModSp. *la pastora, la parienta, la ladrona, la española*), one might very well find, with further investigation, the analogues to which these were associated by either semantic or structural similarity — for example, adjectives of nationality in the case of *la español* > *la española*, nouns denoting occupations in the case of *la pastor, la ladrón* > *la pastora, la ladrona,* etc. This approach may reveal to us the way in which the mind of the speaker of Old Spanish may have worked, while approaching such changes as cases of "leveling across the same grammatical category" will lead nowhere. This is not to say that other types of morphological change do not occur across entire grammatical categories. In the case of **morph-emicization** (i.e., when a phone acquires morphemic status), for example, the new morpheme may be added or deleted across the board in a given grammatical category (see Rini 1995 for a specific example of this type of morphological change). Nonetheless, in this book, the concept of leveling will be confined to the paradigm, such that there will be no need for the term *paradigmatic leveling* (as used by some), except in the case of **extra-paradigmatic leveling** (as defined above), since leveling, by nature, takes place only in the context of the paradigm (be it pronominal, nominal, or verbal). Neither will there be a need for the term *intra-paradigmatic leveling*, since the use of the term **leveling** in this book will necessarily denote "leveling within the same paradigm."

Blending

This process, which results in a **blend** (often referred to as a *lexical blend*), involves a morphological compromise between two forms with identical or similar meaning which are perceived to be in competition with one another. Sometimes the competition between forms is the result of an earlier morphological process. For example, in some varieties of English, non-standard *foots* (which resulted from analogy with *book ~ books*) has blended with the competing standard *feet* to produce *feets*. Sometimes the competition and subsequent blend simply occurs between (near-)synonyms, as in the case of the common non-standard English *irregardless*, the resultant blend of *regardless* and *irrespective* (Hock 1991: 190), or the case of *dethaw*, a blend of *defrost* and *thaw*, or of *ascared*, the common product of children's blending *afraid* and *scared*.

Blending may also result from competition between multiple variants. In an earlier study I have attempted to show that regular phonetic development of Latin CICONIA 'stork' could not have produced OSp. *çigoña*, nor Old and ModSp. *cigüeña*, but only *cegoña*, *ceguña*, *cegoina*, or *cigüena* (the last two with no palatal nasal). Given the heterogeneity of language, it is likely that this word was pronounced in these various ways, and that speakers were therefore exposed to these multiple variants. Such being the case, it is not inconceivable that blending of some of these multiple variants ensued. In this case the blending appears to have been reciprocal, resulting in not one, but two new forms, i.e., **çegoña* X **çigüena* > *çigoña*, *çigüeña* (whereby **çegoña* acquired *çi-* from **çiguena*, while **çiguena* acquired the palatal nasal from **çegoña*).[9]

Finally, blending can be found to be, at times, quite deliberate, as in the following examples: *breakfast* X *lunch* > *brunch*, *guess* X *estimate* > *guestimate*, *information* X *commercial* > *infomercial*, *cafeteria* X *auditorium* > *cafetorium*, *cappuccino* X *frozen* > *frappuccino*, *skirt* X *shorts* > *skort*, Sp. *queso* X *tortilla* > *quesadilla*, *spoon* X *fork* > *spork*.[10]

---

9. For further discussion of this development, see Rini (1993).

10. I am not certain how widespread the use of the term *spork* actually is, but I was told by students in my historical linguistics course (Spring Semester 1998) that this is the common word on grounds here at the University of Virginia for "runcible spoon".

Contamination

This process is like blending in that it results from the interaction of semantically related forms, but, unlike blending, it does not lead to a compromise or hybrid form. Rather, one word will become phonetically more similar to a semantically related word, but without losing its own identity or creating a semantically intermediate form (Hock 1991: 197). For example, since no regular phonological change of /-d-/ > /-l-/ is known to the history of Spanish, it is not unreasonable to assume that Lat. CODA, after shedding its dental consonant, yielding **coa*, was contaminated by semantically related *culo*, producing *cola*. Although Dworkin (1980) calls this a "lexical blend", the word *cola* 'tail' is not a semantic intermediate between original CODA 'tail' and *culo* 'buttocks, ass', whereas the blends *brunch*, *guestimate*, *infomercial*, and *spork* are indeed. Similarly, since Latin /st-/ did not normally evolve to /str-/ in Spanish, it is reasonable to assume that Sp. *estrella* 'star' resulted from contamination of Lat. STELLAM 'star' by ASTRUM 'star'. Again, the concept *"estrella"* is not something in between original STELLAM and ASTRUM.

Another type of contamination has been appropriately termed **serial contamination**. Words that are often said in a series will affect the structure of words that proceed or follow. For example, the /f/ of English *four* is apparently the result of contamination by the /f/ of *five* (cf. Lat. QUATTUOR, Sanskrit *catvaras* vs. Greek *pente*, Sanskrit *pañca*, where /p/ > /ɸ/ > /f/). Similarly, the /o/ of Sp. *cinco* is due to that of *cuatro*, since Lat. QUINQUE would have yielded **cinque* in Spanish (cf. Ital. *cinque*). The pronunciation of Eng. *bologna* as [bəlówni] is no doubt the result of contamination by *salami*, *pastrami*, etc. The oft-cited development of some of the days of the week in Spanish has also involved serial contamination. Straightforward phonological development of Lat. (DIES) LUNAE and (DIES) MERCURII would have yielded **lune* and **mercure*. The forms *lunes* and *miércoles* therefore owe their /s/ to that of *martes*, *jueves*, and *viernes* (< (DIES) MARTIS, JOVIS, and VENERIS) while *miércoles* also owes its stress pattern (and subsequent diphthongization of initial /e/) to that of the other days of the week.

Contamination can also occur between semantic opposites (again, what Malkiel 1951 termed "lexical polarization"). For example, would be **femelle* in English was contaminated by its opposite, *male*, yielding *female*. This cause of contamination is not unlike serial contamination, in that antonyms are often said in close proximity to one another, e.g., *Is that cat a male or female?* (Hock

1991: 197). Old Spanish offers similar examples: OSp. *siniestro* 'left', which would have otherwise been **sinestro* (< Lat. SINISTER), acquired its diphthong from its Old Spanish antonym *diestro*, whose /je/ is etymological (< Lat. DEXTER); likewise, Sp. *nadie* 'no body' owes its structure to Sp. *alguien* 'somebody' (Malkiel 1945).

Sometimes the semantic connection through which contamination occurs is broader than the relationship of synonym or antonym. For example, OEng. *foeder* (MidEng. *fader*) > *father* because of *brother*, a form belonging to the broader word family. Similarly, had the forerunner of Sp. *nuera* 'daughter-in-law' (**NURA* < Clas.Lat. NURUS) not received pressure (quite fittingly) from that of *suegra* 'mother-in-law' (**SOCRA* < Clas.Lat. SOCRUS), the form in modern Spanish would be **nora*. Likewise, Lat. NIVEM 'snow' would have evolved to **neve*, and appears to have acquired its diphthong from its semantically related, quasi-synonym *hielo* whose /jé/ is indeed etymological (< Lat. GELUM, Corominas 1981: 227). However, other terms from the broader semantic field of 'weather' may have also played a role in the shift of **neve* > *nieve*, cf., *niebla* 'fog', *tiempo* 'weather', *cielo* 'sky' (also, diphthongal *llueve* 'it rains', hence diphthongal *nieva* 'it snows').

Finally, contamination can stem from derivatives of a form or forms from the same word-family but which are from outside the paradigm. Such forms by their very nature are semantically related, but unlike the aforementioned cases, they are morphologically similar as well. For example, Penny (1991: 157) points out that a number of infinitives from Old to modern Spanish have acquired in their stem an unetymological atonic diphthong /je/ or /we/, e.g., OSp. *adestrar* 'to train', *atesar* 'to stiffen', *dezmar* 'to decimate, tithe', *desossar* 'to bone (meat)', *engrossar* 'to fatten' > ModSp. *adiestrar, atiesar, diezmar, deshuesar, engruesar* (generally, the diphthongs /jé/ and /wé/ are tonic because they arose phonologically from stressed Latin open /e/ and /o/) At a glance, one might be tempted to attribute the presence of the atonic diphthong to leveling by the etymological tonic one found in the inflected forms of these verbs, i.e., *adiestro* 'I train', *adiestras* 'you train', etc., *atieso* 'I stiffen', *atiesas* 'you stiffen', etc., *diezmo* 'I decimate', *diezmas* 'you decimate', etc., etc. However, a number of other infinitives, e.g., *entregar* 'to hand over', *prestar* 'to lend', *templar* 'to temper', *vedar* 'to forbid', *pretender* 'to intend', *aportar* 'to contribute', *confortar* 'to comfort', *sorber* 'to sip', did not acquire an atonic /je/ or /we/ despite the fact that their inflected forms exhibited in Old Spanish etymological /jé/ or /wé/, e.g. OSp. *entriego* 'I hand over', etc., *priesto* 'I lend', etc., *tiemplo* 'I temper' etc., *viedo* 'I forbid' etc., *pretiendo* 'I intend' etc., *apuerto* 'I contribute' etc., *comfuerto* 'I comfort' etc., *suerbo* 'I sip' etc., etc. On the contrary, these inflected forms were remodeled on, or leveled by, their respective infinitives, i.e., ModSp. *entrego, presto, templo, vedo, pretendo, aporto, comforto, sorbo*, etc. It is therefore more likely that ModSp. *adiestrar, atiesar, diezmar, deshuesar, engruesar* acquired stem diphthongs /je/ and /we/ via contamination by some related form from beyond the verbal paradigm. It so happens that in the word family of each of these infinitives there is a noun or adjective with a tonic, etymological diphthong, e.g., *tieso* 'stiff', *diezmo* 'tenth, tithe', *diestro* 'skilful', *hueso* 'bone', *grueso* 'thick, fat', the probable source of the contamination. Contamination that occurs in this particular context may appear to be closer in nature to leveling than to the other types of contamination exemplified above, but it differs greatly from leveling in that the derived forms involved in the interaction belong to different grammatical categories, e.g., verb and noun, verb and adjective, etc.

Backformation

This morphological change is related to, and perhaps may be considered a subtype of, analogy. However, whereas in analogical change the new form is the synchronically derived form, in backformation, the new form becomes the base form, derived backward from the originally derived, longer form, as shown in example (14), taken from Hock (1991: 204):

(14)   operation   :   orientation
      operate   :   X = orientate (replacing 'orient')

Backformation is often preceded by reanalysis or reinterpretation. The English words *pea* and *cherry* provide good examples of this process. In Old English the word for *pea* was sg. *pise*, pl. *pisan*. The word for cherry was borrowed from the French word, sg. *cerise* ~ pl. *cerises* (cf. Sp. *cereza* ~ *cerezas*). Since the allomorph /-z/ commonly marked plural, the Old English singular *pise* and the French borrowing *cerise*, both exhibiting /-z/, were so reinterpreted and subsequently backformed, perhaps on the model of other vegetables and fruits, as in (15):

(15)   pl.   bean-s   :   rutabaga-s   :   pi-se
      sg.   bean   :   rutabaga   :   X = pi > pea

      pl.   apple-s   :   banana-s   :   ceri-se
      sg.   apple   :   banana   :   X = ceri > cherry

Backformation, though not a common process, is not completely unknown to the history of Spanish. In the nominal paradigm, for example, Latin singular PECTUS, TEMPUS, PIGNUS, and CORPUS yielded the unusual Old Spanish singulars in /s/, *el pechos* 'chest', *el tiempos* 'time, weather', *el peños* 'large rock', *el cuerpos* 'body'(as did Lat. OPUS > OSp. *el huebos* 'the work, deed'). Since in Old Spanish, just as in modern Spanish, /-s/ more often served to mark plural than singular, these nouns were reformed through backformation on the model of nouns such as *libro ~ libros*, etc. as shown in (16), but only after the original singulars in /-s/ were reinterpreted as plurals (ousting whatever descendents there may have been of the original Latin plurals PECTORA, TEMPORA, PIGNORA, and CORPORA):

(16)   *libro-s*:   *pecho-s*   :   *tiempo-s*   :   *peño-s*   :   *cuerpo-s*
       libro   :   X = *pecho*:   X = *tiempo*:   X = *peño*:   X = *cuerpo*

Reanalysis or Reinterpretation

These terms have been used to refer to the process discussed above which precedes the backformation process. The process of reanalysis or reinterpretation may, however, constitute a morphological change in and of itself. For example, in the case of OSp. *el huebos*, which belonged to the same class of nouns as OSp. *el pechos*, *el tiempos*, etc. as discussed above, it was the morphological reflex of the original Latin plural that was reinterpreted as a singular and to which the morpheme /-s/ was added to mark plural, i.e., Lat. pl. OPERA > [ób(e)ra] > *obra* —(reinterpreted as singular)→ *la obra ~ las obras*. Similarly, Lat. sg. FOLIUM ~ pl. FOLIA would have evolved phonetically to **fojo* and *foja* respectively. However, **fojo* never functioned as a singular in Old Spanish, nor *foja* as a plural, since the latter was reanalyzed as a singular and remarked with /-s/ when plural, thus: Lat. pl. FOLIA > *foja* —(reinterpreted as singular)→ OSp. sg. *la foja ~* pl. *las fojas* (> ModSp. sg. *la hoja ~* pl. *las hojas*). What happened here in the evolution of Spanish is currently in progress in American English, as many people, regardless of their level of education, now produce utterances like *"This data is very revealing"* instead of *"These data are very revealing"*. Like other morphological changes, such reanalysis was not regular in the nominal system of Spanish, as one finds in the case of Lat. sg. DATUM ~ pl. DATA, the morphological reflex of the singular remained as the singular, i.e., Lat. DATUM > *el dato* 'datum, a piece of data/information', to which the plural morpheme /s/ was added producing pl. *los datos* 'data, pieces of information'. In at least one case, the original singular vs. plural function has been retained semantically, though morphologically both forms appear to be singulars, i.e., Lat. sg. LIGNUM ~ pl. LIGNA > *el leño* 'log, piece of firewood' ~ *la leña* 'logs, pieces of firewood'.

Morphological Influence

Finally, it should be noted that the role of morphology in the history of Spanish or any other language goes beyond the various types of *morphological change* described above. Very often we find that morphological factors which cannot be described as a particular type of morphological change have played a role in the evolution of a given form. In such cases, I shall refer to the **morphological influence** or the **influence of morphological factors** in a given development, and even more frequently, in the lack of an expected development. We are well aware that synchronically, morphological factors affect the pronunciation of certain words. For example, the vocalic sequence /ua/ is usually realized phonetically as a rising diphthong, i.e., [wá], as in *cuando* [kwán-do], *actual* [ak-twál], etc. In fact, such words are never pronounced with hiatus of this vocalic sequence, i.e., *[ku-án-do], *[ak-tu-ál]. However, an infinitive like *continuar*, for example, may be pronounced either with or without hiatus of the sequence /ua/, thus: [kon-ti-nu-ár] or [kon-ti-nwár]. The reason for this hiatus is the morphological influence of some of the inflected forms of this verb, which carry the phonological stress on the /ú/ and thus exhibit hiatal vocalic sequences, e.g., pres.ind. *continúo, continúas*, etc. A similar example of the influence of morphological factors on the pronunciation of certain vocalic sequences is found in the hiatus of /eu/. Generally, /eu/ is realized phonetically as a descending diphthong, as in *Europa* [eu̯-ró-pa], *Eugenia* [eu̯-hé-nja], never with hiatus *[e-u-ró-pa], *[e-u-hé-nja]. However, the speaker's recognition of the morphemic boundary in *reunir*, i.e., prefix *re-* + *unir*, allows for the pronunciation of this word either with or without hiatus, thus: [re-u-nír] or [reu̯-nír]. Diachronically too, morphological factors can determine the course of phonetic development. For example, in the evolution of words like *doloroso* 'painful' and *oloroso* 'fragrant', one would expected syncope of the pretonic vowel to have occurred (as in *saboroso* > *sabroso* 'flavorful'), followed by epenthesis of a buffer consonant (as in OSp. fut. *saliré* > *salré* > ModSp. fut. *saldré*) or perhaps metathesis of the new consonant sequence, thus: /dol(o)róso/ and /ol(o)róso/ > *[dolróso] and *[olróso]

> **doldroso and **oldroso, or **dorloso and **orloso. However, syncope never occurred in *doloroso* and *oloroso* because of the morphological influence of the respective nouns from which they were derived, i.e., *dolor* 'pain' and *olor* 'smell', which bare the phonological stress on the vowel in question. That fact that syncope was not impeded in *sabroso* may be due to the resulting consonant sequence, i.e., /br/, which, because of its long-time membership in the phonological system concerned, was felt by speakers to be completely natural, whereas /lr/ was not. One may question why the noun *sabor* did not help retain a ModSp. *saboroso, and for such a question we may never have an answer. Nevertheless, whatever the reason may be for the lack of morphological influence of *sabor* on *sabroso*, this would not mean that *dolor* and *olor* did not play a role, perhaps in conjunction with the phonotactically awkward consonant sequence /lr/, in impeding syncope in *doloroso* and *oloroso*.

Another example of morphological influence on phonetic evolution involves the history of the Spanish verbs *creer* 'to believe', *leer* 'to read', and *proveer* 'to provide'. In a separate study, I have suggested that the lack of contraction of /eé/ > /é/ in *creer, leer, proveer* (compare OSp. *seer* 'to be', *veer* 'to see'> ModSp. *ser, ver*) was due to the structure of their respective past participles. In Spanish, infinitives generally exhibit one less syllable than their past participles (e.g., *ir* ~ *ido, hablar* ~ *hablado, comenzar* ~ *comenzado, representar* ~ *representado*, etc.). OSp. *seer* and *veer* fell into this same pattern with their contraction to ModSp. *ser, ver* (i.e., *ser* ~ *sido, ver* ~ *visto*), whereas the contraction of *creer, leer,* and *proveer* would have resulted in a pattern in which the infinitive exhibited not one, but two syllables less than their respective past participles, thus: *creer, leer, proveer* > *crer ~ *creído,* *ler ~ *leído,* *prover ~ *proveído*. The past participle, then, given its close relation to the infinitive, impeded the contraction of /eé/ in these verbs, thus maintaining the general pattern found in all other verbs, i.e., *creer* ~ *creído, leer* ~ *leído, proveer* ~ *proveído*.[11] Morphological factors such as those described here and their role in the evolution of Spanish probably constitutes the area of Spanish historical morphology that has been the least studied of all.

---

11. See Rini (1991) for details.

CHAPTER 2

The Nature of Leveling
in the Old Spanish Verbal Paradigm

As discussed in Chapter 1, leveling is one of the two most systematic types of morphological change (the other being analogy), yet specialists of Spanish historical grammar have not dealt with this phenomenon in any sort of systematic way. On the contrary, leveling has often been invoked, as will be seen below, in a very *ad hoc* fashion. We are therefore without a good explanation for why the Old Spanish infinitives *cobrir* 'to cover', *complir* 'to compile, complete', *sobir* 'to go up', *sofrir* 'to suffer', etc. were leveled to ModSp. *cubrir, cumplir, subir, sufrir*, etc. while *dormir* 'to sleep' and *morir* 'to die' were not. We are also without an explanation for the apparent leveling of /e/ > /i/ from OSp. *aperçebir* 'to warn', *perçebir* 'to perceive', *reçebir* 'to receive', *escrevir* 'to write', *bevir* 'to live' > ModSp. *apercibir, percibir, recibir, escribir, vivir*, when no such leveling occurred in Sp. *concebir* 'to conceive', *decir* 'to say', *medir* 'to measure', etc. One also finds disagreement among scholars regarding the shift of /o/ > /u/ from the Old Spanish preterites *ove, tove* 'I had', *estove* 'I was', *andove* 'I went', *sope* 'I new', *cope* 'I fit' > ModSp. *hube, tuve, estuve, anduve, supe, cupe*. Was it a case of leveling induced by forms with /u/ of the respective paradigms (e.g., *tuvieron, tuviesse*, etc. —leveling→ *tove* > *tuve*, etc.) as some scholars have proposed, or were OSp. *pude* 'I could/was able' and *puse* 'I put' responsible for the change, as other scholars have suggested? These are some of the questions I wish to address in the present chapter through a broad examination of the nature of leveling in Old Spanish.

The Directionality of Leveling in the Old Spanish Verbal Paradigm Distillable from Resistance to Language Shift: The Case of Spanish *dormir*, *morir* (and *podrir*)

If the title of this section is reminiscent of the wonderful titles that accompany the works of the late Yakov Malkiel, it is no coincidence. This section of the present chapter is intended to be, in part, a tribute to the great Berkeley Romanist, who passed away on April 24, 1998. Those who know Professor Malkiel's work very well may have even thought for a moment that I flat out stole one of his titles — particularly if one is familiar with an article he published in Amsterdam's *Neophilologus* only five years before his passing. The 1993 article to which I refer is entitled "Semantic vs. Formal Ingredients Distillable from Resistance to Language Shift: The Case of Spanish *dormir*, *morir*."

Now the similarity in our titles is where the similarity between Professor Malkiel's article and the present analysis ends. I do not believe for one moment that my work could ever compare to that of one of the greatest Romanists of our time: not in his unmatched erudition; not in the marvelous word choice found in his unique style of prose; not in his piercing analyses of, nor the creative solutions he proposed for, the extremely complex problems of historical Romance grammar which he tackled time and again.[1]

The leveling of Old Spanish *cobrir*, *complir*, *sobir*, *sofrir*, etc. > ModSp. *cubrir*, *cumplir*, *subir*, *sufrir*, etc. vis à vis the lack thereof in *dormir*, *morir*, and *podrir* offers specialists of Spanish historical grammar an intriguing conundrum whose solution can reveal some significant facts about the nature of leveling from Old to modern Spanish.

In his 1993 piece, Professor Malkiel observes that there existed in Old Spanish a significant number of /o/-stem *-ir* verbs, shown below in (1); and that all have been eliminated from the Spanish lexicon with the exception of *dormir* 'to sleep' and *morir* 'to die':

(1)   *bollir, cobrir, complir, contir, descobrir, destroir, **dormir**, florir, foir, fondir, **morir**, nozir, ofrir, sebollir, sobir, sofrir, tollir.*

He then points out that these two residual forms resemble one another both semantically and morphologically. Such being the case, he presupposes that one

---

1. For those unfamiliar with Professor Malkiel's life and work (which were basically one and the same), see Dworkin (1998) and Lloyd (1999).

of these factors, semantic or morphological, played a role in the survival of these two infinitives. Hence, the title of his article, again, "Semantic vs. Formal Ingredients Distillable from Resistance to Language Shift: The Case of Spanish *dormir, morir*."

With regard to the semantic affinity between *dormir* and *morir*, Professor Malkiel writes (1993: 395):

> The fact that a certain close affinity prevails, in folk belief no less than in the poetic (and, generally, artistic) elaborations thereupon — in many cultures and in numerous languages alike — between "sleep" and "death" invites no lengthy documentation and requires no heavy-handed explanation. Sleep, after all, involves a fairly brief suspension of consciousness, while death presupposes an indefinite extension of such a period of amnesia.

In terms of their morphological likeness, he observes that *dormir* and *morir* both exhibit, in Old and modern Spanish, a synchronic shift of /o/ → /u/ in various tenses and moods, shown below in (2a); that they agree in their stress-controlled alternation of [o] with [wé] shown in (2b); and that in fact, the morphological parallel between *dormir* and *morir* falls short in only one major respect; namely, the past participle, shown in (2c):

(2) a. Synchronic shift of /o/ → /u/:
        preterite: *durmió, murió; durmieron, murieron*
        pres.subj.:   *durmamos, muramos; durmáis, muráis*
        pres.part.:   *durmiendo, muriendo* (also *durmiente, muriente*).
        imp.subj.:   *durmiese, muriese*, etc.
        OSp.imp.:   *durmiés, muriés; durmié, murié; durmiemos,*
                    muriemos; durmiedes, muriedes; durmién, murién

    b. Stress-controlled alternation of /o/ ~ /ue/:
        duermo, muero ~ *dormimos, morimos*, etc.

    c. Past Participles:
        dormido vs. *muerto*

Professor Malkiel then tells of three ways in which the Old Spanish /o/-stem *-ir* verbs disappeared. Most commonly, /o/ was simply raised to /u/, as shown below in (3a). Alternatively, a few of these verbs shifted to the *-er* conjugation via the so-called inchoative morpheme *-ecer*, as shown in (3b). Finally, a couple of verbs were simply abandoned and substituted with other lexical items, as shown in (3c):

(3)   a.   *cobrir, complir, descobrir, destroir, foir, fondir, nozir, sobir,*
               sofrir, tollir > cubrir, cumplir, descubrir, destruir, fuir, fundir,
               nuzir, subir, sufrir, tullir

      b.   *contir (> cuntir)*   >   *acontecer*
           ofrir   >   *ofrecer*
           florir   >   *florecer*

      c.   *sebollir* 'to bury' —replaced by→ *soterrar,* later *enterrar;*
             bollir 'to boil' (> *bollecer*) —replaced by→ *hervir*

Professor Malkiel then devotes the remainder of the article to demonstrating that, despite almost identical morphological patterns in modern Spanish, throughout their history, *dormir* and *morir* were not always so morphologically similar. Originally, Latin *morior* was deponent, *dormio* was not. Next, in light of the Old Portuguese evidence, *morio probably underwent metathesis to *moiro while *dormio* most likely did not, producing a split between *moiro on the one hand, and *dormo* on the other. As regards the infinitives themselves, *morir* differed from *dormir* in that alongside future *moriré,* there existed for centuries a syncopated *morré,* while nothing similar can be found alongside *dormiré.* However, these differences were eventually eliminated, resulting in the great morphological similarity between the two paradigms described at the beginning of his article.

    Given the "alternating rapprochements and alienations" between *dormir* and *morir* throughout their history, Professor Malkiel concludes: "What lent [*dormir* and *morir*] the necessary strength for such successful resistance on this occasion could not have been their shapes, but solely the affinity, not to say the partial overlap, of their respective meanings" (1993: 400).

    Now then, with all due respect (and I say this over-used phrase with all of its basic, unbleached semantic value), it is difficult to see the reasoning behind Professor Malkiel's argument as regards how or why the semantic connection between these two verbs would have shielded them from a change that affected all other verbs of this category. One concedes that such a semantic link could conceivably have, in the end, led *dormir* and *morir* down the same path — and even add to these *podrir,* thus forming a nice sequence of events, i.e., *dormir* 'to sleep' > *morir* 'to die' > *podrir* 'to rot'. But it seems that some other factor present in one of these verbs would have been necessary to resist the change in the first place. Then, because of the semantic afinity, the other would follow suite (or in this case, not follow the general movement of elimination of /o/-stem

-*ir* verbs). The idea that there is strength in numbers, in this case, a pair of infinitives, does not seem to me to be a sufficient explanation.

Since most of the Old Spanish /o/-stem -*ir* verbs simply exchanged their /o/ for /u/, I would like to reexamine the question of why *dormir* and *morir* did not likewise evolve to **durmir and **murir rather than try to explain why they did not take one of the other two escape routs, (i.e., conversion to **dormecer, **morecer, or total replacement by another lexical item). And rather than concentrating on the *similarities* between the two verbs which did not undergo the change, I would like to approach the problem by examining the *differences* between the paradigms of those verbs which did undergo the change, and those which have not. Let us begin by reexamining the alleged cause of the /o/ to /u/ shift where it did occur.

Most Romance scholars have assumed that the shift of /o/ to /u/ in the infinitives concerned resulted from leveling initiated by the third person singular and plural of the preterite, whose /o/ had already been raised to /u/ by the onglide of the following syllable. Professor Malkiel (1993: 396), for example, in his article, wrote: "*cobrir* 'to cover', with the help of *cubrió*, *cubrieron*, etc., was metamorphosed into *cubrir*..."[2] Penny (1991: 160–61) likewise identifies the /o/ > /u/ shift as "a change which is no doubt assisted by the standardization of /u/ in the 3rd sing. and plur. of the preterite and in the gerund of these infinitives."[3] Such an assumption is easily understood when one compares the preterite paradigm of, for example, OSp. *sobir*, with that of ModSp. *subir*, as in number (4) below (where forms with /u/ appear in bold):

---

2. Malkiel also cited other forms with /u/ from other sections of the paradigm, such as -*iendo*, -*iente*, -*iesse*, and -*iere*, which he believed may have also contributed to the leveling of the infinitives concerned, but he seems to have placed more importance on the preterite forms in /-ió/ and /-ieron/ as one can clearly observe in the foregoing quote.

3. Penny (1991: 160–61) identifies yet another source for the leveling of the /o/-stem -*ir* verbs, i.e., verbs such as *ADDUCIRE > *aducir*, etc., which originally had /u/ in their infinitival stem. In effect, what he proposes here is leveling across a single grammatical category, which has been deemed in the present view to be theoretically invalid. Nevertheless, if such leveling could occur, the question would remain: If other infinitives such as *aducir* were responsible for the leveling of *cobrir*, *complir*, *sobir*, *sofrir*, etc. > ModSp. *cubrir*, *cumplir*, *subir*, *sufrir*, etc. as Penny claims, why were *dormir*, *morir* (and until recently, *podrir*) not also leveled to **durmir, **murir? Again, this example demonstrates the weakness, indeed the invalidity of the notion of leveling across a given grammatical category.

(4)   OSp. *sobir*   ModSp. **subir**
       sobí   *sobimos*   **subí**   **subimos**
       sobiste *sobistes*   **subiste** **subisteis**
       subió **subieron**[4]   **subió**   **subieron**

From such a comparison, one could easily conclude that leveling stemmed from the third person, first spreading to the second and first persons, before ultimately reaching the infinitive, as depicted in number (5), where the hypothetical path of leveling is indicated by arrows and bold print:

(5)   A Hypothetical Path of Leveling of /o/ > /u/:

Early Old Spanish		Old Spanish		Modern Spanish	
sobir		sobir		sobir > **subir**	
				↑	
sobí	*sobimos*	*sobí*	*sobimos*	**subí**	**subimos**
		↑	↑		
sobiste	*sobistes* >	**subiste**	**subistes** >	**subiste**	**subisteis**
↑	↑				
subió	**subieron**	**subió**	**subieron**	**subió**	**subieron**

One might even seek support for such a scenario from general, historical linguistic theory. In Kurylowicz's famous article (1947) on the "laws" of analogy, the second "law" states that analogical developments go in the direction of "basic form" → "derived form", and that the relationship of basic and derived forms is a consequence of their spheres of usage. The form that has a greater sphere of usage is the more "basic" form than the others. Since third person forms are more frequent, i.e., their sphere of usage is greater, then these are therefore the "basic" forms, from which others can be derived. However, one puzzles over the fact that third person *durmió ~ durmieron, murió ~ murieron* did not serve as basic forms from which second and first person forms and, ultimately, newly remodeled infinitives with root morphemes *durm-* and *mur-* could be derived, particularly given that the Old Spanish preterite paradigms of those verbs which underwent the change and those of *dormir* and *morir*, as shown in (6), exhibit no difference whatsoever:

---

4. Occasionally, one even finds in the third person forms whose /o/ has not yet been raised to /u/. For example, in ADMYTE (vols. 0 & 1) one finds *sofrió* 3 times, *sofrieron* 9 vs. *sufrió* 56, *sufrieron* 28. In the Alfonsine corpus, one finds *sofrió* 2 times, *sofrieron* 15 vs. *sufrió* 52, *sufrieron* 5.

(6)   The Preterite of Old Spanish *sobir, dormir, morir*

sobí	*sobimos*	*dormí*	*dormimos*	*morí*	*morimos*
sobiste	*sobistes*	*dormiste*	*dormistes*	*moriste*	*moristes*
subió	**subieron**	**durmió**	**durmieron**	**murió**	**murieron**

It was probably this puzzling diachronic discrepancy that sent Professor Malkiel in search of factors beyond the realm of morphology, though he does not state this in his article.

With regard to the notion of basicness, Hock (1991) makes an observation that may shed light on the problem at hand:

> The inapplicability of Kurylowicz's second 'law' is especially evident in the case of leveling ... closely related languages, starting out from the same Verner's-Law basis, may level in entirely opposite directions. There is thus no predetermined directionality ... the applicability of Kurylowicz's second 'law' of analogy is restricted to certain analogical developments. Most prominanent among these is proportional analogy ... only in proportional analogy does basicness determine possible pivots for change. (Hock 1991: 213–14, 221).

In other words, the directionality of leveling is to date unknown, and might best be described as language- or even case-specific.

Lloyd (1987: 303) observes, contrary to the general belief among hispanists that third person forms were particularly powerful leveling forces in the preterite, that "in the preterite ... we find that the influence of form 1 on form 2, i.e., the basic forms of any dialog, is very strong. In the *-ar* conjugation, form 2 adopted the tonic /-é/ of form 1 and became *-este*...the same vowel is seen in forms 4 and 5, *-emos, -esteis*; and *-emos* is still found in popular Spanish in Castile." What Lloyd has identified here is a case of partial leveling in Old Spanish that radiated outward from the 1st person singular, as indicated by arrows and bold print in (7):

(7)   ***fablé*** →   *fablamos*   ***fablé***   ***fablemos***
       ↓   >

| *fablaste* | *fablastes* | ***fableste*** | *fablastes* |
| *fabló* | *fablaron* | *fabló* | *fablaron* |

The same applies to the *-er* conjugation, where the forms *-ieste, -iemos,* and *-iestes* were leveled by first person /-í/ to *-iste, -imos,* and *-isteis*, as shown in (8):

(8)   Leveling of *-ieste, -iemos,* and *-iestes* by first person *-í*:

Early Old Spanish		Old Spanish		Modern Spanish	
perdí	*perdiemos*	*perdí*→	*perdiemos*	*perdí*	*perdimos*
↓			↘		
perdieste	*perdiestes*	*perdiste*	*perdiestes*	*perdiste*	*perdisteis*
perdió	*perdieron*	*perdió*	*perdieron*	*perdió*	*perdieron*

Lloyd (1987: 308) also believes that the first person singular was the primary leveling force in the evolution of the preterites of OSp. *fazer, venir, poder,* and *poner,* as shown in (9a & b): "The influence of form 1 was sufficient to extend the /u/ and /i/ to other forms so that very early we find *fiziste, fizo, viniste, vino ... pudiste, pudo, pusiste, puso.*"

(9)   a.   Complete leveling in the preterite of OSp. *fazer, venir*

EOSp.	ModSp.	EOSp.	ModSp.
fize	*hice*	*vine*	*vine*
↓		↓	
feziste	*hiciste*	*veniste*	*viniste*
fezo	*hizo*	*veno*	*vino*
fezimos	*hicimos*	*venimos*	*vinimos*
fezistes	*hicisteis*	*venistes*	*vinisteis*
fezieron	*hicieron*	*venieron*	*vinieron*

       b.   Complete leveling in the preterite of OSp. *poder, poner*[5]

EOSp.	ModSp.	EOSp.	ModSp.
pude	*pude*	*puse*	*puse*
↓		↓	
podiste	*pudiste*	*posiste*	*pusiste*
podo	*pudo*	*poso*	*puso*
podimos	*pudimos*	*posimos*	*pusimos*
podistes	*pudisteis*	*posistes*	*pusisteis*
podieron	*pudieron*	*posieron*	*pusieron*

---

5. The evolution of the stem vowel of *pude, pudo,* and *puse, puso,* is a point of historical grammar that is not altogether clear. Some believe that metaphony of final /-i/ was responsible for the /ú/ of the 1st singular, and that this vowel spread to the 3rd singular (Meyer-Lübke 1890:334, Lloyd 1987: 308). Others believe that either the metathesized /u/ of POTUI, POTUIT, POSUI, POSUIT > *POUTI, *POUTIT, *POUSI, *POUSIT, perhaps in conjunction with diphthongization of tonic /ó/, resulted in tonic /ú/ in both the 1st and 3rd singulars (Menéndez Pidal 1941: 318, Penny 1991: 185). This question merits further investigation but lies beyond the scope and purpose of the present discussion.

Lloyd (1987: 308) is more cautious about the possible influence of forms with [j]: "In the plural forms, the endings containing a yod /-ie-/ *may* have changed the stem vowel through the raising effect of a yod on a preceding unstressed vowel, e.g., *feziemos* > *fiziemos, as well as by analogy with the singular* [emphasis added]."

A comparison of the different degrees of leveling in the preterite of cognate Spanish and Portuguese verbs sheds some light on the matter. Hock (1991: 168) points out that morphophonemic alternations which do not signal an important difference in meaning tend to be leveled out. Hence the leveling in the preterite paradigms of Sp. *venir* and *fazer* as shown above in (9) according to Lloyd (1987: 308). Thus we may assume that no significant grammatical meaning was conveyed by the Old Spanish preterite stem of either *venir* or *fazer* and that this function was carried out by the verbal suffix. However, extreme apocope of final /e/ and /o/ of Old Portuguese *fiz(e)* and *fez(o)* resulted in a need to distinguish the first from the third person singular by some other means, that being the root morphemes *fiz-* vs. *fez-*. This important difference in meaning (i.e., grammatical) impeded any such leveling in the singular of this paradigm, so that one now finds in modern Portuguese *eu fiz* vs. *ele/ela fez* (similarly, *eu vim* vs. *ele/ela veio*). In the plural, however, where the verbal suffix, not the stem, conveyed the grammatical meaning, one finds that the type of leveling which occurred in Spanish has also occurred in Portuguese, e.g., *nós fizemos, eles/elas fizeram*. Similarly, *nós viemos, eles/elas vieram*, were leveled by *eu vim*. Thus, although it has been traditionally held that the onglide of the following syllable was responsible for the raising of stem vowel /e/ > /i/ in *venieron* > *vinieron* and *fezieron* > *fizieron* (i.e., [βenjéron] > [βinjéron] and [fedzjéron] > [fidzjéron]), and, there is absolutely no doubt that this yod was capable of such raising (cf. examples of such raising outside of the verbal paradigm, e.g., *deciembre* > *diciembre, encienso* > *incienso*, etc.), the Portuguese evidence reveals that the more active ingredient in the metamorphosis of Sp. *venieron, fezieron* > *vinieron, fizieron* may very well have been the leveling force of the root morpheme of first person *vine* and *fize*. This approach may also explain why the initial raising and subsequent leveling of /e/ > /i/ occurred in the preterite of OSp. *venir* and *fazer* when no such leveling occurred in other second conjugation verbs (e.g., *bebió, bebieron*, not **bibió, *bibieron*, because the 1st sing. was *bebí*, not **bibí*).

I have found in the development of the Old Spanish imperfect indicative another clear-cut example of leveling from the first person singular. The 13th-century imperfect in the second and third conjugations as commonly found in

Alfonsine prose, for example, exhibited one desinence in the first person singular (i.e., etymological /-ía/), and the innovative suffix /-ié/ in all other forms, which, for reasons still unclear to date, never fully supplanted the etymological first person suffix, as exemplified in (10) with third-conjugation OSp. *dezir*:[6]

(10)　13th-century Alfonsine 3rd Conjugation Imperfect Indicative
　　　OSp. *dezir*

dezía	*diziemos*
diziés	*diziedes*
dizié	*dizién*

After the 13th century, however, leveling of the suffixes in /-ié/ by the first person /-ía/ created new variants as shown in (11). Such forms are commonly found, for example, in the *Conde Lucanor* (1335):

(11)

13th century	Post-13th century
dezía	*dezía*
↓	↓
diziés	*dizías*
dizié	*dizía*
diziemos	*dizíamos*
diziedes	*dizíades*
dizién	*dizían*

In other varieties of Medieval Castilian, the first-person suffix exerted pressure on the older, 13th-century /-jé/, producing a new suffix with the stress pattern of the former and the vocalic quality of the latter, i.e., /-íe/,[7] such that one finds a polymorphic state among the post-13th-century paradigms of the Medieval Spanish imperfect indicative as exemplified in (12) again with OSp. *dezir*:

(12)　**dezía**

　　　dizías ~ diziés ~ dezías ~ dezíes
　　　dizía ~ dizié ~ dezía ~ dezíe
　　　dizíamos ~ diziemos ~ dezíamos ~ dezíemos
　　　dizíades ~ diziedes ~ dezíades ~ dezíedes
　　　dizían ~ dizién ~ dezían ~ dezíen

---

6. See Malkiel (1959) for still the best review of the literature on this problem.

7. Lloyd (1987: 361): "Sporadic combinations of the two endings resulted in an occasional *-íe*, with apocope of the final *-e*, e.g., *sey* (Cid 2278) 'he was (staying)' < *seíe*."

Eventually, the forms which were similar to the first person singular came to be preferred to all others, yielding a completely leveled, regularized paradigm in modern Spanish, i.e., *decía, decías, decía, decíamos*, etc. It is entirely possible that the modern paradigm is a continuation of the pre-13th century paradigm (i.e., without the suffix type /-jé/) which simply went out of fashion as regards the written language during the 13th century. And it is not certain whether 14th-century forms such as *dizías, dizía*, etc. were replaced by ModSp. *decías, decía*, etc. on the model of 1st singular *dezía*, or via dissimilation of /i...í/ > /e...í/, e.g., 14th-century *dizías > dezías* > ModSp. *decías*. Nevertheless, it is indisputable that some of the 14th-century forms, namely, those shown above in (11), came about through leveling from the 1st person singular form.

With regard to the present tense indicative, Penny (1991: 151) acknowledges two cases of leveling that stemmed from the first person singular: "In the case of OSp. *oyo* and *fuyo* (MSp. *huyo*), the consonant /ĵ/ was spread analogically from the 1st pers. sing. to the 2nd and 3rd pers. sing. and to the 3rd plur. (*oyes, oye, oyen, fuyes, fuye, fuyen*)." (Although he says that the consonant from the first person singular "was spread analogically", what he means is that the first person form leveled the second singular and third singular and plural forms.)

Now then: If, as the foregoing examples suggest, there was a real tendency for leveling in the Old Spanish verbal paradigm to originate, not from the third person singular and plural, but from the first person singular, then we now have an answer to the question of why *durmió ~ durmieron, murió ~ murieron* did not level the inflected forms of their respective paradigms, nor the infinitives *dormir* and *morir*. In the verbal paradigms where leveling did occur, the source of the leveling can be traced back to the first person singular of a different tense.

Regular phonetic development of the present tense of most /o/-stem -*ir* verbs left paradigms with /u/ in the first person singular, but /o/ in all other forms, as exemplified in (13):

(13)	Early Latin		Late Latin		Early Old Spanish
	/subeo/	>	/subjo/	>	**subo**
	/subis/	>	/subis/		*sobes*
	/subit/	>	/subit/		*sobe*
	/subimus/	>	/subimus/		*sobimos*
	/subitis/	>	/subitis/		*sobides*
	/subiunt/	>	/subent/		*soben*

This first person singular then leveled all other forms of the present tense, as shown in (14):

(14) **subo**   **subo**
      ↓
      sobes   **subes**
      sobe   **sube**
      sobimos   **subimos**
      sobides   **subides** (> **subís**)
      soben   **suben**

Data I have gathered from Alfonsine prose and ADMYTE reveal that, within their respective paradigms, this first person singular form of the present tense was a more powerful leveling force than was the third person singular and plural of the preterite. Observe the percentages of occurrence of /u/- vs. /o/-stem forms in the preterite vs. present tenses of OSp. *complir*, *sobir*, and *sofrir* in (15), as found in the Alfonsine corpus and ADMYTE (vol. 0):

(15)   <u>Leveling of /o/ > /u/ in Preterite and Present of OSp. *complir*, *sobir*, *sofrir*</u>

Preterite:	Alfonsine/ADMYTE			Alfonsine/ADMYTE	
cumplí *subí* *sufrí*	14%	31%	*complí* *sobí* *sofrí*	86%	69%
cumpliste *subiste* *sufriste*	21%	33%	*compliste* *sobiste* *sofriste*	79%	67%
cumplió *subió* *sufrió*	95%	92%	*complió* *sobió* *sofrió*	5%	8%
cumplimos *subimos* *sufrimos*	0%	0%	*complimos* *sobimos* *sofrimos*	100%	100%
cumplistes *subistes* *sufristes*	0%	0%	*complistes* *sobistes* *sofristes*	100%	100%

cumplieron			*complieron*		
subieron	77%	80%	*sobieron*	23%	20%
sufrieron			*sofrieron*		

Present:	Alfonsine/ADMYTE			Alfonsine/ADMYTE	
cumplo			**complo*		
subo	100%	100%	**sobo*	0%	0%
sufro			**sofro*		
cumples			*comples*		
subes	100%	100%	*sobes*	0%	0%
sufres			*sofres*		
cumple			*comple*		
sube	100%	98%	*sobe*	0%	2%
sufre			*sofre*		
cumplimos			*complimos*		
subimos	14%	50%	*sobimos*	86%	50%
sufrimos			*sofrimos*		
cumplides			*complides*		
subides	NA	17%	*sobides*	NA	83%
sufrides			*sofrides*		
cumplen			*complen*		
suben	99%	98%	*soben*	1%	2%
sufren			*sofren*[8]		

---

8. I provide here the actual number of occurrences of the forms presented in this table. The infinitive is first in bold, followed by forms of the present tense, followed by forms of the preterite. The number of occurrences appears in parentheses after each form. Data from Alfonsine prose precede those of ADMYTE (vol.0). In Alfonsine prose, one finds: inf. **complir** (220) ~ **cumplir** (27); pres. *cumplo* (0), *cumples* (6) ~ *comples* (0), *cumple* (97) ~ *comple* (0), *complimos* (0) ~ *cumplimos* (0), *complides* (0) ~ *cumplides* (0), *cumplen* (20) ~ *complen* (1); pret. *complí* (0) ~ *cumplí* (0), *compliste* (3) ~ *cumpliste* (2), *cumplió* (90) ~ *complió* (6), *complimos* (0) ~ *cumplimos* (0), *cumpliestes* (2) ~ *complistes* (0) ~ *cumplistes* (0), *cumplieron* (64) ~ *complieron* (14); inf. **sobir** (42) ~ **subir** (13); pres. *subo* (0), *subes* (0) ~ *sobes* (0), *sube* (449) ~ *sobe* (0), *subimos* (0) ~ *sobimos* (0), *sobides* (0) ~ *subides* (0), *suben* (84) ~ *soben* (0); pret. *sobí* (3) ~ *subí* (1), *sobiste* (8) ~ *subiste* (0), *subió* (11) ~ *sobió* (0), *sobimos* (1) ~ *subimos* (0), *sobistes* (1) ~ *subistes* (0), *subieron* (17) ~ *sobieron* (8); inf. **sofrir** (398) ~ **sufrir** (10); pres. *sufro* (5), *sufres* (2) ~ *sofres* (0), *sufre* (59) ~ *sofre* (0), *sofrimos* (0)

Note that, although the yod of the third-person preterite forms has indeed raised the preceding /o/ to /u/ (though, I would like to emphasize, not in 100% of all cases), these forms have not had as great an impact on the rest of the forms of their paradigms as the first person singular present tense forms have had on theirs. By this stage of the language, present-tense *cumplo*, *subo*, and *sufro* have already leveled all second person singular forms, almost all third singular and plural forms, and some of the first and second persons plural. In light of these data, it makes more sense to attribute the leveling of the infinitives *complir*, *sobir*, and *sofrir*, to the forms *cumplo*, *subo*, and *sufro*, not to the forms *cumplió/cumplieron*, *subió/subieron*, *sufrió/sufrieron*. Moreover, it is probably also the case that the present-tense forms in /u/ leveled the first and second person forms of the preterite. This, by the way, is exactly what happened in the case of OSp. *levar* 'to carry'.

As discussed in Chapter 1, regular phonetic development of Latin LEVARE led to a paradigm with palatalized and non-palatalized lateral consonants in the present, but only non-palatalized forms in the preterite, as shown in (16a), where palatalized forms appear in bold. All forms, including the infinitive, were eventually leveled in favor of the palatalized root allomorph, as shown in (16b):

(16)   a.   Old Spanish *levar*

Present		Preterite	
llevo	*levamos*	*levé*	*levamos*
llevas	*levades*	*levaste*	*levastes*
lleva	***llevan***	*levó*	*levaron*

~ *sufrimos* (0), *sofrides* (0) ~ *sufrides* (0), *sufren* (10) ~ *sofren* (0); pret. *sofrí* (3) ~ *sufrí* (0), *sufriste* (1) ~ *sofriste* (0), *sufrió* (29) ~ *sofrió* (1), *sofrimos* (6) ~ *sufrimos* (0), *sofristes* (0) ~ *sufristes* (0), *sufrieron* (3) ~ *sofrieron* (3).

In ADMYTE (vol.0), one finds: inf. **complir** (268) ~ **cumplir** (65); pres. *cumplo* (1), *cumples* (0) ~ *comples* (0), *cumple* (269) ~ *comple* (9), *cumplimos* (1) ~ *complimos* (0), *complides* (1) ~ *cumplides* (0), *cumplen* (22) ~ *complen* (1); pret. *complí* (5) ~ *cumplí* (0), *compliste* (2) ~ *cumpliste* (0), *cumplió* (63) ~ *complió* (12), *complimos* (1) ~ *cumplimos* (0), *complistes* (1) ~ *cumplistes* (0), *cumplieron* (11) ~ *complieron* (6); inf. *sobir* (109) ~ **subir** (57); pres. *subo* (2), *subes* (3) ~ *sobes* (0), *sube* (95) ~ *sobe* (0), *subimos* (1) ~ *sobimos* (0), *sobides* (2) ~ *subides* (0), *suben* (33) ~ *soben* (0); pret. *subí* (4) ~ *sobí* (3), *subiste* (1) ~ *sobiste* (0), *subió* (154) ~ *sobió* (8), *subiemos* (1) ~ *sobimos* (0) ~ *subimos* (0), *sobistes* (3) ~ *subiestes* (2) ~ *subistes* (0), *subieron* (58) ~ *sobieron* (7); inf. **sofrir** (287) ~ **sufrir** (99); pres. *sufro* (27), *sufres* (9) ~ *sofres* (0), *sufre* (121) ~ *sofre* (3), *sofrimos* (5) ~ *sufrimos* (3), *sofrides* (2) ~ *sufrides* (1), *sufren* (40) ~ *sofren* (1); pret. *sofrí* (3) ~ *sufrí* (1), *sofriste* (0) ~ *sufriste* (0), *sufrió* (50) ~ *sofrió* (4), *sufriemos* (1) ~ *sofrimos* (0) ~ *sufrimos* (0), *sofristes* (2) ~ *sufristes* (0), *sufrieron* (23) ~ *sofrieron* (10).

b. OSp. *levar* > ModSp. ***llevar***

Present:	***llevo*** → *levamos*		***llevo***	***llevamos***
	llevas *levades* >		***llevas***	***lleváis***
	lleva ***llevan***		***lleva***	***llevan***
	↓			
Preterite:	*levé* *levamos*		***llevé***	***llevamos***
	levaste *levastes* >		***llevaste***	***llevasteis***
	levó *levaron*		***llevó***	***llevaron***

I am simply suggesting here that all forms of the /o/-stem -*ir* verbs, including the infinitive, were likewise leveled by forms of the present tense, as shown in (17):

(17) OSp. *sobir* > ModSp. ***subir***

Present:	***subo*** → *sobimos*		***subo***	***subimos***
	subes *sobides* >		***subes***	***subís***
	sube ***suben***		***sube***	***suben***
	↓			
Preterite:	*sobí* *sobimos*		***subí***	***subimos***
	sobiste *sobistes* >		***subiste***	***subisteis***
	subió *subieron*		***subió***	***subieron***

This hypothesis is completely in line with the seventh of Manczak's nine hypotheses regarding the natural tendencies of analogical change, which states that the forms of the present more frequently bring about the remaking of the other tenses than vice versa (Hock 1991: 232).

The present hypothesis explains very neatly why *dormir* and *morir* did not undergo the /o/ > /u/ shift. The first person singular of these two verbs did not yield a stem vowel /u/, because their Latin etyma possessed open, not close /o/. As Professor Malkiel pointed out, DORMIO probably yielded *dormo, while MORIO(R) likely metathesized to *moiro. These two forms subsequently underwent a substitution of /o/ and /oi/ respectively by /we/, yieldeding /dwermo/ and /mwero/ (which thus fell in line with etymological *duermes*, *duerme*, *duermen* and *mueres*, *muere*, *mueren*, as demonstrated in (18a) with *morir*:

(18) a.

Old Latin	Later Latin	Pre-literary Spanish	Old Spanish
MORIO(R)	/mórjo/	/móiro/	*muero*
MORIS	/móres/	/muéres/	*mueres*
MORIT	/móre(t)/	/muére/	*muere*
MORIMUS	/morímos/	/morímos/	*morimos*
MORITIS	/morítes/	/morídes/	*morides*
MORIUNT	/móren(t)/	/muéren/	*mueren*

Had Latin DORMIO and MORIOR possessed a close /o/, and had metathesis of yod not occurred in the first person singular of MORIOR, I believe the development of these two verbs would have followed the path of all other /o/-stem *-ir* verbs, as depicted in the hypothetical development shown in (18b):

(18) b.

Old Latin	Later Latin	Old Spanish	Modern Spanish
**MŌRIRE	**MORIR(E)	**/morir/ ↑	***murir*
**MŌRIOR	**/múrjo/	**/múro/ ↓	***muro*
**MŌRIS	**/móres/	**/móres/	***mures*
**MŌRIT	**/móre(t)/	**/móre/	***mure*
**MŌRIMUS	**/morímos/	**/morímos/	***murimos*
**MŌRITIS	**/morítes/	**/morídes/	***murís*
**MŌRIUNT	**/móren(t)/	**/móren/	***muren*

The only reason *podrir* has been able to escape complete leveling to date in some regions is the fact that speakers probably utter the word *"pudro"* 'I rot' with much less frequency than they utter *cubro, cumplo, subo, sufro,* etc. Hence the slow acceptance of the variant *pudrir*.

I therefore conclude that it is not semantic vs. formal ingredients, but rather, the directionality of leveling in the Old Spanish verbal paradigm which is distillable from resistance to language shift in the case of *dormir, morir* (and *podrir*).

A couple of final points: There is one verb that is conspicuously absent from the list of /o/-stem *-ir* verbs in (1) of this section, namely, Old and ModSp. *oír* 'to hear'. Professor Malkiel excluded it from his general discussion (1993: 397): "If one, then, agrees to disregard the very special case of *oír* (older spelling: *oyr*) 'to hear', which poses unique problems, *dormir* and *morir* emerge from our survey as the sole two important exceptions from an otherwise sweeping tendency to eliminated from the inventory of Spanish verbs those that

reconciled the stem vowel *o* with protracted fidelity to the -*ir* conjugation class."
He explained the dismissal of *oír* from his analysis in a note (1993: 401 n. 6): "In
oír we encounter, for the first time, an *o* traceable, via the reconstructible diphthong *ou*, to a still earlier *au* (Lat. *audire*), as is dramatically confirmed by the
development in Portuguese: *ou-v-ir*. Moreover, the *o*, for once, is not preceded by
any consonant (or consonant cluster)." The reason Professor Malkiel wanted us to
disregard the continued presence of Sp. *oír* is obvious: It does not fit in with his
semantic analysis (i.e., *dormir* 'to sleep' ~ *morir* 'to die' ~ *oír* 'to hear'?)

These two "unique problems", however, do not seem to offer sufficient
grounds for exclusion of this verb from the present analysis. First, since the shift
of /o/ > /u/ occurred from Old to modern Spanish, the origin of the /o/ is irrelevant, as it would have been unknown (or at the very least, unimportant) to the
speakers who participated in the propagation of the shift, unless one were to claim
that speakers possess an inherent knowledge of the historical grammar of their
language (certainly not a claim that Professor Malkiel would have ever made).
Moreover, only if the different origin, i.e., Latin /au/, as opposed to Latin /o/ or
/u/, had had far-reaching effects, i.e., into the medieval period, would such a
distinction become relevant. For example, only if the outcome of /au/ on the one
hand and /o/ and /u/ on the other had been different in Old Spanish, would
speakers have perceived them differently, and perhaps excluded *oír* from the shift
of /o/ > /u/. However, it is doubtful that the *o* of OSp. *oír* (< AUDIRE) represented a
different phonetic realization than, for example, the *o* of OSp. *sobir* (< SUBIRE),
despite the Portuguese evidence (i.e., *ouvir*). On the contrary, Lat. /au/ had closed to
/o/ long before the shift of /o/ > /u/ in Old Spanish /o/-stem -*ir* verbs had begun.

The lack of a consonant or consonant cluster before the /o/ of OSp. *oír* also
seems to be insufficient grounds for its elimination from the present analysis. Yes,
no other verb in (1) of this section begins with the stem vowel. And yes, the only
other verb that does is OSp. *ofrir* 'to offer', which took an alternative escape rout,
i.e., *ofrir* > *ofrecer*. Professor Malkiel therefore may initially appear to have been
justified in discounting OSp. *oír* from the analysis. However, OSp. *foír*, whose
initial consonant became a glotal fricative (i.e., Late-medieval *huír* [hu-ír]) and
then went silent (i.e., ModSp. *huír* [u-ír]) was not eliminated from the shift of /o/
> /u/. If the [f] > [h] > [ø] change occurred before the /o/ > /u/ shift in OSp. *foír*
> ModSp. *huir*, then the /o/ > /u/ shift occurred in this verb without the presence
of an initial consonant. In fact, Dworkin believes the lack of the /o/ > /u/ shift in
Sp. *oír* may be due to the fact that speakers may have strived to avoid homonymy
(or at least near-homonymy) between these two verbs (1995: 538 n.14): "Various

workers have suggested that the presence of *huir* 'to flee' in the late medieval language blocked the transformation of *oír* 'to hear' to expected **uír*; cf. OSp. *complir, sobir, sofrir > cumplir, subir, sufrir*."

There is one verb, however, which underwent the shift of /o/ > /u/ whose stem vowel was not preceded by a consonant or consonant cluster and which Professor Malkiel appears to have overlooked: Sp. *urdir* 'to warp, plot, scheme, lie', the morphological reflex of Lat. ORDIRI 'to begin speaking'. Professor Malkiel may have intentionally excluded Sp. *urdir* from his analysis if he was under the mistaken impression, after consulting Penny (who is indeed cited in note 10 of Malkiel's article), that "in Old Spanish, some O/U verbs (e.g., *escurrir, incurrir, bullir, **urdir**, confundir*) always have stem /u/ [bold added]" (Penny 1991: 161). However, in the *General estoria IV* of the Alfonsine corpus (1280), one finds the following token of *ordir* in (19):

(19)   *Mas por q<ue> la discordia & el mal. siempre an sabor de entrar se de suyo en aq<ue>llas cosas q<ue> ueen q<ue> uan bien. & otrossi en las cosas q<ue> uee<n> estar & ueuir en paz; fueron algunos q<ue> eran sabidores dezir mal & **ordir** lo* (GE4, folio 162v).

Additionally, one finds the third singular preterite *ordió* in the GE1 (4 times), GE4 (twice), LAP (twice), MOA (3 times), PIC (3 times), EE2 (3 times), G2K (3 times), as well as third plural preterite *ordieron* in the GE4 (once) and pluperfect indicative *ordiera* in the G2K (once). Conversely, one finds only *urdió, urdiendo* and *urdiesse* one time each in the EE1, and *urdió* twice again in the GE4, but no occurrence of *urdir* anywhere in the Alfonsine corpus. The evolution of this infinitive therefore followed the same path as the other /o/-stem *-ir* verbs, i.e., OSp. *ordir* > ModSp. *urdir*, and can thus be accounted for within the present theoretical framework, as shown in (20):

(20)

Old Latin	Later Latin	Old Spanish	Modern Spanish
ORDIRI	ORDIR(I)	/ordir/	*urdir*
		↑	
ORDIOR	/úrdjo/	/úrdo/	*urdo*
		↓	
ORDIS	/órdes/	/órdes/	*urdes*
ORDIT	/órde(t)/	/órde/	*urde*
ORDIMUS	/ordímos/	/ordímos/	*urdimos*
ORDITIS	/ordítes/	/ordídes/	*urdís*
ORDIUNT	/órden(t)/	/órden/	*urden*

Nevertheless, even if OSp. *ordir* had not existed, and consequently there were no such verb as ModSp. *urdir*, as far as the inclusion or exclusion of OSp. *oír* is concerned, neither the claim that the lack of an initial consonant (Malkiel 1993: 401), nor the suggested avoidance of (near-)homonymy (Dworkin 1995: 538 n.14) is really necessary if one applies to OSp. *oír* the theoretical approach that I have suggested in the present section.

The regular phonetic development of first person singulars of OSp. *oír* and *foír* resulted in forms with stem vowel /o/ and /u/ respectively, thus: AUDIO > *[óðjo] > [ójo] OSp. *oyo*; but FUGIO > *[fuɣjo] > [fuʝo] OSp. *fuyo*. The present tense paradigms of these two verbs in Early Old Spanish were therefore identical except in the first person singular, as shown in (21):

(21)   EOSp. *oír*   EOSp. *foír*
    oyo   **fuyo**
    oyes   *foyes*
    oye   *foye*
    oímos   *foímos*
    oídes   *foídes*
    oyen   *foyen*

The stem vowel /u/ of first person *fuyo*, like that of *cumplo*, *subo*, *sufro*, etc., would ultimately level the rest of the paradigm, including the infinitive, as in (22):

(22)   EOSp. *foír*   Old and ModSp. *f/huir*
    fuyo   **f/huyo**
    ↓
    foyes   *f/huyes*
    foye   *f/huye*
    foímos   >   *f/huímos*
    foídes   *f/huídes*
    foyen   *f/huyen*

We have already seen how first person singular *fuyo* participated in a partial leveling of its paradigm as regards the palatal fricative: We now witness the complete leveling of *fuyo* as regards the stem vowel.

The only other point in need of an explanation is why the yod of AUDIO did not raise /o/ to /u/ (resulting in **uyo* instead of OSp. *oyo*), while the yod of FUGIO indeed raised /ʉ/ to /u/, yielding OSp. *fuyo*. One possible explanation for OSp. *oyo* instead of the expected **uyo* is, as Penny (1991: 165) states: "because this /o/ developed from AU (e.g., OSp. *oyo* < AUDIO) too late to be affected by the [j] which originally occurred in the verbal ending." If this is true, then Professor Malkiel was very close to the answer, but did not connect this lack of phonetic development in the first person singular of AUDIRE (i.e., AUDIO > [áu̯djo] > [óu̯ǰo] > [óǰo], not **[úǰo]) with the role the first person singular form played in general in the leveling (or not) of the other members of its paradigm (including the infinitive). It is also possible that the raising from [oðjo] > **[uǰo] may have been impeded by an association with the noun *oído* 'ear' (< AUDITU). Whatever the reason for the lack of vowel raising in the development of AUDIO > OSp. *oyo*, the fact remains that two different forms resulted in the first person of OSp. *oír* and *foír*, one with /o/ (OSp. *oyo*), the other with /u/ (OSp. *fuyo*). Had the development of AUDIO also resulted in a form with stem vowel /u/, I suspect that leveling of /o/ to /u/ would have occurred in all forms of this verb as well, as depicted in (23):

(23)	Latin	Early Old Span.		Hypothetical Old and Modern Span.
	AUDIRE	*oyr*	>	***uir**
		↑		
	AUDIO	***uyo**		***uyo**
		↓		
	AUDIS	*oyes*		***uyes**
	AUDIT	*oye*		***uye**
	AUDIMUS	*oímos*	>	***uímos**
	AUDITIS	*oídes*		***uídes**
	AUDIUNT	*oyen*		***uyen**

Now, before reaching some general conclusions on the directionality of leveling, I would like to address a point I made at the beginning of this section: That the present analysis is, in part, intended to be a tribute to the late Yakov Malkiel. One may wonder how the present analysis can be a tribute to Professor Malkiel if I disagree with the fundamental tenet of his 1993 article. I ask the reader's indulgence that I may report the following personal anecdote.

Several years ago, when I was awaiting the appearance of an article I had written on the development of Sp. *conmigo, contigo, consigo*, I came across a footnote in one of Professor Malkiel's articles which made reference to a forthcoming article by him on the same topic. I phoned him. He sent me a copy of his article. When I read it and discovered that we were in total disagreement, I was horrified. I wrote to him and asked if he thought I should retract my article, to which he said in a letter dated October 24, 1989: "I would not, under any circumstances, withdraw it (a hazardous gambit!)."

When my article appeared, I sent Professor Malkiel a reprint of it and apologized for my opposing view, to which he wrote the following in a letter dated February 4, 1991:

Dear Professor Rini,

I am not sure, at present, whether I have acknowledged or more circumstantially answered your December 21 letter, which is unlikely to have reached me before early January.

There is no need for you to worry about the fact that we may have reached somewhat different conclusions regarding the details of the development of (con)migo from MECUM, etc. Disagreements of this sort are perfectly normal and even healthy.

Through a regrettable twist of circumstances I expect to be kept extremely busy for a few months by various deadline-marked projects, so I am not in a position to take up the issue, however stimulating, right now. I am not unlikely to return to it at a later date, though, and can then take into account your experiment with an alternative solution to the problem at hand.

One of those things that keep me so busy at present is, incidentally, an attempt to replace one hypothesis that I formulated forty-five years ago (!) by a more plausible conjecture. Generally speaking, it is fun to tear to pieces one's own earlier thinking: Self-enamored scholars and scientists are almost worthless.

Sincerely,
Yakov Malkiel

So I would like to think that Professor Malkiel would view the present analysis, not as an attack on his 1993 article, but rather, as a continuation of his work on *dormir* and *morir*. For, I am fully aware that I would have never come to the conclusions I have reached here had it not been for Professor Malkiel's initial inquiry into the extraordinary survival of Sp. *dormir* and *morir*, a topic which had never been broached before his 1993 piece.

I now wish to draw some general conclusions regarding the directionality of leveling. First, I would like to point out that, although the present analysis reveals a real tendency for leveling in the Old Spanish verbal paradigm to stem from the first person singular, this observation by no means precludes that leveling may have gone in other directions as well, though further investigation into this matter is certainly welcome. For example, in a significant number of verbal paradigms, the first person singular in Old Spanish appears to have been leveled by the other forms of the paradigm, e.g., OSp. *cozer* 'to cook, boil': *cuego, cuezes, cueze*, etc. > ModSp. *cuezo, cueces, cuece*, etc.; OSp. *esparzir* 'to spill': *espargo, esparzes, esparze*, etc. > ModSp. *esparzo, esparces, esparce*, etc.; OSp. *tañer* 'to touch': *tango, tañes, tañe*, etc. > ModSp. *taño, tañes, tañe*, etc.; OSp. *plañir* 'to lament': *plango, plañes, plañe*, etc. > ModSp. *plaño, plañes, plañe*, etc.; OSp. *ceñir* 'to gird': *cingo, ciñes, ciñe*, etc. > ModSp. *ciño, ciñes, ciñe*, etc. One must ask, however, whether the modern Spanish first person singular forms resulted from leveling by the other inflected forms of the paradigm, or whether these new forms (i.e., *cuezo, esparzo, taño, plaño, ciño*), because of their very low frequency of use, were simply remodeled on the basis of the infinitive, in which case we would identify the infinitive as the source of leveling. The same question may be raised in the case of OSp. *meresco* 'I deserve', *conosco* 'I know', and *nasco* 'I am born', whose change to *merezco* [mereθko], *conozco* [konoθko], and *nazco* [naθko] respectively have been traditionally attributed to leveling by all other inflected forms of the present tense indicative paradigm, which exhibited *ç* [ts] in Old Spanish, later *z* [θ], e.g., OSp. *mereçes, mereçe*, etc.; OSp. *conoçes, conoçe*, etc.; *naçes, naçe*, etc. Penny (1991: 155) takes this view: "the /s/ of *meresco, -a*, etc., was replaced by the /ts/ of *mere(s)çes*, etc." However, the acquisition of unetymological [θ] in ModSp. *merezco, conozco*, and *nazco* might just as well have originated from the leveling force of their respective infinitives, which also exhibited *ç* in Old Spanish, i.e., OSp. *mereçer, conoçer, naçer* (—leveling→) *meresco, conosco, nasco* > *merezco, conozco, nazco*.

Notwithstanding the possibility of the infinitive as the source of leveling of the foregoing first person singular forms, we may not want to rule out altogether the possibility of the directionality of leveling originating in other inflected forms of the paradigm, particularly if we take into account examples from other languages. For instance, in some varieties of Black English, second person singular *you is*, clearly leveled by third person singular *he is*, probably occurs with more frequency than the alternative *you am*, the result of leveling from *I am*. And there is no question that the common American English *aren't I*, replacing *am I not*, is the result of leveling from second person singular *aren't you*. In light of this last example from American English, perhaps we might want to allow, at least for the history of Spanish, that leveling may have also gone in the direction of second person singular (—leveling→) first person singular, since, as Lloyd (1987: 303) has pointed out, these are the two basic forms of any dialogue. It therefore does not seem unreasonable that in some cases the first person leveled the second, while in other cases, the second leveled the first. This may be what happened in the abovementioned cases of Sp. *merezco, conozco, nazco,* and even *cuezo, esparzo, taño, plaño, ciño,* though further evidence would be needed to acertain that it was indeed the second person singular and not the infinitive, as suggested above.

Though interaction between the first and second persons singular may lead to leveling of the other form, it is not necessarily the case that leveling will proceed smoothly, or in any sort of a unilinear fashion. Rather, other factors may alter slightly the path of the leveling during the process. For example, though we might schematize the leveling process as a kind of domino effect, as exemplified in (24a) with the preterite of Old Spanish *fazer,* the textual evidence from ADMYTE (vol. 0) shown in (24b) suggests that in this case the leveling force of the first person singular was initially greater on the third person singular *fezo* than on the second person singular *feziste.* Whereas at this stage of the language second person *feziste* still outnumbers its leveled allomorph *fiziste,* in the third person, leveled *fizo* clearly predominates over non-leveled, nearly extinct *fezo* (actual number of occurrences appears after each form, followed by the percentage of occurrence in parentheses):

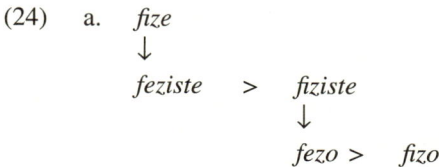

(24)　a.　*fize*
　　　　　↓
　　　　feziste　>　*fiziste*
　　　　　　　　　　　↓
　　　　　　　　fezo >　*fizo*

　　　b.　The Singular of the Preterite of OSp. *fazer* in ADMYTE vol. 0.
　　　　　fize
　　　　　feziste 63 (77.8%) ~ *fiziste* 18 (22.2%)
　　　　　fezo 117 (3.7%) ~ *fizo* 3,074 (96.3%)

　　　c.　Stage One　　　　　　　Stage Two　　　　　　　Stage Three
　　　　　fize (—continues→)　*fize* (—continues→)　*fize*
　　　　　↓　　　　　　　　　　↓
　　　　　　　　　　　　　　　feziste >　　　　　　*feziste* ~*fiziste*
　　　　　fezo >　　　　　　*fezo* ~ *fizo* >　　　(*fezo*) ~ *fizo*

The reason for the more advanced (and therefore, presumed earlier) stage of leveling from the first to the third person singular is probably that the third person form is the only other form of the paradigm which, like the first person, is disyllabic, and therefore bears the phonological stress on the stem, not the suffix. Since the leveling element of first person *fize* is the tonic stem vowel /í/, it should come as no surprise that a form with a similar structure, i.e., exhibiting a tonic stem vowel, would be the first form of the paradigm to be leveled. One might therefore represent the leveling process in this case, not as the domino effect in (24a), but rather as shown in (24c), where different forms are leveled at different stages (the path of leveling is shown in bold). Stage three of (24c) is intended to represent the stage of development according to the data from ADMYTE (vol. 0) shown in (24b), where leveling has produced by this point in time both *fiziste* and *fizo*, though the latter occurs with much more frequency *vis à vis* its non-leveled allomorph than does the former. The plural forms which did not exhibit a yod in their desinence (i.e., *fezimos* and *fezistes*), like second person singular *feziste*, lagged a bit behind the third singular in the leveling process, as the data from ADMYTE (vol. 0) show in (25):

(25)   The Plural of the Preterite of OSp. *fazer* in ADMYTE vol. 0.
   fezimos 27 (38.6%) ~ *fiziemos* 35 (50%) ~ **fizimos** 8 (11.4%)
   fezistes 65 (62.5%) ~ *fiziestes* 37 (35.5%) ~ **fizistes** 2 (2%)
   fizieron 991 (91.8%) ~ *fezieron* 89 (8.2%)

The preterite tense of *poder* and *poner*, according to the data from ADMYTE (vol. 0) in (26), exhibit an even more advanced stage of leveling in the third singular *vis à vis* the second singular and first and second persons plural, i.e., no occurrence of the expected **podo and **poso,[9] despite a predominance of second persons singular *podiste*, *posiste*, first persons *podimos*, *posimos*, and second persons plural *podistes*, *posistes*:

---

9. If, as stated in note 6, the formation of *pude* and *puse* was due metaphony of final /-i/ (Meyer-Lübke 1890: 334, Lloyd 1987: 308), then we may conclude that these leveled an earlier *podo and *poso (unattested, but possible forerunners of *pudo* and *puso*). However, if Lat. POTUI, POTUIT, POSUI, POSUIT developed to *POUTI, *POUTIT, *POUSI, *POUSIT via metathesis of /u/ (Menéndez Pidal 1941: 318, Penny 1991: 185), then the regular phonetic development of these may have led to *pude*, *pudo*, *puse*, *puso*, thus eliminating the need to account for third person *pudo* and *puso* via leveling from *pude* and *puse*. Since this matter of historical phonology remains unresolved, I have allowed for the possibility that leveling may have occurred here.

(26)   The Preterite of OSp. *poder* and *poner* in ADMYTE vol. 0.
pude 79 (100%)
podiste 13 (76.5%) ~ *pudiste* 4 (23.5%)
pudo 699 (100%) ~ *podo* 0
podimos 3 (100%) ~ *pudimos* 0
podistes 8 (100%) ~ *pudistes* 0
pudieron 282 (72.3%) ~ *podieron* 108 (27.7%)

puse 47 (100%)
posiste 11 (64.7%) ~ *pusiste* 6 (35.3%)
puso 824 (100%) ~ *poso* 0
posimos 10 (83.3%) ~ *pusimos* 2 (16.7%)
posistes 7 (87.5%) ~ *pusistes* 1 (12.5%)
pusieron 282 (81.5%) ~ *posieron* 64 (18.5%)

Finally, despite the example from Black American English of *you is* (presumably leveled by third person *he is*), I would not hasten to identify any third person form, singular or plural, as the source of any cases of leveling in the Old Spanish verbal paradigm, particularly in light of examples from that same variety of English such as *he do*, *she say*, etc., which appear to be the result of leveling from first person *I do*, *I say*, etc. (perhaps in conjunction with second person *you do*, *you say*, etc.). Other varieties of American English also exhibit such forms and more. For example, even among speakers who never say *he do*, *she do*, it is not uncommon to hear them utter *he don't*, *she don't* (i.e., contracted versions of *he do not*, *she do not*), clearly the result of leveling by *I don't*, *you don't* (and perhaps of extra-paradigmatic leveling as well by *I won't*, *you won't*, *he won't*, *she won't*).[10] In any event, there is more evidence against than there is for such a directionality of leveling in Old Spanish, and, moreover, such an assumption, as seen in the present analysis of Sp. *dormir* and *morir*, has often led scholars astray in their diachronic linguistic inquiries. I do not exclude the possibility, however, that such a directionality of leveling may be the tendency in other languages, given the language-specific nature of leveling, as hinted at by Hock (1991: 213).

---

10. Again, I wish to credit my son, Marcus, for bringing to my attention the examples *he/she don't* which, according to him, are often uttered by both African-American and Non-African-American classmates.

Old Spanish *ove, tove, estove, andove, sope, cope* > Modern Spanish *hube, tuve, estuve, anduve, supe, cupe*

Spaulding (1943: 114) offered three possible explanations for the change of /o/ > /u/ in OSp. *ove, tove, estove, andove, sope, cope*:

> The use of *u* has been variously explained as due to association with the *u* of *-ude* (*pude*, O. S. *estude*, O. S. *andude*) and *puse*; as beginning in the third person plural, where the presence of a *yod* (e.g., *sopieron*) acted to make closer the vowel of the syllable preceding, from the third person the *u* spread to the remaining persons and numbers; as resulting from the confusion in unstressed syllables (e.g., *sopiste, sopimos, sopistes, sopieron*) of *u* and *o*, then it spread to those forms in which the stem vowel is stressed (e.g., *sope, sopo*).

Like many other developments in the history of Spanish, one finds no consensus among the leading scholars regarding this point of Spanish historical grammar. For example, Alvar and Pottier (1983), Penny (1991), and Lathrop (1996) subscribe to one of the three hypotheses described by Spaulding, while Lloyd (1987) suggests something entirely new.

The last of the three hypotheses described by Spaulding, that /o/ first shifted to /u/ in unstressed syllables and then spread to stressed ones, can be quickly dismissed in light of some textual evidence. Data gleaned from ADMYTE (vol. 0) reveal that the use of stem vowel /u/ is actually higher in stressed stems, i.e., *uve/uvo, tuve/tuvo, estuve/estuvo, anduve/anduvo, supe/supo, cupe/cupo* occur at a rate of 11% (vs. 89% for their counterparts in /ó/), while *uviste/uvimos/uvistes, tuviste/tuvimos/tuvistes, estuviste/estuvimos/estuvistes,* and *anduviste/anduvimos/anduvistes, supiste/supimos/supistes, cupiste/cupimos/cupistes* occur at a rate of only 7% (vs. 93% for their counterparts in /o/). If the change had begun in the unstressed forms and spread to the stressed ones, one would expect a higher rate of occurrence of /u/ in the unstressed forms in the texts included in ADMYTE (vol. 0).

Penny (1991: 186) subscribes to the view which maintains that in later Old Spanish, the semivocalic onglide [j] of forms such as *ovieron, toviera, sopiesse, ploguiere*, etc. occasionally raised the /o/ of the preceding syllable to /u/, yielding *uvieron, tuviera, supiesse, pluguiere*, etc., thus likening this vowel inflection to that found in weak preterites (e.g., **dormió > durmió, *dormieron > durmieron*, etc.). By the 16th century, the latter forms totally ousted the former, and the /u/ of these forms "is then rapidly extended to those forms whose ending had never contained [j], so that *ove > uve, sopiste > supiste, tovimos > tuvimos*, etc."

(Penny 1991: 186). Alvar and Pottier (1983: 270) also adopt this view: "la *u* de *hube, -o* procede de las personas en que, etimológicamente, aparece (*hubieron*)."

The initial problem with this hypothesis is that, as demonstrated quite clearly above, leveling does not appear to proceed from third-person forms, at least in the cases from Spanish analyzed thus far. Moreover, vocalic inflexion by yod is characteristic of the 3rd conjugation only. The question therefore remains: Why would [j] have raised /o/ to /u/ in these verbs, all of which belong to the second conjugation (with the exception of first-conjugation *estar* and *andar*), but not in other verbs of the second conjugation? That is, why not *comió* > **cumió, *comiera* > ***cumiera, comiesse* > **cumiesse, etc., or *llovió* > **lluvió and *lloviendo* > **lluviendo, especially in light of the high back vowel of the substantive *lluvia*? These theoretical problems notwithstanding, I have put this hypothesis to the test and have found that there appears to be some evidence to support the contention that the yod of these forms indeed raised /o/ to /u/.

The data in (27) for the paradigms of *aver, tener, estar, andar, saber* and *caber* were gathered from ADMYTE (vol. 0). These data are divided in the case of each verb into (a) preterite forms whose stems lack [j], (b) preterite third person forms (whose stems contain [j]), and (c) third person singular forms of the imperfect subjunctive, pluperfect indicative, and future subjunctive (which also contain [j]):

(27)   AVER
    (a) ove   103 ~ uve   7
           oviste   29 ~ uviste   1
           ovo   1,994 ~ uvo   90
           ovimos   9 ~ uvimos   0
           ovistes   12 ~ uvistes   2

                2147   100
               (96%)   (4%)

    (b) ovieron   608 ~ uvieron   41
               (94%)   (6%)

    (c) oviesse   499 ~ uviesse   125
           oviera   157 ~ uviera   20
           oviere   326 ~ uviere   2

               982   147
              (87%)   (13%)

TENER

(a)	tove	19	~	tuve	13
	toviste	3	~	tuviste	1
	tovo	399	~	tuvo	52
	tovimos	2	~	tuvimos	0
	tovistes	2	~	tuvistes	0

425	66
(87%)	(13%)

(b)	tovieron	124	~	tuvieron	7
		(95%)			(5%)

(c)	toviesse	81	~	tuviesse	38
	toviera	24	~	tuviera	1
	toviere	59	~	tuviere	2

164	41
(80%)	(20%)

ESTAR

(a)	estove	7	~	estuve	5
	estoviste	2	~	estuviste	0
	estovo	118	~	estuvo	45
	estovimos	1	~	estuvimos	0
	estovistes	2	~	estuvistes	0

130	50
(72%)	(28%)

(b)	estovieron	24	~	estuvieron	16
		(60%)			(40%)

(c)	estoviesse	39	~	estuviesse	32
	estoviera	3	~	estuviera	3
	estoviere	8	~	estuviere	3

50	38
(57%)	(43%)

ANDAR

(a)

andove	1	~	anduve	3
andoviste	0	~	anduviste	0
andovo	20	~	anduvo	19
andovimos	1	~	anduvimos	0
andovistes	0	~	anduvistes	0

22	22
(50%)	(50%)

(b)

andovieron	6	~	anduvieron	14
	(30%)			(70%)

(c)

andoviesse	7	~	anduviesse	5
andoviera	1	~	anduviera	0
andoviere	2	~	anduviere	0

10	5
(67%)	(33%)

SABER

(a)

sope	13	~	supe	14
sopiste	2	~	supiste	1
sopo	593	~	supo	146
sopimos	1	~	supimos	0
sopistes	2	~	supistes	0

611	161
(79%)	(21%)

(b)

sopieron	183	~	supieron	62
	(75%)			(25%)

(c)

sopiesse	162	~	supiesse	78
sopiera	15	~	supiera	13
sopiere	33	~	supiere	7

210	98
(68%)	(32%)

CABER

(a)	cope	0	~	cupe	0
	copiste	0	~	cupiste	0
	copo	8	~	cupo	3
	copimos	0	~	cupimos	0
	copistes	0	~	cupistes	0

	8	3
	(73%)	(27%)

(b)	copieron	0	~	cupieron	1

(c)	copiesse	1	~	cupiesse	0
	copiera	0	~	cupiera	1
	copiere	6	~	cupiere	0

	7	1
	(87.5%)	(12.5%)

Regarding these data, one observes that although forms with /o/ predominated in all of the foregoing paradigms, forms with /u/ (vis à vis their counterparts in /o/) occurred at a higher percentage rate in the third person plural preterite than in preterites which lacked [j]. The combined occurrences of *uvieron, tuvieron, estuvieron, anduvieron, supieron,* and *cupieron* total 471 (17%) vs. *ovieron, tovieron, estovieron, andovieron, sopieron,* and *copieron* 2,368 (83%), as compared to combined occurrences of yod-less *uve, uviste, uvo, uvimos, uvistes, tuve, tuviste,* etc., *estuve, estuviste,* etc., etc. which total 402 (11%) vs. *ove, oviste,* etc., *tove, toviste,* etc., etc. 3,343 (89%). One also observes that in the imperfect subjunctive, pluperfect indicative, and future subjunctive, the percentage of forms in /u/ was even higher, i.e., *uviesse, uviera, uviere, tuviesse, tuviera, tuviere, estuviesse, estuviera, estuviere, anduviesse, anduviera, anduviere, supiesse, supiera, supiere, cupiesse, cupiera, cupiere* total 330 (19%) vs. *oviesse, oviera, oviere, toviesse, toviera, toviere, estoviesse, estoviera, estoviere, andoviesse, andoviera, andoviere, sopiesse, sopiera, sopiere, copiesse, copiera, copiere* 1,423 (81%).[11]

Evidence from *The Electronic Texts and Concordances of the Prose Works of Alfonso X, El Sabio* (Kasten et al 1997) further supports this hypothesis. In

---

11. The slightly lower percentage rate in the third person plural preterites (17%) vs. (19%) in other forms with [j] may be due to morphological influence of the corresponding preterite singulars, i.e., *ovo, tovo, estovo,* etc., which contain no yod.

addition to only one example of *supo* in the 14th-century *General estoria VI*, one finds *supieron* and *cupiessen* one time each in the *General estoria V* (13th-14th century), and three more occurrences of *supieron*, two of *supies* (i.e., *supiesse* with apocope of /-e/) and one each of *tuvies* (i.e., *tuviesse* with apocope of /-e/) *tuviessen*, and *tuvieron* in the 14th-century *General estoria II*. One might therefore conclude that the higher percentage rate of occurrence of /u/ in forms with [j] means that the change began in these forms. Yet, despite this textual evidence, other evidence from the history of Spanish complicates the matter.

As seen above, in cases where [j] clearly inflected the preceding /o/ to /u/, i.e., some forms of third conjugation verbs, e.g., *durmió, durmieron, durmiendo, durmamos* (< *[durmjámus] < DORMIAMUS), *durmáis* (< OSp. *durmades* < *[durmjátis] < DORMIATIS), no permanent leveling of the first and second person forms occurred, i.e., *dormí, dormiste, dormimos, dormistes*, not **durmí, **durmiste, **durmimos, **durmistes. According to Penny (1991: 182), one occasionally finds in Old Spanish forms such as *durmí, durmiste, durmimos,* and *durmistes*. It might appear as though these forms resulted from the leveling forces of *durmió, durmieron* etc. (though one could adopt the view that they are blends of etymological *dormimos, dormistes* and innovative *durmiemos, durmiestes*). Nevertheless, such forms were extremely rare. In the case of OSp. *dormir*, for example, no occurrence of **durmí, **durmiste, **durmimos, **durmistes appears in either volume of ADMYTE (nor does *durmieste, durmiemos, durmiestes*) though one indeed finds *dormí* 6 times, *dormimos* 11 (*dormiste* 0, *dormistes* 0). In the case of OSp. *morir*, one example of *muristes* appears in ADMYTE (vol. 0), and six examples of *murí* appear in ADMYTE (vol. 1), though the forms with stem vowel /o/ are more common (in vols. 0 & 1, one finds: *morí* 21, *moriste* 3, *morimos* 7, *moristes* 3). These rare forms with /u/ when no [j] is present indicate an attempt at leveling the paradigm, which ultimately failed, as such forms were eventually abandoned for those with stems in /o/. So the question remains: Why would forms such as *uvieron, tuvieron, supieron*, etc. be capable of leveling /o/ > /u/ permanently in the other forms of their paradigms when *durmieron, murieron*, etc., could not do the same to *dormí, dormiste*, etc.?

It seems that, even if one concedes that [j] was a contributing factor in the raising of /o/ > /u/ in the third person plural preterite, the imperfect subjunctive, the pluperfect indicative, and the future subjunctive of *aver, tener, estar, andar, saber*, and *caber* as the textual evidence from ADMYTE (vol. 0) and the 13th-century Alfonsine texts suggests, and even if one grants that the change may have begun in forms with [j], it is not likely that [j] alone caused the shift from

/o/ > /u/ in the rest of the paradigm. Rather, in light of our earlier discussion of the impact of the first person singular on other forms in the paradigm of various verbs during various periods in the history of Spanish, it seems that the shift of *oviste* > *hubiste*, *ovo* > *hubo* etc., *toviste* > *tuviste*, *tovo* > *tuvo* etc., *sopiste* > *supiste*, *sopo* > *supo*, etc., etc. would have been the result of leveling by the first person forms *uve*, *tuve*, *estuve*, *anduve*, *supe*, and *cupe*. But the question remains: What could have caused the initial shift of /o/ > /u/ in the first person singular?

Lloyd (1987: 366) provides an alternative solution to those described by Spaulding (1943: 114): "The development of the /o/ verbs to uniform preterites with the stem-vowel /u/ may be related to a general movement of sound symbolism." Lloyd explains that verbs of the 3rd conjugation tend to have high vowels in their stems and function as action verbs, whereas those of the 2nd conjugation tend to have mid-vowels in their stems and often function as non-action verbs (i.e., as stative and auxiliar verbs). Lloyd (1987: 366) therefore concludes: "What appears to have happened in the development of modern Spanish out of the medieval system is the association of high vowels with perfective aspect, and, as a consequence, the generalization of the high vowels in the stem of the rhizotonic verbs." This proposal could explain why /o/ would have shifted to /u/ in the first person singular, and subsequently throughout the paradigm of these verbs, without attributing the change to *pude* and *puse*, and to the even more unlikely metaphonic effect of [j] in the 2nd conjugation.

While I agree with Lloyd's proposal in principle, I believe that morphological factors had a hand in creating the association of the high vowel /u/ with perfective aspect. After all, Lloyd (1987: 366) invokes morphological factors in the case of verbs which replaced /e/ with /i/ in their perfect indicative forms (e.g., *veno*, *veniste* > *vino*, *viniste* through leveling by *vine*), which in effect helped to provide the model for the verbs which allegedly underwent the phonosymbolic shift of /o/ to /u/.

Lathrop (1996: 180), who subscribes to the first hypothesis mentioned by Spaulding (1943: 114), writes: "The *u* of these two verbs [*pude* and *puse*] was very powerful, and caused all of the verbs in the preceding section [*ove*, *tove*, *cope*, *sope*, *estove*, *andove*] to exchange their etymological *o* for an analogical *u*." However, this scenario would constitute a case of leveling across a single grammatical category, which in the present view of morphological change is theoretically unacceptable, since leveling, by nature, is paradigmatic (i.e., intraparadigmatic). Furthermore, Lathrop does not say why the /u/ of *pude* and *puse* would have been so powerful. If one were to accept, for the sake of argument, that leveling across one grammatical category is theoretically possible, it would still remain unclear how a minority of forms (i.e., *pude, puse*) would have leveled the majority (*ove, tove, cope, sope, estove, andove,* and rarer *plogue*). One might attempt to explain the leveling of the majority by the minority by noting that preterite forms of *poder* and *poner* were more frequent than most of the preterite forms of the verbs that underwent the shift (e.g., in ADMYTE vol. 0, stems in *pus-* total 1,162, stems in *pud-* total 1,064 vs. *sop-/sup-* 1,017, *tov-/tuv-* 622, *estov-/estuv-* 220, *andov-/anduv-* 64, *cop-/cup-* 12). However, following such a line of reasoning falls short in explaining this change since the preterite root of *aver* is the most frequent of all of these forms, e.g., *ov-/uv-* 2,896 (and in fact surpasses in frequency the total number of occurrences of *pus-* and *pud-* combined), yet this lexical morpheme too underwent the shift. These insurmountable difficulties bring to the fore the weakness of approaching this problem with the notion that leveling can occur across a single grammatical category.

There is independent evidence, however, that *pude* and *puse* affected the development of some verbs, as Penny (1991: 185–86) clearly points out: "The first [*puse*] serves as the model for analogical OSp. *respuse* (Latin perf. RESPONDI) 'I replied', while the second [*pude*] is the model for the following Old Spanish restructured preterites: *estude* 'I was', *andude* 'I went', **tude* (implied by OSp. fut. subj. *tudiere*) 'I had'." But OSp. *respuse* and *estude* most likely resulted, not from any leveling forces of *puse* and *pude*, rather, as Penny states, from analogy with these verbs.

As discussed in Chapter 1, analogy, like other morphological changes, occurs between forms that already share some similar feature or features. That is, in morphological change (whether we are speaking of leveling, analogy, blending, or contamination), forms which are already structurally (i.e., morphologically), syntactically, and/or semantically similar to one another become even more similar to each other in their phonetic and morphological make up (Hock 1991: 167). For example, in the case of OSp. *respuse*, one notes a structural similarity between the root of Lat. (RES-)PONDERE 'to reply' and PONERE 'to put' which no doubt led to the genesis of OSp. *respuse* on the basis of OSp. *puse*, despite the fact that there is no semantic connection between the two verbs. With regard to modern Spanish, Penny (1991: 186) further states that "MSp. *repuso* 'he replied', may be a descendant of OSp. *respuso* 'id.', curiously influenced by the pret. of *reponer* 'to replace')." But again, the influence of *reponer* on *responder* must be due to the structural similarity of the two: *re(s)pon(d)er*. The analogy would have occurred as shown in (28):

(28)   *(re)-poner*   :   *re(s)-pon(d)er*
       (re)-puse   :   X = *re(s)puse*

The structural similarity between the two forms can be at times quite minimal. Take the case of unetymological OSp. *fuxo* 'he fled' (cf. Latin FUGIT) which may have resulted from analogy based on the structural similarity between the desinence of its infinitive *foír* and that of etymological *destroír*, as depicted in (29):

(29)   *destroír*   :   *foír*
       destruxo   :   X = *fuxo*

In the case of *pude* and *estude* in (30), the connection was likely a syntactic one, since both *poder* and *estar* could function as auxiliary verbs, though the fact that both verbs exhibited perfects with dental consonants introduces here a structural similarity as well:

(30)   *poder*   :   *estar*
       pude   :   *estide* ~ X = *estude*

Analogy, in fact, played a major role in the formation of many of the strong perfects under examination here.

It is well known that after Latin perfect HABUI suffered metathesis of labio-velar /w/ and ensuing regular phonetic changes of /au/ > /o/, /b/ > /β/, and /-i/ > /-e/ yielding OSp. *ove* (i.e., [abwi] > [aubi] > [oβe]), Latin perfect TENUI was completely abandoned for analogically remodeled *tove* as shown in (31) because of the semantic similarity between the two verbs, i.e., HABERE 'to have' and TENERE 'to have, hold, posses', and because they were syntactically similar as well (both served as auxiliaries with the past participle):

(31)   *aver*   :   *tener*
       ove   :   X = *tove*[12]

Latin STETI yielded OSp. *estide* (whose stem vowel /í/ must be analogical to

---

12. Latin TENUI would have never developed to *tove* through regular phonetic development (i.e., [tenwi] > *[teuni]? > *[teune]?). Alvar and Pottier (1983: 270) suggest that TENUI, by analogy with HABUI, was replaced by *TEBUI, which underwent metathesis to *TEWBI and subsequently yielded *tove*. While the hypothetical *TEBUI and *TEWBI are not completely implausible reconstructions, the suggestion that /ew/ resulted in /o/ through regular phonetic development is not convincing (cf. /ew/ > /u/ in ModSp. *Europa*, dialectally [u-ró-pa]). It seems more likely that TENUI, on the basis of HABUI, would have been remodeled as *TABUI (> *TAUBI > *tove*).

that of *vine* and *fize* since regular phonetic development would have yielded *estiede*, cf. 3rd sg. *estiedo* Malkiel 1980). It is therefore generally accepted that OSp. *estove*, like OSp. *tove*, was remodeled on the basis of OSp. *ove* as shown in (32), though no reason is ever given for the connection between HABERE and STARE. I would like to suggest here that the link between these two verbs was syntactic — *estar*, like *aver*, functioned as an auxiliary; HABERE + past participle, STARE + present active participle. A semantic factor may have also been partially involved in the connection between these two verbs — in the third person singular *aver* functioned as an impersonal verb of existence, i.e., *ovo* 'there was/were', and similarly, *estovo* 'it was (there)':

(32) | *aver* | : | *estar* |
      | *ove* | : | X = *estove* |

It should be noted that the genesis of *estove* may have been later than that of *tove*, or at least it was not strongly propogated early on, judging by the fact that the former is relatively rare in the earliest texts. For example, one finds *tovieron* a total of 307 times in the *Estoria de Espanna I*, the *Estoria de Espanna II*, the *General estoria I*, and the *General estoria IV*, as compared to one occurrence of *estovieron* (in the *Estoria de Espanna I*). Likewise, *tovo* is found 409 times in the same texts, while no occurrence of *estovo* is found at all. In the 15th-century *General estoria V*, *estovo* is found only twice, *estovieron* once, and *estovimos* once. The most common form of the preterite of *estar* in the 13th and early-14th centuries is etymological *estide*, which began to receive competition from *estude*, the allomorph which arose through analogy with *pude* as shown above in (30). In the *Estoria de Espanna I*, the *Estoria de Espanna II*, the *General estoria I*, and the *General estoria IV*, *estido* is found 90 times, *estidieron* 45, *estudo* 23, and *estudieron* 23. One notes that allomorphs *estide/estude* were then joined by the rare *estode* (which appears as *estodiessen* in the 13th-century *Libro de saber de astronomía* and as *estodieron* 6 times in the *Estoria de Espanna II*).

OSp. *andar* appears to have followed the developmental path of *estar*. It is very likely that OSp. *andove* owed its morphological make up to OSp. *estove* as in (33), since it too functioned as an auxiliary for the present active participle:

(33) | *estar* | : | *andar* |
      | *estove* | : | X = *andove* |

Also like *estude* (analogically extended from *pude*), one finds *andude*, as in (34):

(34) *poder*   :   *estar*   :   *andar*
      pude   :   estude   :   X = *andude*

Evidence to support this scenario is found in the fact that the Old Spanish variant *andide* was undoubtedly created in imitation of etymological *estide*, as were others, most likely because of semantic and structural similarities. Compare in (35) another verb of motion, somewhat structurally similar to *estar*, namely, *entrar*, and structurally similar *demandar*, perhaps falsely reanalyzed as *dem* + *andar*:

(35) *estar*   :   *andar*   :   *entrar*   :   *demandar*
      estide   :   X = *andide*   :   X = *entride* :   X = *demandide*

But again, *andove*, like *estove*, was not abundant in the earliest period of Old Spanish, as the textual evidence shows a preponderance of *andide* and *andude*. In the entire Alfonsine corpus, one finds only one occurrence of the stem *andov-*, as *andouo*, in the 15-century *General estoria V*, whereas in the *Estoria de Espanna I*, the *Estoria de Espanna II*, the *General estoria I*, and the *General estoria IV*, for example, one finds *andido* 70 times, *andidieron* 44, *andudo* 24, and *andudieron* 43. Also, like the rare *estode*, one finds *andodieron* once in the *Estoria de Espanna II*.

The forms *sove* (of *seer*), *crove* (of *creer* and *cresçer*), and *atrove* (of *atrever*) have also been explained as analogical imitations of OSp. *ove* (Penny 1991: 185), but again, no reason is ever given for their alleged association with this verb. It seems that a connection with *estar* as in (36) would have first been made in the case of *seer* on semantic grounds — *estar* 'to be (standing)' ~ *seer* 'to be (seated)':

(36) *estar*   :   *seer*
      estove   :   sove

Next, in imitation of *seer*, speakers would extend analogically -*ove* to *creer* as in (37) because of the structural similarities between it and *seer* (the infinitives themselves, as well as their past participles *seído*, *creído*), as seen above in the unquestionable case of *responder* and its association with *(re)poner*:

(37) *seer*   :   *creer*
      sove   :   crove

OSp. *cresçer* would then adopt the same form as in (38) because of the same structural similarity:

(38)   *creer*   :   *cre(ç)er*
       crove   :   *crove*

And finally, OSp. *atrever*, admittedly only minimally similar in structure to *creer* and *cresçer* (the common factors being a *muta cum liquida* cluster and a vocalic pattern /e...é/), apparently followed the lead of these verbs, giving rise to *atrove* as shown in (39), though perhaps association of medial -*v*- of the infinitive with that of *ove*, etc. played a role in the genesis of this form:

(39)   *creçer*   :   *atrever*
       crove   :   *atrove*

The forms *estove* and *andove* became increasingly popular after the 13th century, though they did not immediately oust earlier *estide*, *estude*, and *andide*, *andude*, thus producing a state of polymorphism. Speakers of Castilian in the Middle Ages therefore experienced a period in which they were exposed to these multiple variants, if indeed they themselves did not vacillate between innovative *estove*, *andove*, and older *estide/estude/(estode)*, *andide/andude/(andode)*. This polymorphic situation was conducive to the introduction at this point of yet another morphological process, namely, blending. Blending, as discussed and defined in Chapter 1, is a morphological compromise between two forms with identical or similar meaning, which are perceived as being in competition with each other; the competition between the multiple variants is often the result of other morphological processes, like analogy (Hock 1991: 189). Lloyd (1987: 365) suggests just this regarding the creation of *andudo* when he describes "the compromise form that blended *andido* and *anduvo* into *andudo* (possibly supported by *pudo*)." However, since *andudo* is attested much earlier than *anduvo* (and even *andovo*), it makes more sense to suggest that *andudo* resulted from analogy with *poder* and *estar* as shown earlier in (34). Nevertheless, I believe that the basis of Lloyd's tenet, that multiple variants blended to create an innovative form, is correct. I would therefore like to suggest here that innovative *estove* and *andove* were blended with older, but still extant, *estude* and *andude*, resulting in *estuve* and *anduve*.[13]

---

13. Hanssen (1913: 115) believed that different forms merged or blended to form new ones, though he was not clear about whether *estuve* resulted from a blend of *estude* and *estove*, or *pude*, *puse* and *estove*. Under "Confusión de las Categorías Enumeradas", which include *pude*, *puse*, etc., *ove*, *tove*, etc., *estide*, *andide*, etc., *crove*, *sove*, etc., he wrote: "Se forman diferentes combinaciones. Por ejemplo, el pretérito de *estar* tiene en lo antiguo las siguientes formas: *estide*, *estude*, *estove*, *estode*, *estuve*."

The forms *estuve* and *anduve* (along with still extant allomorphs *estude* and *andude*) would then exert pressure on *ove* as depicted in (40), via the same syntactic connection that originally led to the remodeling of *estide/estude* and *andide/andude* as *estove* and *andove* respectively:

(40)   *estar*   :   *aver*
       estove ~ *estuve*   :   *ove* ~ X = *uve*

Next, given the structural similarities between the infinitive *aver* on the one hand, and *saber* (and *caber*) on the other, the pattern *aver*: *ove* ~ *uve* would produce new allomorphs for *saber* and *caber* as follows in (41):

(41)   *aver*   :   *saber*   :   *caber*
       ove ~ *uve* :   *sope* ~ X = *supe*[14] :   *cope* ~ X = *cupe*[15]

As a result of this development, forms with allomorphs in /u/ now outnumbered those forms with stem vowel /o/: *pude*, *puse*, *estuve* ~ (*estude*), *anduve* ~ (*andude*), *uve* vs. *tove*. Add to these, those Old Spanish perfect indicative forms which descended from Latin with /u/ already in their stem, e.g., ADUXI > *aduxe* (*aduzir*), CONDUXI > *conduxe* (*conduzir*), COGNOVI/*COGNOVUI > *conuve* (*conosçer*), DESTRUXI > *destruxe* (*destroír*), and any verb remodeled on the basis of these, e.g., *fuxe* (*foír*). With alternations between *estove* ~ *estuve* ~ (*estude*), *andove* ~ *anduve* ~ (*andude*), *ove* ~ *uve*, *sope* ~ *supe*, *cope* ~ *cupe*, it would not be long until speakers of Medieval Spanish began to alternate as well, between *tove* ~ *tuve*, especially given its semantic connection to *aver*. With no such alternation in the cases of *puse* and *pude*, and perhaps with the aid of the phonosymbolic factor suggested by Lloyd, the ultimate triumph of *estuve*, *anduve*, *uve*, *supe*, *cupe*, and *tuve* over allomorphs with stem vowel /o/ is not surprising.

Thus according to the foregoing theoretical diachronic sketch of the shift

---

14. Penny (1991: 164) recognizes the importance of the structural similarity between *aver* and *saber* in a discussion of the formation of *sé*: "The form *sé* is best explained as an analogical imitation of *he*, due to the considerable structural similarity between the verbs *haber* and *saber*..."

15. The [p] of ModSp. *cupe* and *supe* is the expected outcome in Castilian, where sonorization of Latin /-p-/ > Castilian /-b-/ was blocked by the semivowel of the diphthong [au̯] at the stage */kau̯pi/, */sau̯pi/ (< *CAPUI, SAPUI). Compare sonorization of /-p-/ > /-b-/ where /-p-/ is truly intervocalic, as in the infinitives: CAPERE, SAPERE > *caber*, *saber*. By the time the [au̯] had closed to [o] (as found in OSp. *cope*, *sope*), the sound change /-p-/ > /-b-/ was no longer operant.

from /o/ > /u/ in these verbs, *estuve* and *anduve* were the first to acquire /u/, followed by *uve*, *supe* and *cupe*. Textual evidence supports this proposed series of events. In a sample of forms with tonic stem vowels (i.e., first and third person singular) from ADMYTE (vol. 0), *anduv-* and *estuv-* are found to occur with respect to their counterparts *andov-* and *estov-* at a higher degree of frequency than any of the other verbs involved in the change, e.g., *anduve/ anduvo* 51%, *estuve/estuvo* 29% vs. *cupe/cupo* 27%, *supe/supo* 21%, *tuve/tuvo* 13%. One assumes that when a new variant is introduced into an existing system it competes with the older form or forms for some time. At first, the new form will occur less frequently than the older ones. Over time, it will gradually become more accepted and therefore occur more and more frequently, until eventually it becomes more frequent than the older forms. Finally, the innovative form will become the preferred one, and the others will be left in the past. If this assumption is true, then the higher degree of frequency of forms with /ú/ may mean that these forms were introduced into the system before the others. Thus the higher percentage rates of *anduv-* and *estuv-* may mean that these two verbs were indeed first in line in the chain of events. The other verbs fall in line in the expected order, with the exeption of *aver*, i.e., *uve/uvo* (4%) vs. *ove/ovo* (96%), and the reversed order of *andar* and *estar*. But the relatively low percentage rate of *uv-* (4%) as compared to *cup-* (27%), *sup-* (21%) and *tuv-* (13%) does not necessarily mean that *ov-* was not affected by *estuv-* and *anduv-* before *sop-* and *cop-* acquired *sup-* and *cup-* as suggested above. It could very well be that *ov-* indeed acquired its allomorph *uv-* earlier than did *sop-* and *cop-*, but that the diffusion of /u/ in the preterite paradigm of *aver* was slowed down by the very high frequency of occurrence of this verb. Regarding frequency and morphological change, Penny (1991: 101) writes: "The more frequent a set of forms, the less likely it is to be affected by analogy." In the sample taken from ADMYTE (vol. 0), *ov-* occurred 2,097 times, while the others occurred much less frequently: *sop-* 606, *tov-* 418, *estov-*125, *andov-* 21, *cop-* 8. Likewise, the higher frequency of *estov-* vis à vis *andov-* could perhaps explain why the frequency of *anduv-* (51%) is higher than that of *estuv-* (29%). The same can be said for the low number of occurrences of *cop-* (8) vis à vis *sop-* (606) which accounts for the higher degree of frequency of *cup-* (27%) than of *sup-* (21%). Finally, the slow acceptance of *uve* in general can be seen in the still low frequency of *uv-* (3%) vs. *ov-* (97%) in ADMYTE (vol. 1), while all other stems in /ú/ have increased in popularity: *sup-* (72%), *anduv-* (66%), *cup-* (55%), *estuv-* (32%), *tuv-* (20%).

To conclude: There appears to be some truth to the first two hypotheses described by Spaulding (1943: 114) at the beginning of this chapter. Textual evidence seems to indicate that the change of /o/ > /u/ may have begun in the third person plurals *estuvieron, tuvieron, supieron*, etc. However, there is no evidence that the /u/ of these forms spread to the others — to the contrary, there is plenty of evidence from the observations of the directionality of leveling in Old Spanish that the change was carried to completion only when the first person singulars *estove, tove, sope*, etc. shifted to *estuve, tuve, supe*, etc. The present view attributes the shift in the first singulars, not to the influence of *pude* and *puse* as one of the traditional views maintains, but primarily to the blending of multiple variants within the same paradigm, i.e., *estude* X *estove* > *estuve*, etc. The form *puse* played virtually no role in the development of these verbs, while *pude* was found to have played a minimal role (i.e., only as base form 1 in the case of *estude* and *andude*). Finally, it is conceded that the phonosymbolic factor introduced by Lloyd (1987: 366) may have aided in the final decision between forms with /o/ and forms with /u/, but is not viewed here as the cause of the change.

Old Spanish *aperçebir, perçebir, reçebir, escrevir, bevir* > Modern Spanish *apercibir, percibir, recibir, escribir, vivir*: A Case of Leveling or Reanalysis?

It is difficult to account for the pretonic /i/ in the modern Spanish infinitives *apercibir, percibir, recibir, escribir, vivir* in light of the pretonic /e/ of ModSp. *concebir* and *decir*. This contrast presents a particularly perplexing puzzle for specialists of the history of Spanish, given that the early history of all of these infinitives is virtually identical. The ancestral forms of these infinitives originally belonged to the third conjugation in Latin, but then shifted to the fouth i.e., CONCIPERE, PERCIPERE, RECIPERE, DICERE, SCRIBERE, VIVERE > *concipire, *percipire, *recipire, *dicire, *scribire, *vivire.[16] Then, at some point along the continuum from Spoken Latin to Old Spanish, these infinitives (i.e, either Spoken Latin *concipire, *percipire, *recipire, *dicire, *scribire, *vivire, or Early OSp. *conçibir, (a)perçibir, reçibir, dizir, escrivir, bivir*) underwent a fairly powerful phonological process whereby the atonic stem vowel /i/ dissimilated from the tonic infinitival vowel /í/, yielding OSp. *conçebir,*

---

16. This shift has been attributed to the high stem vowel /í/ of the inflected forms, as in DICO, DICIS, DICIT, etc. (Lloyd 1987: 283–84).

(a)perçebir, reçebir, dezir, escrevir, bevir.[17] The effects of this particularly powerful dissimilatory tendency, which may be formulized as /i/.../í/ > /e/.../í/ (Penny 1991: 159), can also be found in grammatical categories other than the verb, e.g., Lat. VICINU 'neighbor' > OSp. *vezino,* Lat. VINDEMIA 'vintage' > **vindimia > vendimia.* Dialectically, one also finds *civil* 'civil' > *cevil, milicia > melicia* (García de Diego 1951: 129). During the Middle Ages, allomorphs without a dissimilated stem vowel do appear in the case of some verbs (e.g., *reçibir, escrivir, bivir),* though dissimilated *conçebir, (a)perçebir, reçebir, dezir, escrevir, bevir* were clearly preferred in the early period.

Those verbs which did not undergo permanently the /e/ > /i/ change, i.e., ModSp. *decir, concebir,* generally appeared as *dezir* and *conçebir* in Old Spanish, though occurrences of *conçebir* are extremely rare. For example, in Royal and non-Royal Scriptorium Alfonsine prose, one finds *dezir* 3,399 times (99.6%) vs. *dizir* 15 times (0.4%); *conçebir* 1 vs. *conçibir* 0.

The extent to which Old Spanish variants with stem vowel /e/ outnumbered those with stem vowel /i/ in those verbs which underwent the /e/ > /i/ change is as follows in 13th-century Royal Scriptorium Alfonsine prose texts (number of occurrences appears in parentheses): *aperçebir* (6) ~ *aperçibir* (0), *perçebir* (3) ~ *perçibir* (0), *reçebir* (312) ~ *reçibir* (3), *escrevir* (88) ~ *escrivir* (73), *bevir* (167) ~ *bivir* (11). In the 14th-century texts analyzed for this study,[18] one finds the following: *aperçebir* (9) ~ *aperçibir* (0), *perçebir* (2) ~ *perçibir* (0), *reçebir* (187) ~ *reçibir* (42), *escrevir* (35) ~ *escrivir* (64), *bevir* (180) ~ *bivir* (5). In 15th- and 16th-century texts,[19] one finds: *aperçebir* (0) ~ *aperçibir* (0), *perçebir* (2) ~ *perçibir* (0), *reçebir* (69) ~ *reçibir* (2), *escrevir* (95) ~ *escrivir* (12), *bevir*

---

17. In the development of Lat. VIVERE, a consonantal dissimilation also occurred, i.e., *v-vir > b-vir* (Malkiel 1975) such that one finds four variants in Old Spanish: *vivir, vevir, bivir,* and *bevir.* In 13th-century Alfonsine prose, forms with initial *v-* outnumber those with consonantal dissimilation by a margin of 190 (64.4%) to 105 (35.6%). In post-Alfonsine works, the trend is reversed. In the 14th-century texts analyzed for this study, forms with *b-* outnumber those with *v-* 112 (91.8%) to 10 (8.2%), and in the 15th and 16th centuries, 226 (90.4%) to 24 (9.6%).

18. These texts include 14th-century Royal and non-Royal Scriptorium Alfonsine prose texts, as well as the *Cauallero Çifar* (Olsen 1984), the *Cuento de Tristán de Leonis* (Corfis 1985), the *Obra completa de Juan Manuel* (Ayerbe-Chaux 1986), and the *Libro de buen amor* (Mignani et al 1977).

19. These texts include the *Libro de las doñas* (Lozano 1992), *Historia del gran Tamerlán* (Rodríguez et al 1986), *Tratado de patologia general* (Herrera 1987), *Ordenanzas reales* (Corfis & Petit 1990), *Corbacho* (Naylor 1983), *Arte Cisoria* (O'Neill 1987), *Cancionero de las obras de Juan del Enzina* (Temprano 1983), *Claros varones de Castilla* and *Letras* (Dangerfield 1986), *Defenssa de virtuossas mugeres* (Montoya 1992), *Cancionero Castellano* (Black 1985).

(128) ~ *bivir* (115).[20] The percentage rate of occurrence of these variants over the course of these three centuries according to textual evidence is shown in (42):

		13th century	14th century	15th/16th centuries
(42)	*aperçebir*:	100%	100%	100%
	aperçibir:	0%	0%	0%
	perçebir:	100%	100%	100%
	perçibir:	0%	0%	0%
	reçebir:	99%	82%	97%
	reçibir:	1%	18%	3%
	escrevir:	55%	35%	89%
	escrivir:	45%	65%	11%
	bevir:	94%	97%	53%
	bivir:	6%	3%	47%

In view of the foregoing data, one notes the following important facts: (a) The change from OSp. *aperçebir* and *perçebir* to ModSp. *apercibir* and *percibir* is a late development; (b) Despite the fluctuation in the popularity of *reçibir* and *escrivir* after the 13th century, they have clearly made their entrance into the system by the 14th century, particularly in the case of *escrivir*; (c) Though already rivalled by *bivir*, OSp. *bevir* predominates during the 13th and 14th centuries, after which *bivir* experiences a sudden surge in popularity.

From the 16th century onward, *bivir*, *escrivir*, and *reçibir* continued to increase in popularity until totally ousting older *bevir*, *escrevir*, and *reçebir*. Also, at some point after the 16th century, ModSp. *apercibir* and *percibir* made a sudden appearance, perhaps following the lead of *reçibir*, given the fact that all three shared a root morpheme (i.e., (*a*) + *per-*, *re-* + -*çebir* > -*cibir*).

In view of the foregoing brief outline of the histories of these infinitives, one might ask the following questions: What could have caused structurally similar verbs whose histories began in identical fashion to go eventually in seemingly opposite directions? What forces could have aided OSp. *aperçebir*, *perçebir*, *reçebir*, *escrevir*, and *bevir* in overcoming the powerful dissimilatory factor of /i/.../í/ > /e/.../í/, and why were such factors unsuccessful in the case

---

20. Although no occurrence of *aperçebir* was found in the 15th- and 16th-century texts analyzed here, its existence may be inferred by the frequent occurrence of the past participle *aperçebido*.

of OSp. *conçebir* and *dezir*? A satisfactory answer to these questions has not been forthcoming in the literature on the history of Spanish. For example, no reasonable explanation can be found in Menéndez Pidal (1941), García de Diego (1951), Alvar and Pottier (1983), Lapesa (1983), Lathrop (1984, 1996), or Lloyd (1987). Menéndez Pidal (1941: 272–75), for example, only comments that "estos dos verbos [*bevir* and *escrevir*] no prosperaron sino entre el vulgo" and that "**recipio**, a pesar de su hermano *concebir*, hizo todas sus formas con *i*" marking the forms *recibir, recibimos, recibiste*, etc. as analogues of *vivir, vivimos, viviste*, etc., and *escribir, escribimos, escribiste*, etc. His implication is that the latter are the "correct" outcome because Latin had /i/ in the stem and that the temporary /i/.../í/ > /e/.../í/ shift was eventually overcome (but by what factor he does not say) except among the *vulgos*. García de Diego (1951: 129) later made no advance whatsoever. One only notes an obvious 20th-century bias from his statement: "Hay algunos casos de disimilación entre vocales, sobre todo en el caso *i-i*, **dicere** vulg. *dicir* culto *decir*...**scribere** *escribir* ant. y vulg. *escrebir*, **vivere** *vivir* ant. y vulg. *vevir*." He does not explain why the modern forms in each case won out, nor why *decir* should be considered "culto" while *escrebir* and *vevir* "vulgar". If disimilation is a regular change, and *escrebir* and *vevir* are therefore considered "vulgares", then so should *decir*. Only Penny (1991: 159–60) recently and Hanssen (1913: 96) earlier in the 20th century attempt to provide an explanation.

Penny (1991: 159–60) attributes the shift of OSp. *escrevir, bevir*, and *reçebir* > ModSp. *escribir, vivir*, and *recibir* to learned influence:

> Occasionally, however, learned influences have overcome this dissimilatory force in the early modern period, since the most usual Old Spanish forms *escrevir* (< SCRIBERE) and *bevir* (< VIVERE) were replaced, in educated usage, in the Golden Age by *escribir* and *vivir*, forms no doubt felt to be in closer accord with their etyma. Similarly remodelled is one E/I verb, RECIPĬRE, which in Old Spanish most frequently appeared as *recebir*, but which adopted the stem-vowel /i/ (*recibir*) in more recent times, in imitation of RECĬPERE [with Ĭ = [i], not [i̯]].

And further on he adds (1991: 190):

> Variation between /e/ and /i/ was at that time [sixteenth century] largely resolved in favour of /e/, at least in part due to the dissimilatory interaction between stem-vowel and infinitival vowel ... , whence MSp. *decir, medir, sentir,* but with infrequent exceptions like MSp. *escribir, recibir* (OSp. also *escrevir, recebir*) due to learned interference stemming from the form of corresponding Latin verbs (SCRIBERE, RECIPERE, etc., read aloud with stem /i/).

Penny's proposal is not totally unreasonable, since it constitutes a fairly common type of morphological change. In effect what he is suggesting is blending of the Old Spanish (or popular) and Latin (or learned) forms in each case, i.e., OSp. *escrevir* X Lat. SCRIVERE > ModSp. *escribir*, OSp. *bevir* X Lat. VIVERE > ModSp. *vivir*, OSp. *reçebir* X Lat. RECIPERE > ModSp. *recibir*. And while I agree with Penny that *escribir* and *vivir* would have been felt to be more in line with their Latin counterparts by educated writers of the Golden Age, Penny's proposal does not explain why Lat. CONCIPERE and DICERE did not cause OSp. *conçebir* and *dezir* to shift to *concibir and *dicir in modern Spanish. Surely these Latin verbs, especially DICERE, would have been as well known to educated speakers as Lat. SCRIBERE, VIVERE, and later, RECIPERE. Moreover, one would expect influence of Lat. VIVERE on OSp. *bevir* to affect not only the pronunciation, but also the spelling of the verb, such that one should find an increase of forms with initial *v-* along with the increase of forms with the stem vowel /i/. But according to the data from texts analyzed for this study, when the frequency of *bivir* had increased from 3% in the 14th century to 47% in the 15th and 16th centuries, forms with initial *b-* still outnumbered those with initial *v-*, 90.4% vs. 9.6% respectively (see note 16). And what about the other verbs involved in the change? Does the same explanation, i.e., influence from (AD)PERCIPERE apply to *apercibir* and *percibir*? It seems that these two Latin verbs would have been less common during the Golden Age than DICERE (and even CONCIPERE), yet OSp. *aperçebir* and *perçebir* indeed shifted to *apercibir* and *percibir*. Clearly, some other factor or factors had to be involved in the overpowering of the dissimilation of /i/.../í/ > /e/.../í/.

Perhaps this was simply a case of leveling. The phonological change of /i/.../í/ > /e/.../í/ brought about assymmetry between the infinitive and some inflected forms of the paradigm. Observe in (43) the disruption of symmetry as exemplified in bold print in the following paradigms of the present indicative:

(43)   Early Old Spanish   Medieval Spanish
        reçibir   >   **reçebir**

        reçibo   *reçibimos*   >   *reçibo*   **reçebimos**
        reçibes   *reçibides*   >   *reçibes*   **reçebides**
        reçibe   *reçiben*   >   *reçibe*   *reçiben*

From Medieval to modern Spanish, symmetry has been restored to its original state, as it had been in Early Old Spanish as shown in (44):

(44)   Medieval Spanish   Modern Spanish
        reçebir   >   *recibir*
        reçibo   ***reçebimos***   >   *recibo*   *recibimos*
        reçibes   ***reçebides***   >   *recibes*   *recibís*
        reçibe   *reçiben*   >   *recibe*   *reciben*

Based on what we have seen thus far in this chapter with regard to the direction-ality of leveling in the Old Spanish verbal paradigm, one might be tempted to suggest that first person *reçibo, bivo, escrivo*, etc. leveled *reçebir, bevir, escrevir*, etc. Hanssen (1913: 96), by the way, made this very suggestion earlier this century: "Otros [verbos] han generalizado la *i*: *vivir, escribir, recibir*, etc." We saw in the cases of OSp. *cobrir, complir, sobir, sofrir*, for example, that the leveling which reached the infinitive was based on the first person singular of the present indicative, i.e., *subo* (—leveling→) *sobir* > *subir*, etc. It appears that we have the same conditions in the verbs under consideration here. In fact, verbs such as *sobir* and *reçebir* displayed similar patterns as shown in (45), not only in the present indicative, but also in the preterite, where the third person singular and plural forms exhibited vocalic inflexion by yod:

(45)   <u>Present and Preterite Indicative of Old Spanish *sobir* and *reçebir*</u>
        pres.ind. ***subo***   *sobimos*   ***reçibo***   *reçebimos*
                   subes   *sobides*   *reçibes*   *reçebides*
                   sube   *suben*   *reçibe*   *reçiben*

        pret.   *sobí*   *sobimos*   *reçebí*   *reçebimos*
                   sobiste   *sobistes*   *reçebiste*   *reçebistes*
                   subió ***subieron*** ***reçibió*** ***reçibieron***

However, the leveling found to have occurred from the present indicative to the preterite in the case of *cobrir, complir, sobir, sofrir*, etc., indeed did not occur in the case of *reçebir*. While preterite *subí* was found in Old Spanish, no occur-rence of **reçibí* appears in the Alfonsine corpus (only *recebí*, three times, in the *Estoria de Espanna I*, and the *General Estoria I, IV*), and in ADMYTE (vols. 0 & 1), only three occurrences of *reçibí* are found vs. 29 occurrences of *reçebí*, and all three appear in the *Esopete Historiado*, copied, at the latest, in 1482. This observation reveals the fact that the /i...í/ > /e...í/ change and the /e...í/ pattern was too powerful to be overcome by simple leveling.

Even if one were to find that *reçibo*, etc., had indeed leveled the corre-sponding preterite forms in Old Spanish, the question would still remain: Why not ModSp. *dicir and *concibir because of *digo* and *concibo*? Moreover, there were (and still are) many verbs that displayed alternation between pretonic /e/ of the infinitive and /i/ of inflected forms, e.g., OSp. *deçir* 'to descend', *ceñir* 'to gird', *feñir* 'to knead' *comedir* 'to govern', *fenchir* 'to swell', *medir* 'to measure', *pedir* 'to ask for' etc., yet these verbs were not permanently leveled to **diçir, **ciñir, **fiñir, **comidir, **finchir, **midir, **pidir, etc. It should also be noted that in the case of *dezir*, most Spanish philologists believe that the past participle *dicho* was leveled by the /i/ of inflected forms such as Spoken Latin *dico, *dices, etc., since Lat. DICTUM would have otherwise evolved to **[detʃo] (i.e., [dȋktum] > [dektu] > [deχto] > [deȋto] > [deȋtjo] > [deȋtʃo] > **[detʃo]). Why was the past participle leveled, but not the infinitive? In view of the leveling of *dicho*, it is even more difficult to understand why some verbs would have been leveled while *dezir* was not. Although leveling has been shown to be the cause of the remaking of some infinitives, e.g., *sobir* > *subir*, *levar* > *llevar*, we are still without an explanation for why OSp. *aperçebir, perçebir, reçebir, escrevir,* and *bevir* would have been leveled while other infinitives were not, if we only consider inflected forms of the verbal paradigm as potential leveling factors.

Perhaps one might suggest that there were different factors in the case of each verb that aided in the shift of /e/ > /i/. For example, in the case of OSp. *bevir*, contamination by the nouns *vida* 'life', and *viveza* 'liveliness' (the latter attested in the *Estoria de Espanna II*), as well as the adjective *bivo/a-s* 'alive', none of which ever suffered the change of /i/ to /e/ in their root morphemes, may have combined with the leveling forces of the stem /i/ of inflected forms (and possible influence from learned VIVERE) to complete the shift of /e/ > /i/. Perhaps this is why one finds instances of *bivir* earlier than *apercibir, percibir,* and *recibir*, which had no such corresponding forms. In the case of OSp. *escrevir*, perhaps a contributing factor was the past participle *escri(p)to/a*, together with its nominal derivatives, *escri(p)tura* and *Escri(p)tura* (the latter = *Biblia*), *escriba, escribano*, none of which, possessing only /o/, /a/, or /u/ after the stem /i/, ever suffered dissimilation of /i/ > /e/.

A justifiable appeal to the past participle and its derivatives may be made on the grounds that the infinitive and participle share certain features: (a) Both are verbal elements; (b) Both of these verbal elements occur with auxiliaries in very similar syntactic structures, e.g., *he de escribir la carta* 'I have to write the letter', *he escrito la carta* 'I have written the letter'; (c) The participle, whether used with the auxiliary *haber*, or whether functioning as an adjective with the auxiliary *estar*, is frequently used in conjunction with an auxiliary-infinitival construction, e.g., *No he escrito la carta todavía, pero voy a escribirla ahora* 'I haven't written the letter yet, but I'm going to write it now', and *La carta no está escrita, todavía tengo que escribirla* 'The letter isn't written, I still have to write it'; (d) Throughout the history of Spanish (and Romance in general), infinitives have often been restructured on participial bases, e.g., inf. CANERE 'to sing', p.p. CANTUM > inf. *cantar*; inf. UTI 'to use', p.p. USUM > inf. *usar*; inf. VOMERE 'to vomit', p.p. VOMITUM > inf. *vomitar*; ModSp. inf. *freír* 'to fry', p.p. *frito* > inf. *fritar* (dialectal, e.g., Medellín, Colombia); and (e) The infinitive may be nominalized, bringing it into close association with nominal derivatives, e.g., *El escribir es un arte* 'Writing is an art', *La escritura del escribano es ilegible* 'the (hand)writing of the scribe is illegible'. Given the close relationship between infinitive and participle engendered by the aforementioned common denominators, it should not seem unreasonable to include as a primary factor the influence of the high front /i/ of the participle *escri(p)to/a* and its derivatives, *E/escri(p)tura, escriba, escribano*, in the process which ultimately reshaped OSp. *escrevir* as ModSp. *escribir* (The same account would apply to ModSp. *describir* and its participle *descrito*). The fact that other verbs which exhibited the /e/.../í/ pattern and had no /i/ in the lexical morpheme of their participle did not undergo the shift from /e/ > /i/, e.g., *medir ~ medido, pedir ~ pedido*, etc., supports, in an inverse manner, the proposal for *escrevir ~ escri(p)to > escribir ~ escrito*.[21] Perhaps this is why one finds a significantly elevated number of occurrences of *escribir* already in 13th-century Alfonsine prose.

But again, OSp. *dezir* complicates the problem for OSp. *bevir* and *escrevir*. The past participle *dicho* and its derivatives, which functioned as nouns and adjectives (e.g., *dicho* 'saying', *dicha* 'happiness, good fortune', *dichero* 'one who uses oportune sayings', *dicharacho* 'a vulgar saying', *dichoso* 'lucky', *desdichado* 'unfortunate, unhappy', *dicharachero* 'propensity to use vulgar sayings'), should have matched the contaminating and leveling forces of *vida*, *viveza, bivo/a-s*, and *escri(p)to/a*, etc., if indeed these were responsible for the leveling of *bevir > vivir* and *escrevir > escribir*. Moreover, no such factors can be cited to account for the leveling of *aperçebir, perçebir, reçebir* — their past

---

21. There are some cases where the participle indeed had /i/ in the stem, but no shift of /e/ > /i/ occurred in the infinitive. Witness *freír ~ frito*, OSp. *reír ~ riso*. In these cases, such influence from the participles may have ultimately been resisted to avoid hiatal ***friír and ***riír or even subsequent contraction of these to ***frir and ***rir.

participles were *aperçebido*, *perçebido*, and *reçebido* respectively. There must therefore be another factor, heretofore undiscovered, which led to the replacement of OSp. *aperçebir*, *perçebir*, *reçebir*, *escrevir*, and *bevir* by their modern Spanish counterparts.

The few scholars who have previously attempted to explain this problem have overlooked the fact that these Old Spanish verbs possessed root allomorphs with non-dissimilated stem vowels in the synthetic future and conditional, i.e., *aperçibir-*, *perçibir-*, *reçibir-*, *escrivir-*, and *bivir-*.[22] These allomorphs are actually relics of Early Old Spanish which, during the passage from analytic to synthetic structures, were never subject to the dissimilatory factor /i...í/ > /e...í/ since the originally stressed /í/ became atonic before the dissimilation process could take effect, e.g., EOSp. *reçibír é* > *reçibiré*. Proof that tonic infinitival /í/ became atonic and was therefore rendered incapable of causing dissimilation of the original pretonic /i/ lies in the fact that infinitival /i/ was often syncopated during the passage from analytic to synthetic structures (i.e., tonic vowels are never syncopated), e.g., EOSp. *reçibír é* > *reçibiré* > *reçib(i)ré* > *reçibré*. In *The Electronic Texts and Concordances of the Prose Works of Alfonso X, El Sabio* (1997) one finds the following non-dissimilated, syncopated and non-syncopated future and conditional root allomorphs (number of occurrences in parentheses): *aperçibr-* (3), *reçibir-* (2), *reçibr-* (63), *escrivir-* (37), *bivir-* (43), *bivr-* (54). Speakers were probably cognizant of the fact that analytic structures constituted synchronically a decomposition of a synthetic structure (though, diachronically, the synthetic structure was a composition of earlier analytic elements). For example, speakers no doubt realized that an expression such as *non veer lo é* 'I shall not see him' was simply another way (analytic) of saying *non lo veré* (synthetic), and that the two verbal constructs, *veer...é* and *veré*, were closely related to one another, though slightly different in their structure. During the earliest period of Old Spanish, structures such as synthetic, non-dissimilated *lo reçibiré* coexisted with analytic, dissimilated *reçebir lo é* and *quiero reçebirlo*. It is therefore not inconceivable that non-dissimilated allomorphs would have spread, syntagm by syntagm, first competing with, until totally ousting, dissimilated infinitives, as depicted in the hypothetical five-stage sequence of events in (46):

---

22. Penny (1991: 177) does recognize the existence of these root allomorphs, but does not incorporate them into his explanation of *recibir*, *escribir*, etc.

(46) Stage One   Stage Two   Stage Three
      lo reçibiré   *lo reçibiré*   *lo reçibiré*
      reçebir lo é   *reçebir/reçibir lo é*   *reçebir/reçibir lo é*
      quiero reçebirlo   *quiero reçebirlo*   *quiero reçebir/reçibirlo*

      Stage Four   Stage Five
      lo reçibiré   *lo reçibiré*
      reçibir lo é   *reçibir lo é* (eventually extinguished)
      quiero reçebir/reçibirlo *quiero reçibirlo*

This hypothesis explains why *dezir* was never permanently "leveled" to **dicir*. That is, none of the verbs in question (i.e., *apercibir, percibir, recibir, escribir, vivir*) suffered leveling. Rather, the structure of these verbs can be explained as having resulted from morphological reanalysis. The future and conditional root allomorph of *dezir* was *dizr-*, a form exhibiting a phonetic structure which would not have adapted well to analytic structures, i.e., *dizré* > **dizr lo é* and **quiero dizr*.

In the case of *conçebir*, one may still ask why futures and conditionals such as *conçib(i)ré* and *conçib(i)rié-/ía* did not spread to **conçibir lo é* and **quiero conçibirlo*. One possibility is that only the most frequent verbs, primarily *escrivir-* and *reçib(i)r-*, were involved in the aforementioned syntagmatic diffusion — as seen above, in the entire Alfonsine corpus *conçebir* occurs only once in analytic structures (*General estoria I*), and the root allomorphs *conçibr-* occurs only three times (*Estoria de Espanna I, General estoria I, General estoria VI*). Thus highly frequent *escrivir-* and *reçib(i)r-* may have been the leader words in the entire diffusion process. The intrusion of these allomorphs into syntagms originally occupied by *escrevir* and *reçebir* would set up a state of allomorphy in which speakers vacillated between two verbs exhibiting vocalic patterns of /(C)-e-C-e-C-í-C/ and /(C)-e-C-i-C-í-C/ (where C = consonant or consonants). A comparison of the infinitives concerned reveals immediately a difference in the quality of the vowel which precedes the stem vowel between those which underwent the change (*aperçebir, perçebir, reçebir, escrevir*) and that which did not (*conçebir*). The structure of the former may be formulized as /(a)–(C)-e-C-e-C-í-C/. On the other hand, *conçebir* displayed the pattern /C-o-C-e-C-í-C/. With the merger of /b/ and /β/, all of these verbs, except *conçebir*, would have been brought even closer into line with one another, displaying a general pattern which may be formulized as /(a)–(C)-e-C-e-b-í-r/. The morphological factors involved in the history of *escrevir* (i.e., *escri(p)to/a, escri(p)tura, Escri(p)tura,* *escriba, escribano*) may have led to a definitive preference for the allomorph *escrivir*, which, in effect, produced a shift from /e-C-e-b-í-r/ to /e-C-i-b-í-r/. Following suit, the broad pattern /(a)–(C)-e-C-e-b-í-r/ would shift to /(a)–(C)-e-C-i-b-í-r/, and any verbs belonging to that category (i.e., *aperçebir, perçebir,* and *reçebir*) would inevitably be swept up in the change. *Conçebir*, with its own pattern of /C-o-C-e-b-í-r/, would thus be left out. The replacement of OSp. *bevir* by *bivir*, which may not have been part of the aforementioned chain reaction, was probably motivated by factors involving homonymy and near-homonymy with OSp. *bever* 'to drink'.[23]

    This account is consistent with the textual evidence provided at the beginning of this chapter regarding (a) the absence of *apercibir* and *percibir* during the Middle Ages, (b) the early appearance of *reçibir* and *escrivir* (due to frequent occurrence of fut./cond. root allomorphs *escrivir-* and *reçib(i)r-*), and (c) the elevated number of occurrences of *escrivir* in analytic structures in the 14th century (due to influence of p.p. *escri(p)to/a*, nouns *escri(p)tura, escriba,* etc.). The present analysis also accounts for the divergent paths these verbs took after beginning their evolution in identical fashion, whereas attributing the change examined here to leveling or learned influence leaves many questions unanswered.

---

23. See Rini (1997a) for details.

CHAPTER 3

Phonological or Morphological Change?

On some points of Spanish historical grammar, one finds that while most scholars acknowledge that a phonological change has occurred, the door has been left open for the possibility that the change was a morphological one. Take, for example, the case of the development of the various Old Spanish future/ conditional stems of *poner*, *tener*, and *venir*. The passage from analytic to synthetic structures and the ensuing syncope of the infinitival vowel left stems with the consonant sequence /nr/, which was "phonotactically unacceptable in Old Spanish" (Penny 1991: 176).[1] From the phonotactically awkward *ponr-*, *tenr-*, and *venr-* arose the following allomorphic sets, thus facilitating the articulation of the sequence /nr/: (1) *pondr-/tendr-/vendr-*, (2) *porn-/tern-/vern-*, (3) *ponrr-/tenrr-/venrr-*, and (4) *porr-/terr-/verr-*. The first set suffered epenthesis of /d/; the second, metathesis; the third, strengthening of /r/ to /r̄/. Lloyd (1987: 312) believes that the fourth set is a continuation of the third with loss of the nasal, while Penny (1991: 176) believes these resulted from a direct assimilation of /n/ to /r/. In either case, they both agree that *porr-/terr-/verr-* resulted from some type of phonological change. Alvar and Pottier (1983: 251–52), on the one hand, mention the phonological process of assimilation, but, on the other,

---

1. The syncope of the intertonic infinitival vowel in *poneré* > *ponré*, *teneré* > *tenré*, and *veniré* > *venré*, etc. is the expected development of these forms (and others like them, e.g., *comeré* > OSp. *combré*), since, from Latin to Old Spanish, all intertonic vowels, except /a/, were syncopated. In fact, Old Spanish had many more syncopated futures (and conditionals) than does modern Spanish (some exhibiting epenthetic consonants) — in effect, any verb in the future or conditional could undergo syncope. Lloyd (1987: 311–12) cites the following attested Old Spanish forms which no longer exist in the modern language: *bevrá, vivrán, movrás, concibredes, recibrían, ardrá, eñadrá, entendremos, prendría, perdrás, comidrás, consintrás, mentrién, partremos, repentremos, ferredes, conquerrá, parrás, combré, doldrá, faldrá, moldrié, remandrá, falleztrá, conoztría, bendizdré, yazdré*. According to Lloyd (1987: 367): "Only those verbs whose frequency of use was very high managed to keep the sycopated forms." For more on syncope in Old Spanish, see Harris-Northall (1990).

allow for the possibility of a morphological change as well — analogy with verbs whose syncopated stems resulted in *-rr-*, e.g., *quererá > querrá, morirá > morrá, ferirá > ferrá, parirá > parrá*. In this particular case there may be no way to discern whether these future/conditional forms in *-rr-* resulted from phonological or morphological phenomena, though the strengthened form *verrá* 'verá' found in Berceo (clearly analogous with those forms in *-rr-*) may clue us in.

In other cases, scholars are completely polarized in their views about whether a given change is phonological or morphological in nature. Take, for example, the reduction of the Old Spanish segment *-iell- > -ill-* (as in OSp. *aniello* 'ring' > ModSp. *anillo*, OSp. *castiello* 'castle' > ModSp. *castillo*, OSp. *Barbadiello* > ModSp. *Barbadillo*, etc.). Alarcos Llorach (1968: 144) suggested that if the vocalic sequence /ie/ in this segment maintained its earlier stress pattern, i.e., realized phonetically [íe], the reduction of *[íeλo] > [íλo] via syncope would easily follow (whereas [jéλo] > [íλo] is more difficult to envisage and thus less convincing). Lloyd (1987: 317), following Malkiel (1976), rejects this proposal on the grounds that it is most doubtful that /ie/ was still realized [íe] at the time of the reduction of *-iell- > -ill-*, and therefore touts the virtues of incorporating morphological factors:

> A purely phonetic explanation lacks something. A more plausible account is the one that looks beyond the narrow phonetic circumstances in which the change occurs. The first thing to be noted is that the combination /ieḷ/ is found in the diminutive suffix *-iello* < Late Lat. -ELLU. Since the other diminutive suffixes *-ito, -ico, -ín* existed in competition with *-iello*, it is far more likely that the substitution of /i/ for /ie/ was due to the analogical influence of the other suffixes which are all distinguished by the presence of tonic /í/. The peculiar phonetic circumstances were at most a supplementary factor.

In his review of Lloyd (1987), Hartman (1989: 146–47) vehemently rejects the role of morphology in this particular case and appeals to a different phonologically based solution:

> [T]he appeal to morphological analogy rings hollow ... in the change of *-iell-* to *-ill-* ... First L[loyd] presents a fully phonological proposal by Alarcos Llorach (1968), which depends on the suggestion that the /i/ of the diphthong, in its early existence, may have been stressed. This implausible view then in effect serves as a straw-man argument, obliged to make way for one based on the semantic affinity of the diminutive suffix *-iello* with three other diminutives having stressed /í/. No consideration is given to the possibility that the modern /í/ may simply be derived by phonological rule from the medieval /é/,

as the latter may have been raised by the flanking pair of palatal segments. By favoring the semantic/morphological scenario, L obscures the phonological affinity of *-iell-* > *-ill-* with *-ies-* > *-is-* (e.g. OSp. *aviespa* > Mod. *avispa*), which in turn obliges him to qualify the latter change as "not very clear" (318).

Although Hartman makes a good point regarding the *-ies-* > *-is-* change and the light it can possibly shed on the *-iell-* to *-ill-* problem (cf. OSp. *priessa* > ModSp. *prisa*, OSp. *priesco* > ModSp. *prisco*, OSp. *riestra* > ModSp. *ristra*, OSp. *viéspera* > ModSp. *víspera*), in Lloyd's defense, one should point out that his uncertainty about the phonological reduction of *-ies-* > *-is-* is based on the stubborn persistence of *-ies-* in ModSp. *fiesta* and *siesta*, as well as OSp. *finiestra* (add to these OSp. *diestro* and *siniestro*). Hartman's phonological explanation of raising "by the flanking pair of palatal segments" fails to explain why these words never underwent reduction to **fista, **sista, **finistra, **distro, **sinistro. In the case of *-iell-* > *-ill-*, then, there may not be any way to prove whether phonological or morphological factors were more likely responsible for the change.

While the foregoing discussion may appear trivial in that it concerns a minor point of Spanish historical grammar, specialists in the history of Spanish can also be found to be in such disagreement about some of the more important developments. The reduction of the Old Spanish suffixes *-ades*, *-edes*, *-ides* (and *-odes* of *sodes*), which resulted in both a set of singulars *-ás*, *-és*, *-ís*, *-os* and plurals *-áis*, *-éis*, *-ís*, *-ois*, is one example. First, while the loss of /d/ has traditionally been assumed to be the result of a straightforward sound change, Dworkin (1988a) has suggested a scenario that constitutes a morphological change. Second, after the loss of /d/, Penny (1991: 138–40) deems the ensuing vocal development in both singulars and plurals a purely phonological change while Lloyd (1987: 359) invokes morphological factors. In this particular case, further investigation and closer philological work has led to an answer to the problem.[2]

Resolving such issues is important, not only in that we attain a clearer picture of the historical development of Spanish, but also, for the advancement of linguistic theory. Determining whether a linguistic change is the result of phonological or morphological phenomena is important in that it contributes to

---

2. For more on the loss of /d/, see Chapter 4 of this book. For a complete analysis of the vocalic formation of the second person plural suffixes after the loss of /d/, see Rini (1996).

our general understanding of how language changes. Yakov Malkiel has been a pioneer in this regard. As is well known among Spanish philologists, he has suggested on numerous occasions that phonological change may have had its origin in morphological factors, or that morphological factors may control sound change (see, for example, Malkiel 1968, 1969a, 1969b, 1970, 1971, 1976, 1980, 1981, 1982). Some have followed his lead — primarily, his most successful students (such as Lloyd and Dworkin mentioned above), though not exclusively (cf. Penny 1993). Yet, it is my opinion that, despite the efforts of Malkiel and his followers, the role of morphology in the history of Spanish is still underrated — far too many points of historical grammar have simply been assumed to be the result of sound change. The following cases are perfect examples.

The Effects of Morphology on Sound Change in the Paradigm: The /ee/ > /e/ Sound Change and Old Spanish *veer*.

In Chapter 2 we saw some of the problems involved in arriving at an accurate analysis of the morphological changes that occur in the verbal paradigm. In the present section of this chapter, I would like to demonstrate that it is not always clear whether the changes that occur in a given paradigm are truly due to morphological change, or if they are actually the result of phonological change. Consider, for example, the case of the Old Spanish preterite desinence -*este* of the -*ar* conjugation, as found in verse (4a) of the *Libro de buen amo* (ed. Joset 1974): "Señor, tú que *libreste* a [la] santa Susaña" which alternated with -*aste*, as found in verse (3a): "Señor, tú que *sacaste* al profeta del lago"). The perfect tense paradigm preserved in Classical Latin was comprised of the forms demonstrated with the verb AMARE in Stage One of (1). The verbal suffixes exhibit symmetry in that all contain -V- (realized phonetically [-w-]). It is fairly certain that, during the course of time, not all six suffixes underwent the same phonological change. In order to arrive at the Old (and modern) Spanish forms shown in Stage II of (1), one must assume that (a) in the first singular only -V- was lost; (b) in the third singular, posttonic /i/ was syncopated; and (c) in the other forms, the entire syllable, -VI- or -VE-, was dropped. After the loss of -V- in the first singular, mutual assimilation of /á/ and /i/ yielded /é/ (cf. Lat. LAICU(S) 'layman' > *leigo* > *lego*), while in the third singular, mutual assimilation of /á/ and /w/ resulted in /ó/ (cf. Lat. TAURU(S) 'bull' > *toro*):

(1)   The Development of Latin AMARE in the Perfect Tense

Stage One			Stage Two
AMA(V)I	>	*amei	>	amé
AMA(VI)STI			>	amaste
AMAV(I)T	>	*amaw(t)	>	amó
AMA(VI)MUS			>	amamos
AMA(VI)STIS			>	amastes
AMA(VE)RUNT			>	amaron

The question regarding the genesis of the Old Spanish variant -este now arises: Is this form the result of leveling from the first person singular amé (as discussed in Chapter 2), or did -este develop alongside -aste through the same phonological process which produced the first singular suffix -é? It is not inconceivable, with what we now know about language variation in society, that in the speech of some inhabitants of Central Iberia, -AVISTI suffered the loss of the syllable -VI-, while in the speech of some, only the bilabial was eliminated, leading to a phonolgical development like that of the first singular, i.e., -A(V)ISTI > *-aiste > *-eiste > -este (like -A(V)I > *-éi > -é).

In theory, either account is possible, even plausible. However, closer philological examination of the available evidence can help determine whether -este truly arose through phonological or morphological change, and thus provide us with a more accurate history of this particular form. Upon further investigation, one finds that, although Classical Latin preserves trisyllabic -AVISTI, disyllabic -ASTI is documented in the very earliest literary sources (Lloyd 1987: 99). Given that Latin was carried to Iberia well before the Classical period, it is more likely that -ASTI, not -AVISTI, was the Hispano-Latin second person perfect desinence. If this was in fact the case, then we may conclude with certainty that OSp. -este was indeed a product of leveling, and thus a morphological, not a phonological change. In light of the attested -ASTI, but no attestation of *-AISTI (< -AVISTI), it is not surprising that Spanish philologists are in general agreement regarding the morphological genesis of OSp. -este (cf. Alvar and Pottier 1983: 272–73; Lloyd 1987: 303, 364; and Penny 180–81). In other cases, however, one cannot always find such a consensus among scholars. Consider the case of the evolution of OSp. veer 'to see'.

The development of all but the first person singular of the present indicative paradigm of OSp. veer offers specialists of Spanish historical linguistics an example of a change which is not easily discernible as being either a case of phonological or morphological change. On the surface, it appears as though the modern Spanish paradigm resulted from a straightforward phonological process, i.e., the contraction of /ee/ > /e/ (shown in bold), in (2):

(2)   Old Spanish   Modern Spanish
       veer   [βeér]   >   [ber]   *ver*
       vees   [βées]   >   [bes]   *ves*
       vee   [βée]   >   [be]   *ve*
       veemos   [βeémos]   >   [bemos]   *vemos*
       veedes   [βeéðes]   >   [βéðes] > [béi̯s] >   *veis*
       veen   [βéen]   >   [ben]   *ven*

And so it has been assumed. Penny (1991: 163), for example, recently refers to the "late medieval contraction of /ee/ to /e/" and provides the diachronic equations "*veer > ver, vees > ves, veemos > vemos, veedes > veis,* etc." Alvar and Pottier (1983: 164) also view this evolution as the result of a straightforward phonological process: "En la edad de oro, este verbo se conjugaba con un doble paradigma: *veo, ves, ver* y *veo, vees, veer,* que acabó fundiendo las *ee* en una *e* (*veemos, veeis, veen > vemos veis, ven*)." This, of course, is a reasonable assumption, given that, throughout the history of Spanish, the vocalic sequence /ee/ has been known to contract regularly to one. Most recently, however, Lathrop (1996: 155) points out that the ultimate reshaping of the inflected forms of the modern Spanish paradigm could have been the result of a morphological change: "When the infinitive [*veer*] simplified to *ver,* the other forms made an analogical change to conform to the new infinitive." This seems to be an equally reasonable assumption. After all, we are dealing with a change in a verbal paradigm, one of the primary environments in which morphological change usually operates. So, what was originally a rather transparent phonological change has now become complicated by the possible role of morphological factors.

The development of this paradigm is further complicated by Craddock's (1994: 89) observation of the behavior of /ee/ and its contraction to /e/ under different phonological conditions. There have been differences of opinion regarding the questions of when and why the contraction occurs, but Craddock (1994: 89) has linked the relative date of contraction to a conditioning factor of stress, observing in examples like Latin SIGILLUM 'stamp' > OSp. *seello* vs. Latin DIGITUM 'finger' > *dedo* that the contraction occurred "late if the second

[/e/] was stressed, early if the first was stressed."[3] The examples in (3) added to Craddock's support his observation:

(3) First /e/ stressed, i.e., /ée/ > /é/, early contraction:

DIGITUM >	*[déjedo] >	*[déedo] >	dedo (not **deedo)
COMEDERE >	*[koméðer] >	*[koméer] >	comer (not **comeer)
PEDEM >	*[péðe] >	*[pjée] >	pie (not **piee)

Second /e/ stressed, i.e., /eé/ > /é/, later contraction:

SIGILLUM >	*[sejéllo] >	OSp. seello >	ModSp. sello
VIDERE >	*[βeðér] >	OSp. veer >	ModSp. ver
SEDERE >	*[seðér] >	OSp. seer >	ModSp. ser

I might add here the observation that if neither of the two vowels was stressed, the contraction occurred early in most cases, as shown in (4):

(4) Neither /e/ stressed, i.e., /ee/ > /e/, usually early contraction:

VIGILARE >	*[βejelár] >	*[βeelár] > velar
CONTIGESCERE >	*[kontejetsér] >	*[konteetsér] > OSp. conteçer
RIGESCERE >	*[rejetsér] >	*[areestér] > *[aretsér] > arrecir
*SEDENTARE >	*[seðentár] >	*[seentár] > sentar
but, *IMPEDESCERE >	OSp. empeeçer ~	OSp. empeçer

Some lexical items have not yet undergone the contraction, e.g., ModSp. creer, leer, poseer, and proveer.[4] However, if the stress of the second /e/ of these verbs is eliminated (as in the ModSp. future and conditional), the two /ee/'s indeed contract to one, as shown in (5):

(5) Loss of stress in /eé/, i.e., /eé/ → /ee/ → [e]:

/kreér/ + /émos/	→	/kreerémos/	→	[krerémos]
/leér/ + /émos/	→	/leerémos/	→	[lerémos]

---

3. Regarding the /ee/ > /e/ change, early-20th century opinion held that factors such as frequency of occurrence and learned influence determined the outcome of the contraction. For example, Menéndez Pidal (1941: 83–4) wrote: "la fecha depende del mayor o menor uso que desgasta las palabras; así videre hacía antiguamente veer, pero ya al fin de la Edad Media se decía ver, mientras el menos usado proveer conserva hasta hoy mismo su hiato . . . leer conserva firmemente su hiato, como más culto que ver."

4. See the discussion of **Morphological Influence** in Chapter 1 for a summary and Rini (1991) for details about the lack of contraction in these verbs.

| /kreér/ + /íamos/ | → | /kreeríamos/ | → | [kreríamos] |
| /leér/ + /íamos/ | → | /leeríamos/ | → | [leríamos][5] |

In the case of the paradigm of Lat. VIDERE > OSp. *veer*, then, one would expect, after the loss of medial /-d-/, the contraction of /ee/ to have occurred in the 2nd and 3rd singular and 3rd plural (given that these forms exhibited /ée/), but not in the 1st and 2nd persons plural, nor in the infinitive (given that these forms exhibited /eé/) as depicted in bold in the hypothetical diachronic equation in (6):

(6)   Latin

VIDERE	>	[βe$^\delta$ér]	>	[βeér]			*veer*
VIDEO	>	[βéjo]	>	[βéo]			*veo*
VIDES	>	[βé$^\delta$es]	>	[βées]	>	[βés]	****ves*
VIDET	>	[βé$^\delta$e]	>	[βée]	>	[βé]	****ve*
VIDEMUS	>	[βe$^\delta$émos]	>	[βeémos]			*veemos*
VIDETIS	>	[βe$^\delta$édes]	>	[βeédes]			*veedes*
VIDENT	>	[βé$^\delta$en]	>	[βéen]	>	[(én]	****ven*

Yet a search through a significant number of early Old Spanish texts turns up no evidence of the expected /ée/ > /é/ change in the paradigm of OSp. *veer* before the 14th century. For example, in the 13th-century Royal Scriptorium texts of Alfonso X, one finds *vees* 60 times ~ *ves* 0, *vee* 81 ~ *ve* 0, and *veen* 72 ~ *ven* 0. Even in post-13th century non-Royal Scriptorium Alfonsine texts, one finds only one example each of *ves* and *ve*. Even more perplexing is the discovery that the change which is not expected to be found in the earliest stages of the languages, i.e., /eé/ > /é/, had in fact begun by the 13th century, as one finds a state of allomorphy in the first and second persons plural of this paradigm in 13th-century Royal Scriptorium Alfonsine prose: *veemos* 36 (75%) vs. *vemos* 12 (25%), and *veedes* 23 (52%) vs. *vedes* 21 (48%). These same patterns are found in other early texts as well. For example, in the *Poema de mio Cid* (ed. Smith 1983, Waltman 1972), the *Poema de Fernán González* (ca. 1250), the *Gran Conquista de Ultramar* (1295), the *Crónica de veinte reyes* (ca. 1252–1350), and the *Sumas de la Historia Troyana* (ca. 1300–1350), one finds a combined total of

---

5. Dalbor (1980: 183) states: "Identical vowels, both of which are *unstressed*, are usually realized as just one short vowel both in careful and rapid speech: **la abriré** [la-βri-ré], **creeré** [kre-ré], **lo odiaba** [lo-ðjá-βa]."

vees 5 ~ *ves* 0, *vee* 3 ~ *ve* 0, *veen* 3 ~ *ven* 0 vs. *veemos* 4 ~ *vemos* 3, and *veedes* 9 ~ *vedes* 23. One begins to wonder if Craddock's observation is truly valid, or if some factors have disrupted the natural course of the /ee/ > /e/ sound change in this particular paradigm. Since the data regarding OSp. *veer* paradoxically show the opposite results of what Craddock's observation would predict, perhaps we ought to put to the test the validity of this observation by taking a look at the outcome of DIGITUM and SIGILLUM in the same texts.

The data regarding DIGITUM gleaned from the Alfonsine corpus show that, as Craddock had claimed, the contraction of /ée/ > /é/ was complete by the 13th century, such that one does not find a single example of **deedo* or **deedos*, only *dedo* and *dedos* (353 occurrences). In the case of SIGILLUM and contraction of /eé/ > /é/, Craddock's claim is accurate, though not 100%, as the contraction appears to have already begun, though minimally, as *seello* and *seellos* combine for 37 occurrences (95%) vs. two of *sellos* (5%). I decided to test further the validity of Craddock's observation by examining the behavior of other lexical items, namely Latin FIDEM 'faith' and PEDEM/-S 'foot/feet' for /ée/ > /é/, and SEDERE 'to be (seated)' for /eé/ to /é/. The results were identical to those found with DIGITUM and SIGILLUM. For example, as in the case of DIGITUM > *dedo*, after the loss of /-d-/ from FIDEM and PEDEM/-S, the phonetic realizations *[fée] and *[pjée(s)] apparently underwent the contraction to [fé] and [pjé(s)] early, as one finds *fe* (271 occurrences), *pie* (249 occurrences), and *pies* (352 occurrences), but no occurrence of **fee*, **piee*, or **piees* in 13th-century Alfonsine prose.[6] And like SIGILLUM > *seello* (95%) ~ *sello* (5%), in the case of SEDERE > *seer* (> *ser*), one finds in 13th-century Alfonsine prose *seer* 2,638 times (95%) ~ *ser* 143 (5%).[7]

Based on Craddock's observation as tested with the independent lexical items DIGITUM > *dedo*, FIDEM > *fe*, PEDEM/-S > *pie(s)*, SIGILLUM >

---

6. In post-13th-century Alfonsine prose, the same trend continues with the exception of one example of *fee* in the *General Estoria VI* (14th century): *fe* (98 occurrences), *fee* (1 once) vs. *fees* (zero); *pie* (139 occurrences), **piee* (zero), *pies* (148 occurrences), **piees* (zero). The lone example of *fee*, if not an erratum, may have acquired its additional final /-e/ via the influence of Latin FIDEM, which occurs in the Alfonsine corpus 25 times.

7. Some might wish to attribute some of the occurrences of monosyllabic *ser* to the hypothetically reconstructed etymon *ESSERE. However, in a separate article (Rini 1997b), I have advanced arguments for a single etymon, namely SEDERE, for modern Spanish *ser*.

seello/sello, and SEDERE > *seer/ser*, one would expect to find in the development of the 13th-century paradigm of *veer* the straightforward phonological development of /ée/ and /eé/ to have led to 100% occurrence of the contraction in forms whose etyma exhibited /ée/, but only occasional contraction (i.e., 5%) in those forms which exhibited /eé/, as depicted in (7):

(7)   <u>Hypothetical 13th-c. Paradigm of OSp. *veer*</u>
   veo   *veemos (95%) / *vemos (5%)
   *ves (100%)   *veedes (95%) / *vedes (5%)
   *ve (100%)   *ven (100%)

But in reality, what we have found is the paradigm shown in (8):

(8)   <u>Actual 13th-c. (Alfonsine) Paradigm of OSp. *veer*</u>
   veo   veemos (75%) / vemos (25%)
   vees (100%)   veedes (52%) / vedes (48%)
   vee (100%)   veen (100%)

Thus it remains to be explained why the forms *vees*, *vee*, and *veen* have resisted the regular phonological change of /ée/ > /é/, and why the reduction of *veemos* and *veedes* to *vemos* and *vedes* respectively had already begun at this early stage of the language.

One possible explanation for why *vees*, *vee*, and *veen* resisted the contraction of /ée/ > /é/ is that they received support from forms with the stress pattern /eé/, i.e., *veemos*, *veedes* (as well as the infinitive itself, *veer*). This explanation is weakened, however, by the fact that the reduced allomorphs, *vemos* and *vedes* had already begun to appear at this time: That is, why then were *vees*, *vee*, and *veen* not remodeled as *ves*, *ve*, and *ven* on the basis of *vemos* and *vedes*? Another possible explanation is that the atonic /e/ was likely felt to be part of the plural morpheme, i.e., phonetically, [βées], [βée], [βéen] (no contraction) because morphemically, /βé-es/, /βé-e/, /βé-en/. Evidence that speakers indeed recognized this morpheme boundary is found in the fact that they often inserted an unetymological antihiatic yod in the infinitive, i.e., *veyer* (Lloyd 1987: 235). But again, this cannot be the only reason, since the same recognition of the morpheme boundary in /βe-emos/ and /βe-edes/ did not impede the creation of disyllabic allomorphs *vemos* and *vedes*. Perhaps the answer to why *vees*, *vee*, and *veen* were able to resist the phonological rule /ée/ > /é/ may lie in an understanding of why *veemos* and *veedes* contracted to *vemos* and *vedes* against the phonological rule that /eé/ was to be maintained. In order to understand what gave rise to the allomorphs *vemos* and *vedes*, let us look at the history of the infinitive itself, which, like *veemos* and *veedes*, exhibited the /eé/ stress pattern.

Latin VIDERE, through regular phonetic development, yielded OSp. *veer* (i.e., /βidere/ > [βeδér(e)] > [βe(δ)ér] > [βeér]). This infinitive evolved in two different syntactic environments: (a) analytic structures in which the infinitives followed prepositions and auxiliary verbs (e.g., PRO + VIDERE > *por veer*, POTET + VIDERE > *puede veer*), and (b) structures which were passing from analytic to synthetic in nature, i.e., future and conditional, in which the infinitives preceded the auxiliary HABERE (e.g., VIDERE + HABET/HABEBAT > *verá/vería*).

OSp. *veer*, containing the sequence /eé/, would have evolved in analytic structures as shown in (9) in much the same way as did lexical items like SIGILLUM → > *seello*). With phonological stress on the second of the two like vowels, i.e., *-eér*, it was normally maintained as a disyllabic infinitive:

(9)   [non póte(t) βidér(e)] > [non póde βe(δ)ér] > [non pwéδe βeér]

Conversely, during the passage from analytic to synthetic future and conditional structures in general, it is conceivable that the phonological stress of the infinitive could have been displaced to the radical morpheme (though perhaps downgraded to secondary stress), e.g., *CANTARE HABET /kantáre hábet/ > *[kantár(e) á(be)] > *[kàntará]. In the case of the syntagm VIDERE HABET, this shift in stress would have converted the original vowel sequence /eé/ to /èe/, quite similar in structure to /ée/ as depicted in (10):

(10)   VIDERE HABET /βidére hábet/ > [βe(δ)ér(e) á(βe)] > [βeér á] > *[βèerá]

Thus, like /ée/ of *[déedo] (> [dedo] OSp. *dedo*), /èe/ of *[βèerá] would contract early, yielding [βerá] *verá* already in the earliest period of Old Spanish.

It is also entirely possible that the stress on the infinitive of analytic *[βeér á] may have been lost altogether once the synthesis of the two forms had begun, leaving only one stress, on the auxiliary. Thus during the passage from analytic to synthetic future and conditional structures, the atonic nature of the two contiguous like vowels would have led to their inevitable contraction: [βeér á] > [βeerá] > [βerá]. Therefore, whether the root morpheme bore a secondary stress (i.e., /èe/) or not (i.e., /ee/), one can expect the contraction of these two vowels to have occurred early.

Textual evidence bears out the foregoing hypothetical scenario. In the *Auto* *de los reyes magos* (Menéndez Pidal 1978), *La fazienda de ultra mar* (Lazar 1965), the 13th-century Royal Scriptorium texts of Alfonso X and post-13th-century Alfonsine manuscripts, i.e., *Estoria de Espanna II*, and the non-Royal Scriptorium *General estoria II, V,* and *VI* (Kasten et al. 1997), the *Libro del cauallero Çifar* (Olsen 1984), *Libro de buen amor* (Mignani et al. 1977), *La dança general de la muerte* (Sola-Sole 1981), and the *Arcipreste de Talavera* (De Gorog and De Gorog 1978), monosyllabic *ver* predominates in synthetic structures: *ver-* 454 vs. *veer-* 1. The one example of *veer* in a synthetic structure most likely represents a relic of an earlier system, representing the stage right before the contraction of the two like vowels became obligatory, perhaps when (and if) the first of the two vowels still bore a secondary stress, i.e., *[βèerá]. Observe this example in (11) from the *General Estoria IV*, together with the syntactic variation of analytic and synthetic futures, which almost seems to capture the change in progress:

(11)   Sinon **veer** lo **an** por so saber (GE.IV 23v 39)   [βe-ér-lo-án]
       Mas pero non le **veeran** (GE.IV 68r 72)   [nón-le-βè-e-rán]
       Los omnes locos non la **veran** (GE.IV 262v 91) [nón-la-βe-rán]

This development in synthetic structures produced a state of allomorphy for this infinitive, i.e., *veer* for analytic structures, and *ver-* for synthetic structures. It would not be long before the monosyllabic future and conditional allomorph *ver-* spread to analytic structures, since speakers were well aware of the fact that, *veer lo an*, for example, was simply a decomposition of *lo verán* (not unlike the spread of the non-dissimilated future/conditional stems *reçib(i)r-*, etc. to analytic structures as discussed in Chapter 2). It comes as no surprise, therefore, that disyllabic *veer*, though the predominant allomorph in analytic structures, is rivaled by monosyllabic *ver* already in 13th-century texts: *veer* 398 (76%) vs. *ver* 123 (24%). Compare in (12) the percentage of occurrence of these infinitival allomorphs with the corresponding inflected forms in 13th century Alfonsine prose:

(12)   *veer* (76%) / *ver* (24%)
            veo   *veemos* (75%) / *vemos* (25%)
            vees (100%) *veedes* (52%) / *vedes* (48%)
            vee (100%)   *veen* (100%)

The similarity in the frequency of occurrence between infinitival allomorphs *veer/ver* on the one hand and inflected *veemos/vemos* on the other is striking. In light of these data, one might suggest that the unusually early reduction of *veemos* and *veedes* > *vemos* and *vedes* may have been due to a restructuring on the basis of the monosyllabic allomorph *ver*, which would thus constitute a morphological, not a phonological change.[8]

The similarity in the data between *veer/ver* and *veemos/vemos* in 13th-century Alfonsine prose appears to be no small coincidence. In post-13-century Alfonsine prose, the same trend continues. One finds an almost identical ratio of occurrence between the infinitival allomorphs and the 1st person plural: *veer* 247 (70%) vs. *ver* 107 (30%), compared with *veemos* 11 (69%) vs. *vemos* 5 (31%). In the second person plural, the disyllabic allomorph continues to gain popularity, as it surpasses the trisyllabic allomorph: *veedes* 14 (32.5%) vs. *vedes* 29 (67.5%). The forms *vees*, *vee*, and *veen*, on the other hand, still predominate, as one finds *vees* 24 vs. *ves* 1 (*Estoria de Espanna II*, 14th century), *vee* 28 vs. *ve* 1 (*General Estoria V*, 15th century), and *veen* 19 vs. **ven* 0.

The question now remains: Why were *veemos* and *veedes* restructured on the basis of the infinitival allomorphs *veer/ver*, while *vees*, *vee*, and *veen* were not? One might consider, as alluded to above, the factor of stress: the only difference between these two sets of inflected forms. Since the reduction arose in the category of infinitive, which exhibited the stress pattern /eé/, only those forms with this stress pattern, i.e., *veemos* and *veedes*, would be restructured morphologically on the basis of this new state of allomorphy, i.e., through analogy with the infinitival variants /βeér/ ~ /βer/ as in (13):

(13)	variant 1	*veer*	:	*veemos*	:	*veedes*
	variant 2	*ver*	:	X = *vemos*	:	X = *vedes*

Conversely, *vees*, *vee*, and *veen* remained stable with the support of the stress pattern of the first singular /βéo/, which, like *vees*, *vee*, and *veen*, possessed a tonic radical vowel. Thus, while this change produced a fluctuation and asymmetry within inflected forms of the paradigm, it in effect gave rise to a symmetrical

---

8. In the case of the second person plural, reduced *vedes* and non-reduced *veedes* are found at an almost equal rate of occurrence, and thus reduced *vedes* is more frequent than the reduced infinitival allomorph *ver* and first person *vemos*. One possible explanation for the higher percentage rate of occurrence of reduced *vedes* (48%) vis-à-vis *ver* (24%) and *vemos* (25%) is that perhaps the use of *veedes* as a singular and consequent association with disyllabic *vees* compelled speakers to reduce the trisyllabic form to a disyllabic one (i.e., disyllabic *vedes* was more in line with disyllabic *vees* than was trisyllabic *veedes*). However, further investigation into the singular vs. plural use of *vedes* ~ *veedes* would be required before reaching any firm conclusion on this matter.

pattern within the entire paradigm as regards the pattern of stress as shown in (14) in bold:

(14)   /éV/   vs.   /eé/   ~   /é/
       /βéo/   /βeér/   ~   /βer/
       /βées/   /βeémos/   ~   /βemos/
       /βée/   /βeédes/   ~   /βedes/
       /βéen/

Thus one discovers in the present analysis that the vocalic sequence /ee/ has exactly opposite outcomes depending on whether it followed the phonological or morphological rule. Whereas the phonological rule as first adduced by Craddock (1994) can be written as /ée/ > /é/ early, /eé/ > /é/ later, the morphological rule revealed in the present analysis as it applies to the paradigm of OSp. *veer/ver* is as follows: /eé/ > /é/ early, /ée/ > /é/ later.

The forms *vees*, *vee*, and *veen* would begin to be remodeled to their modern state only after *ver* had become a significant rival to *veer*. For example, in the *Libro de las doñas* (1448), one finds *veer* 20 ~ *ver* 15, and consequently, allomorphy in the second person singular, i.e., *vees* 18 ~ *ves* 7 (though the 3rd person remains unaffected, i.e., *vee* 40 ~ *ve* 0, *veen* 20 ~ *ven* 0). Similarly, in the *Libro del Cauallero Çifar* (copied late-14th- early-15th century), one finds *veer* 3 ~ *ver* 62, *vees* 5 ~ *ves* 2, but *vee* 10 ~ *ve* 0, *veen* 6 ~ *ven* 0. And the *Cuento de Tristán de Leonis* (ca. 1390–1410) offers *veer* 7 ~ *ver* 44, *vees* 1 ~ *ves* 1, but *veen* 2 ~ *ven* 0. The process was clearly slow going, as one can find texts produced well into the 15th century which exhibit a preponderance, or even exclusive use of monosyllabic *ver*, yet still offer examples, however sparse, of *vees*, *vee*, and *veen*: witness the *Cancionero de Baena* (ca. 1425) *veer* 10 ~ *ver* 76, *vees* 12 ~ *ves* 6, *vee* 7 ~ *ve* 0, *veen* 5 ~ *ven* 4; the *Cancionero de París* (ca. 1470) *veer* 1 ~ *ver* 18, *vees* 2 ~ *ves* 3, *vee* 1 ~ *ve* 1; the *Imitatio Christi* (1490) *veer* 0 ~ *ver* 12, *vees* 4 ~ *ves* 1, *vee* 5 ~ *ve* 0, *veen* 3 ~ *ven* 0; the *Tratado de amores de Arnalte y Lucenda* (1491) *veer* 0 ~ *ver* 20, *vees* 4 ~ *ves* 2; the *Cancionero Castellano Misceláneo* (copied ca. 1450–1500) *veer* 0 ~ *ver* 6, *vees* 0 ~ *ves* 2, *vee* 1 ~ *ve* 1, *veen* 0 ~ *ven* 2. It was not until sometime during the 16th century, after disyllabic *veer* had long been forgotten, that *vees*, *vee*, and *veen* were able to overcome the influence of /βéo/ and undergo complete restructuring on the basis of monosyllabic *ver*, as the *Historia de las Amazonas* (ca. 1550) reveals, while showing in the third singular what is surely one of the last glimpses of the Old Spanish forms in /ée/: *veer* 0 ~ *ver* 31, *vees* 0 ~ *ves* 14, *vee* 1 ~ *ve* 1, *veen* 0 ~ *ven* 1. In the case of *veemos* and *veedes*, the first to acquire restructured, reduced allomorphs, the former appears to have persisted as long as *veer* was still on the scene, while the latter is absent from texts after the late-14th or early-15th century: witness the *Libro del Cauallero Çifar* – *veemos* 3 ~ *vemos* 1, *veedes* 17 ~ *vedes* 11; the *Cuento de Tristán de Leonis* – *veedes* 1 ~ *vedes* 19; the *Cancionero de Baena* – *veemos* 6 ~ *vemos* 6, *veedes* 0 ~ *vedes* 23; the *Cancionero de París* – *veemos* 2 ~ *vemos* 0, *veedes* 0 ~ *vedes* 5; the *Imitatio Christi* – *veemos* 1 ~ *vemos* 4, *veedes* 0 ~ *vedes* 1; the *Historia de las Amazonas* – *veemos* 0 ~ *vemos* 3, *veedes* 0 ~ *vedes* 3.

The development of this paradigm, then, apparently had little to do with the late medieval phonological contraction of /ee/ > /e/, as many scholars have assumed to this point in time, and everything to do with the reduction of the infinitive *veer* > *ver*, as Lathrop (1996) had suspected. The linguistic change in this one Old Spanish paradigm demonstrates quite clearly the potential impact of morphology on sound change.

The /ée/ > /éi/ Change: Sound Change or Backformation?[9]

Menéndez Pidal established in the early-20th century the following "sound law": "La -*E* se hace -*i* cuando queda en hiato con la vocal tónica" (1941: 79). Applied to the vocalic sequence /ée/, this law would require the outcome /éi/. This sound law, however, like all others, was based on the available data in the form of Latin etyma and corresponding Romance morphological reflexes. Witness Latin BOVEM 'ox', GREGEM 'herd', LEGEM 'law', REGEM 'king', which, after the loss of their medial consonant (and diphthongization of /ǫ/ > /ue/ in BOVEM) first yielded *buee*, *gree*, *lee*, *ree* (forms which, according to Menéndez Pidal, are preserved in Old Leonese), and later *buey*, *grey*, *ley*, *rey*, according to the law.

The problem with establishing this sound law, however, is that unlike a transparent diachronic equation such as Latin ACUTUM 'accute, sharp' > Sp. *agudo*, about which no one would dispute that Latin /k/ and /t/, being intervocalic, voiced to /g/ and /d/ respectively, 19th-century Romanists were not at all in agreement about the development of the Spanish nouns, *buey*, *grey*, *ley*, and *rey*.

---

9. This section is a shortened, yet revised, version of parts of the discussion found in Rini (1998a). It is not a straightforward reproduction of that article.

Diez (1844:267) believed that Latin REGEM, for example, would have first lost its final syllable, and that the velar consonant would have then undergone palatalization and vocalization under the influence of the preceding vowel, i.e., REGEM > *REG > *rey*. Cornu (1880:71) disagreed, suggesting instead, that final /e/ would have been retained and transformed to /i/ under the influence of the preceding velar, which may have palatalized and then fused with the final high vowel, and that the outcome would have been disyllabic, i.e., REGEM > *REGE > *REGI (or *REYI) > *reï*. In complete contrast with these two views, Meyer-Lübke (1890:272) believed that the velar consonant played no part whatsoever, that it would have been lost altogether, and that the unstressed /e/ in contact with the stressed /é/ would simply become /i/, i.e., REGEM > *RE(G)E > *ree* > *reï*. It should be noted, however, that Meyer-Lübke, like Cornu, believed that the outcome was disyllabic.

In the early-20th century, there was no more agreement than there had been in the previous century. Hanssen (1903, and later in 1913) insisted that Latin REGEM would have developed to *REYE, and that apocope (or syntactic syncope) of final /-e/ would then yield *rey*, i.e., REGEM > *REYE > *rey(e)* > *rey*. By contrast, Menéndez Pidal (1904, 1908, and ultimately in 1941) attempted to refine Meyer-Lübke's view and, as mentioned above, established his "sound law" which maintained that after the loss of the velar consonant, the unstressed /e/ would become a semivocalic offglide in contact with the preceding stressed /é/, just as it would with a stressed /á/ or /ó/, i.e., through loss of hiatus, i.e., REGEM > *RE(G)E > *ree* > *rey*. Thus, unlike Cornu and Meyer-Lübke, Menéndez Pidal believed that the outcome would be monosyllabic.

Hanssen's view has been repeated by Bourciez (1956), and in part, by Lloyd (1987), though most modern Spanish philologists subscribe to the diachronic equation proposed by Menéndez Pidal. Despite the general consensus, I do not believe that the matter has ever been completely resolved.

Menéndez Pidal sought support for his sound law in the apparent phonological development of the Old Spanish second person verbal suffix -*edes,* which, after the loss of its medial dental consonant, yielded diphthongal -*éis* in Standard Castilian, as in OSp. *tenedes* 'you have' > *tenees* > ModSp. *tenéis.* The problem with this source of support, however, is that it is not altogether certain that diphthongal -*éis* resulted from a straightforward phonological process. In fact, many scholars, from the 19th century to present, which include Cuervo (1893:120), Hanssen (1913: 94–95), De Souza (1964: 11–13), Fontanella de Weinberg (1976: 250), Lapesa (1983: 259, 389), and Lloyd (1987), have held the view that normal phonetic development would have reduced OSp. *-edes* to the monophthongal variant *-és*, and that diphthongal *-éis* must be the result of a morphological development (most likely an analogue of *-áis* < reduced *-ades*). Textual evidence supports this view, since the earliest cases of reduced *-edes* involve monophthongal *-és*, not diphthongal *-éis*. For example, Dworkin (1988b) cites monophthongal *abés, abrés, andarés, darés, podrés, querés, tenés*, and *yrés* from late-14th century *Libro de buen amor*, and early-15th century *Dança general de la muerte* and *Libro rimado de palacio* (see Chapter 4 for full details). Of particular significance is the fact that in the *Dança*, *-edes* appears as monophthongal *-és* in the late-14th century manuscript, while not until the 1520 edition (Sevilla) does diphthongal *-éis* replace its monophthongal forerunner (e.g., *avéys, avréys, daréys, podéys, tenéys, diréys, yréys*). If diphthongal *-éis* resulted from morphological rather than phonological phenomena as the chronology of the foregoing textual evidence suggests, then the diphthongal suffix can no longer be applied to support the contention that *buey, grey, ley,* and *rey* resulted from a straightforward phonological process.

The /ée/ > /éi/ law is further weakened by other examples, given above in the discussion of OSp. *veer* > ModSp. *ver*, which demonstrate the fact that throughout the history of Spanish, hiatus of the sequence /ee/ has been resolved by the contraction of the two vowels into one. It is the indisputable fact that /ee/ will eventually contract to /e/, unless some factor impedes the contraction, that makes the development of Sp. *buey, grey, ley,* and *rey* an intriguing problem for Spanish philologists. One would expect Latin BOVEM, GREGEM, LEGEM, and REGEM, to have suffered the same contraction of /ee/ > /e/ after the loss of their medial consonant. And given that /ee/ tended to contract early when the first vowel was stressed, the Latin etyma should have evolved directly into Old Spanish as monosyllabic, monophthongal forms, as depicted in (15):

(15)	BOVEM	>	[bóβe]	> [bwée]	>	*[bwé]	*bue*
	GREGEM	>	[gréɣe]	> [grée]	>	*[gré]	*gre*
	LEGEM	>	[léɣe]	> [lée]	>	*[lé]	*le*
	REGEM	>	[réɣe]	> [rée]	>	[ré]	**re**

There is in fact evidence that this scenario actually happened in the evolution of these four nouns in Early Castilian. Corominas (1981:900), for example, states with regard to *rey* that: "La variante *re* [i.e., monophthongal] abunda en la época arcaica", hence the unastericized **re** in bold print above (and the single asterisk on **bue*, **gre*, **le*, indicating that they are unattested, but may have indeed existed).

But these nouns were formed in the plural in Old Spanish, not only as *bueyes, greyes, leyes,* and *reyes,* but also as *bueys, greys, leys,* and *reys,* which seem to provide further evidence that the original sound law is valid. Based on these items, one could posit the following diachronic equations in (16):

(16)   BOVES   >   [bóβes]   >   [bwées]   >   [bwéi̯s]   OSp. *bueys*
       GREGES   >   [gréɣes]   >   [grées]   >   [gréi̯s]   OSp. *greys*
       LEGES   >   [léɣes]   >   [lées]   >   [léi̯s]   OSp. *leys*
       REGES   >   [réɣes]   >   [rées]   >   [réi̯s]   OSp. *reys*

In fact, these Old Spanish plurals have been viewed by some recent scholars as the regular development, while the formation of the modern Spanish plurals (*bueyes, greyes, leyes, reyes*) has been charged to a restructuring process on the basis of the singulars. A problem arises, however, when one takes a closer look at the textual evidence.

According to the phonologically-based view, one should expect to find *bueys, greys, leys,* and *reys* in the earliest texts, followed by a gradual increase of *bueyes, greyes, leyes,* and *reyes,* since the former allegedly resulted from regular phonetic change while the latter were allegedly restructured throughout the course of the Middle ages. However, the textual evidence does not support this scenario. In fact, the textual evidence seems to indicate that disyllabic *bueyes, greyes, leyes,* and *reyes* are every bit as old as, if not older than, monosyllabic *bueys, greys, leys,* and *reys.* For example, in the Alfonsine *Libro de las leyes,* a book dealing with laws, it is significant that one finds 98 occurrences of the form *leyes,* but not a single occurrence of monosyllabic *leys.*[10] And the earliest attestation of any of these forms that I have been able to find is *bueyes,* which appears twice in a legal document dating from the late-12th century:

> Que quien laurare con **bu[e]yes** tan bien de la uilla como de las aldeas, cada ayno de un almud de trigo; qui laurare con un buey, de medio; aquel qui no ouiere **bueyes**, de al ospital sobredicho de los captiuos quoatro dineros quadayno. (Menéndez Pidal 1966, *DL,* #305 [1184])
> [Whosoever may work with oxen in the village as well as in the towns, may he give each year an "almud" of wheat; whoever will work with one ox, half (an almud); he who will not have oxen, may he give to the abovementioned hostal of the captives four "dineros" (= units of money) each year.]

---

10. For more on the textual evidence and other problems concerning a phonological approach to these plurals, see Rini (1998a).

To account for monosyllabic *bueys*, *greys*, *leys*, and *reys*, one might suggest that these were reformed on the basis of the singulars (Hanssen 1913: 71). But this brings us right back to the question of how the singulars *buey*, *grey*, *ley*, and *rey*, were formed in light of the regular /ée/ > /e/ change.

The original sound law describing a word-final sequence of /-ee/ is made suspect by only one example adduced thus far, i.e., the monosyllabic, monophthongal attestation, *re*. In fact, another grammatical category, the Old Spanish informal imperatives, *¡crey!* 'Believe!', *¡ley!* 'Read!', *¡sey!* 'Be!', and *¡vey!* 'See!' (of *creer, leer, seer,* and *veer*), seems to give credibility to the /ée/ > /éi/ sound law. Based on these items, one could posit the diachronic equations shown in (17):

(17) CREDE > [kréðe] > [krée] > [kréi̯] OSp. *crey*
      LEGE   > [léɣe]   > [lée]   > [léi̯] OSp. *ley*
      SEDE   > [séðe]   > [sée]   > [séi̯] OSp. *sey*
      VIDE   > [βéðe]   > [βée]   > [βéi̯] OSp. *vey*

Perhaps we have here a case where /ée/ in final position become a diphthong, but in word-medial position contract to /e/. One could conclude that these Old Spanish imperatives, as well as the singular nouns *buey*, *grey*, *ley*, and *rey* underwent regular phonetic development, and that the monosyllabic Old Spanish plurals, *bueys*, *greys*, *leys*, and *reys* were formed on the basis of the singulars, i.e., *buey*, *grey*, *ley*, and *rey*, + allomorph /-s/. There is, however, some evidence which complicates the development of the singular nouns and informal imperatives.

In addition to the attested monophthongal *re*, consider the development of Latin FIDEM and PEDEM. After the loss of medial /-d-/, these two lexical items clearly underwent the contraction of /ee/ > /e/ as shown in (18) and as discussed above with regard to OSp. *veer*:

(18) FIDEM > *[féðe] > *[fée] > [fé]   Old and ModSp. *fe*
      PEDEM > *[péðe] > *[pjée] > [pjé] Old and ModSp. *pie*

If one is to uphold the view that *buey, grey, ley,* and *rey* (as well as imperatives *crey, ley, sey,* and *vey*) are straightforward phonological developments, then one has to explain why the intermediate stages in the development of *fe* and *pie* (i.e., disyllabic *[fée] and *[pjée]), did not also undergo semi-vocalization, yielding forms such as **fey* and **piey* in some varieties of Old (or modern Spanish) as depicted in (19):

(19)   FIDEM > *[féðe]   > *[fée]   > **[féi̯]   Old or ModSp. **fey
      PEDEM > *[péðe]   > *[pjée] > **[pjéi̯] Old or ModSp. **piey

Given the unquestionable regularity of the contraction of /ee/ > /e/ (or of any two contiguous like vowels for that matter), perhaps one would do well to consider anomolous the examples which *appear* to show semi-vocalization instead of contraction in word-final position. I believe that the solution to the enigmatic development of Sp. *buey, grey, ley,* and *rey,* can be found in the development and morphological structure of their disyllabic plurals, *bueyes, greyes, leyes,* and *reyes.* All previous treatments, because of their emphasis on sound change and sound laws, have overlooked the role morphological factors may have played in the formation of these nouns (as well as that of the four verbs *crey, ley, sey,* and *vey*).

According to Craddock's observation regarding the relative chronology of the contraction of /ée/ > /é/, one would expect the plurals BOVES, GREGES, LEGES, and REGES, to have suffered an early contraction of /ée/ > /e/ after the loss of their medial consonant (since the first /e/ was stressed), yielding monosyllabic, monophthongal forms, as depicted in (20):

(20)   BOVES   > [bóβes]   > [bwées] >   **[bwés]   **bues
      GREGES > [gréɣes] > [grées] >   **[grés]   **gres
      LEGES   > [léɣes]   > [lées] >   **[lés]   **les
      REGES   > [réɣes]   > [rées] >   **[rés]   **res

However, because of certain morphological factors, the contraction of /ée/ > /e/ would have been resisted. We have already seen above in the case of the paradigm of OSp. *veer* how morphological factors affected the results of the /ée/ > /e/ sound change. In the case of these four nouns, the atonic /e/ was likely felt to be part of the plural morpheme, i.e., phonetically, [bwées], [grées], [lées], [rées] (i.e., no contraction) because morphemically, /bué-es/, /gré-es/, /lé-es/, /ré-es/.

This morphologically motivated resistance in the plurals would have allowed /bué-es/, /gré-es/, /lé-es/, and /ré-es/ to exist long enough with hiatal vocalic sequences to acquire an antihiatic yod as shown in (21):

(21)   [bwées] >   [bwéjes]
         [grées] >   [gréjes]
         [lées]   >   [léjes]
         [rées]   >   [réjes]

It is entirely possible that speakers originally perceived the morphemic boundary of [bwées], [grées], [lées], [rées] between the atonic /e/ and /s/, i.e., morphemically /buee-s/, /gree-s/, /lee-s/, /ree-s/ in light of disyllabic singulars such as /buee/, /gree/, /lee/, /ree/ (cf. OLeon. *buee, gree, lee, ree*). However, once the contraction of /ée/ > /é/ began to diffuse to these nouns, perhaps reaching the singulars first creating allomorphs such as /buee/ ~ /bue/, /gree/ ~ /gre/, /lee/ ~ /le/, /ree/ ~ /re/, the morphemic boundary would have been reinterpreted as /bué-es/, /gré-es/, /lé-es/, /ré-es/ on the basis of the new, monosyllabic singulars.

It is also possible that the medial consonant was never completely lost in three of these four nouns. While Meyer-Lübke, Menéndez Pidal, and those who follow these two posit a direct loss of the velar in the development of both singular and plural of GREGEM, LEGEM, and REGEM, Lloyd (1987: 248), like Hanssen (1913), believes that the loss of the Latin voiced velar /g/ would have left behind, at least temporarily, a trace of a palatal glide, as shown in (22):

(22)	GREGEM	>	[gréɣe]	>	*[gréi̯e]
	GREGES	>	[gréɣes]	>	*[gréi̯es]
	LEGEM	>	[léɣe]	>	*[léi̯e]
	LEGES	>	[léɣes]	>	*[léi̯es]
	REGEM	>	[réɣe]	>	*[réi̯e]
	REGES	>	[réɣes]	>	*[réi̯es]

These forms would have provided the model for the acquisition of the antihiatic yod in BOVE(S) after the loss of its intervocalic bilabial fricative, thus: [bóβe]/ [bóβes] > [bwée]/[bwées] > *[bwéi̯e]/*[bwéi̯es].

Lloyd points out, however, that "[t]his palatal was then absorbed by the vowel and disappeared completely" and gives the example of DIGITUM > *dedo*. But the main difference between this palatal [i̯] (< Latin voiced velar /g/) in the singulars (*[gréi̯e], *[léi̯e], *[réi̯e]) on the one hand, and in the plurals (*[gréi̯es], *[léi̯es], *[réi̯es]) on the other, is that in the plurals the palatal is found at the morphemic boundary, while in the singulars it is not. In the plurals, the absorbtion of the palatal [i̯] into the preceding /é/ would have been resisted, and its articulation strengthened, while in the singulars, the palatal [i̯] would have been absorbed into the preceding vowel since there would have been no morphological pressure to retain it. These different outcomes between singular and plural are depicted in (23):

(23)	*[bwéi̯e]	>	*[bwée]	>	*[bwé]
	*[bwéi̯es]	>	[bwéǰes]		

*[gréi̯e]	>	*[grée]	>	*[gré]	
*[gréi̯es]	>	[gréǰes]			
*[léi̯e]	>	*[lée]	>	*[lé]	
*[léi̯es]	>	[léǰes]			
*[réi̯e]	>	*[rée]	>	[ré]	
*[réi̯es]	>	[réǰes]			

Whether the palatal [i̯] (< Latin voice velar /g/) was indeed absorbed by the preceding vowel in the plurals under scrutiny and later replaced by the antihiatic yod, or whether the original palatal [i̯] remained and strengthened to a full-fledged palatal obstruent (i.e., [ǰ]), it seems reasonable to conclude, taking into account the role of morphology in the evolution of these forms, that the regular development of BOVES, GREGES, LEGES, and REGES would have been [bwéǰes], [gréǰes], [léǰes], [réǰes], i.e., those forms which we now know in modern Spanish. The textual evidence cited earlier supports this conclusion.

Once the disyllabic plurals were established, one might suggest that the singulars arose through a morphological reanalysis of these plural forms, i.e., morphemically, /buéǰ-es/, /gréǰ-es/, /léǰ-es/, /réǰ-es/, backforming and producing singulars /buéǰ/, /gréǰ/, /léǰ/, /réǰ/ following the established pattern of other plural vs. singular nouns where the allomorph /-es/ marked plural, as in (24):

(24)   <u>leon-es</u>   :   <u>español-es</u>   :   <u>rey-es</u>
      <u>leon</u>   :   <u>español</u>   :   X = <u>rey</u>

Furthermore, these plurals may have been realized phonetically with the palatal element spreading across the syllabic boundary, i.e., *[bwéi̯-ǰes], *[gréi̯-ǰes], *[léi̯-ǰes], *[réi̯-ǰes]. Lloyd (1987: 356) writes: "with glide elements, there is a strong phonetic tendency to spread the glide over two syllables when it appears between vowels." Barrutia and Schwegler (1994: 21) recognize: "la articulación … de segmentos fónicos como los que encontramos en <u>leyes</u> o <u>mayo</u> puede ser muy variada dentro de un mismo dialecto (y aún dentro de un mismo hablante) … (la variante [[léi̯-ǰes], [mái̯-ǰo]] es particularmente interesante porque contiene un sonido adicional — un tipo de 'puente fónico' en forma de deslizada (i.e., [j] o [i̯]) — que no se representa al nivel ortográfico)." This appears to be particularly true when the preceding vowel is tonic, as in the case of /buéǰes/, /gréǰes/, /léǰes/, and /réǰes/. From phonetic realizations such as *[bwéi̯-ǰes], *[gréi̯-ǰes], *[léi̯-ǰes], *[réi̯-ǰes], backformations with the palatal offglide could have easily arisen, as shown in (25):

(25) /buéǰes/ > *[bwéi̯-ǰes] (pl.) → [bwéi̯] (sg.) > /buei/
      /gréǰes/ > *[gréi̯-ǰes] (pl.) → [gréi̯] (sg.) > /gréi/
      /léǰes/   > *[léi̯-ǰes] (pl.)   → [léi̯] (sg.)   > /léi/
      /réǰes/   > *[réi̯-ǰes] (pl.)   → [réi̯] (sg.)   > /réi/

In this manner, the formation of the singulars *buey*, *grey*, *ley*, and *rey* may be charged to both morphological and phonological factors, but not to a straightforward phonological development alone.

The Old Spanish imperatives, *crey*, *ley*, *sey*, and *vey* can also be explained in this manner, i.e., as backformations of Early Old Spanish negative imperatives *creyas*, *leyas*, *seyas*, and *veyas*, as in (26):

(26) | Negative Imperative | | | Affirmative Imperative |
      |---|---|---|---|
      | /non kréǰas/ | > | *[non kréi̯-ǰas] | → [kréi̯] |
      | /non léǰas/ | > | *[non léi̯-ǰas] | → [léi̯] |
      | /non séǰas/ | > | *[non séi̯-ǰas] | → [séi̯] |
      | /non βéǰas/ | > | *[non βéi̯-ǰas] | → [βéi̯] |

In the *Libro de buen amor*, for example, one finds the form *sey* in the following verse: *Non le seas mintroso, **sey** le muy verdadero* (MS G 561-1, Mignani et al. 1977). At an earlier stage of the language, such an utterance would certainly have been realized as **Non le **seyas** mintroso, **sey** le muy verdadero* (cf. the abundant attestations of *seya*, etc., in the *Glosas Emilianenses* and *Silenses*, Menéndez Pidal 1950: 359); and it is therefore not inconceivable that in such an utterance the latter affirmative imperative was backformed from the former negative imperative.

Viewing these four nouns and four verbs in terms of reanalysis of the plurals followed by backformation allows one to explain why Latin FIDEM developed to [fé] and not to ****fei**. Since FIDEM 'faith' is essentially a singular idea, this form had no plural such as ****feyes** from which to acquire through backformation the palatal offglide.[11] In the case of Latin PEDES > (*[pjées]>)

---

11. For example, no occurrence of any plural form such as *fees* or ****feyes** is found in the entire corpus of Alfonsine prose. Only one example occurs in ADMYTE vol. 0: *e quebrantamos las fees a las nuestras mugeres* (*Historia Troyana*). It is not until later in the history of Spanish that one finds more examples of the plural *fees*, though it is still relatively infrequent when compared to singular *fe*. For example, ADMYTE vol. 1 shows only five occurrences of *fees* as compared to 1,243 of singular *fe*.

[pjes], the acquisition of an antihiatic glide at the stage *[pjées] may have been thwarted by the presence of the onglide of the root morpheme (i.e., via dissimilation, i.e., *[pjées] > *[pjéjes] > *[pjées]), leading eventually to the contraction of *[pjées] > [pjes]. It is also possible that *pies* is simply sg. /pie/ + the plural allomorph /-s/.

The Portuguese nouns *grei*, *lei*, *rei* and their plurals *greis*, *leis* and *reis* may appear to provide evidence for a /ée/ > /éi/ change in Western, and therefore perhaps in Central, Iberoromance. However, given the tendency of /ee/ > /e/ in this language as well (cf. PEDEM > *pe*, FIDEM > *fe*, as well as OPtg. *creer*, *leer* > ModPtg. *crer*, *ler*), it would not be unreasonable to assume that these nouns in /-ei/ in this language resulted from the same process described above for Castilian. The ultimate preference for plurals in /-éis/ is completely in line with the general preference for descending diphthongs in this language. Alternatively, one could account for these Western forms through a different morphological analysis. Given that Latin open /o/ did not diphthongize in this language, BOVEM and BOVES would develop through regular phonological change to *boe* ~ *boes* and later, through reduction of hiatus, to *boi* and *bois*. On the model of these, the semantically related GREGEM ~ GREGES 'herd(s)' would follow suit via analogy as depicted in (27), during a period in which hiatal *boe* and diphthongal *boi* were co-existent variants (cf. the co-existing variants *boe* ~ *boy* in Old Leonese, Pensado 1988: 216):

(27)   variant 1:   <u>*boe*</u> :   <u>*gree*</u>
        variant 2:   *boi* :   X = *grei*

Then, structurally similar *lee* and *ree* would follow the lead of *gree*, as shown in (28):

(28)   variant 1:   <u>*gree*</u>   :   <u>*lee*</u>   :   <u>*ree*</u>
        variant 2:   *grei*   :   X = *lei* :   X = *rei*

The Portuguese plurals can be accounted for in this mannar as well as shown in (29):

(29)   variant 1:   <u>*boes*</u> :   <u>*grees*</u>   :   <u>*lees*</u>   :   <u>*rees*</u>
        variant 2:   *bois* :   X = *greis* :   X = *leis* :   X = *reis*

Given that the Western forms can be accounted for through morphological processes, they can provide absolutely no solid evidence for a phonological change of /ée/ > /éi/ in this language, or in Castilian.

The skeptic may doubt that a singular can be derived from a plural, given that the former is much more frequent in occurrence than the latter. And in the case of these four Spanish nouns, the singular indeed occurred with significantly greater frequency (see data in Rini 1998a). Nevertheless, some of these nouns appeared in their plural form in important, highly visible syntagms, e.g., *los reyes magos* 'the three Wise Men', also, *las leyes del regno* 'the laws of the land' (hence the Alfonsine *Libro de las leyes* 'The Book of Laws', not *Libro de la ley*). Moreover, as discussed in Chapter 1, the process of reanalysis followed by backformation of a singular noun from its plural is not unknown to Spanish or other languages (cf. OSp. singular *el tiempos*, *el cuerpos*, reanalyzed as plural *los tiempos*, *los cuerpos*, from which new singular *el tiempo*, *el cuerpo* were derived; also, cf. Fr. *le château* < OFr. pl. *les châteaux* ~ sg. *le châtel*; and Engl. *pea* < MidEngl. pl. *pise*).

The developed of these nouns, in both the singular and plural, may be summarized as in (30) with the noun REGEM ~ REGES, according to the present analysis:

(30)   REGEM > /réi̯e/ > /rée/ > /ré/ EOSp. re > re ~ rey > OSp. rey (+ pl. /s/)
                                                ↑   ↓
        REGES > /ré-(i̯)es/ > /ré-ĵes/ OSp. *reyes* (analyzed /reĵ-es/) > reyes ~ reys

In light of the present analysis, one may conclude that the sound law /ée/ > /éi/ is merely an illusion: The nouns *buey*, *grey*, *ley*, *rey* and their plurals, and the Old Spanish imperatives *crey*, *ley*, *sey*, *vey*, all of which on the surface appear to be the result of sound change, were actually the products of morphological change. This analysis resolves the difficulty of explaining why the vocalic sequence /ée/ would have produced both /é/ and /éi/ in identical phonetic environments. When a sound change /A/ > /B/ can be attributed incontrovertibly to phonological processes, perhaps we should question whether or not some factor extraneous to the phonological system, morphological or other, is at work when in some cases /A/ appears to have given rise to /C/, instead of simply assuming that the /A/ > /C/ change was also the result of a phonological process.

The *Voseo* Imperatives: Sound Change or Morphemicization?

The development of the Latin imperatives in -TE (originally plural) yielded two results in modern Spanish: (a) forms which retain a phonetic remnant of Latin /t/, e.g., AMATE 'Love!' > *amad*, PONETE 'Put!' > *poned*, VENITE 'Come!' > *venid*; and (b) forms which do not, e.g., AMATE > *amá*, PONETE > *poné*, VENITE > *vení*. The former function as the standard Peninsular informal plurals, while the latter predominate as singulars in *voseante* regions of America, and as plurals in Peninsular Spanish when followed by *os*, e.g., *¡Levantaos!* 'Get up! (pl.)'.

The development of both sets of imperatives has been traditionally viewed as a straightforward phonological change. Regarding the forms which retain /d/, for example, Lloyd (1987: 315) writes: "In general, the imperative forms developed as one would expect with regular phonetic change. Thus . . . -TE > -d." Indeed the development of these forms is quite clear, as Penny (1991: 139) points out: "Pre-literary Spanish gives glimpses of forms like *cantade* (< CANTATE), which most frequently lost their /-e/ and provided the predominant medieval and modern form *cantad*." The development of the second set, however, is less transparent. De Souza (1964: 4–5) posits two possible chronologies after the voicing of Latin intervocalic /t/: (a) Loss of /-d-/ followed by vocalic simplification, e.g., AMATE > *amade* > *amae* > *amá*; and (b) Loss of final /-e/ followed by loss of final /-d/, e.g., AMATE > *amade* > *amad* > *amá*. De Souza not only posits two different hypothetical scenarios, but also believes that both may have actually occurred: "de ser así, las formas que llamamos simplificadas [i.e., *-á*, *-é*, *-í*] podrían provenir de dos soluciones originariamente divergentes" (1964: 4).

To date there is no consensus on which of the two hypothetical scenarios, if not both, is more representative of the historical linguistic reality. In the two most recent historical grammars of Spanish, one finds opposing views. Lloyd (1987: 360) follows the view that the loss of final /-d/ followed the loss of final /-e/: "In much of American Spanish it [i.e., /-d/] disappeared, leaving the imperative for *vos* as a stressed vowel, *-á*, *-é*, *-í*." Penny (1991: 139), on the other hand, subscribes to the chronology in which loss of intervocalic /d/ is followed by a simplification of the remaining vocalic sequences: "[P]re-literary *cantade* was probably also the ancestor (via loss of /d/ and assimilation /áe/ > /á/) of the frequent golden Age imperative *cantá* (similarly *meté*, *salí*)."

There is evidence which appears to suggest a longer retention in some varieties of Ibero-Romance of final /-e/ and loss of /d/ when intervocalic in pre-literary imperatives such as *cantade*. Menéndez Pidal (1941: 281): "El leonés aún hoy conserva la *-e*: *dade*, *fazede*, *salide*, forma que, naturalmente, existió también en el castellano primitivo, y de la cual derivan *dai*, *facei*, *sali*, vulgares en ciertas partes de Castilla y muy usadas en leonés, gallego y portugués." García de Diego (1951: 180) similarly states: "En el antiguo estado -te -*de* se perdió en ciertas zonas la *d* antes que la *e* y se originaron *llorai, tenei, decí*." But the existence of such forms does not prove that the forms we now know as the *voseo* imperatives descended from those in which the loss of /-d-/ preceded the loss of /-e/. Granted, a form like **cantade* could have first evolved to **cantae*, after which the loss of hiatus would produce *cantai*. But how would this form have yielded *cantá*, as Penny has proposed? There is no evidence of any phonological change of /ai̯/ > /a/ in the history of Spanish. Penny (1991: 139) tries to circumvent this difficulty by suggesting that, rather than a loss of hiatus, assimilation of atonic /e/ to tonic /á/ occurred in a form like **cantae*. However, this proposal lacks support from any evidence, be it dialectal, textual, or theoretical. If this vocalic sequence had truly undergone progressive assimilation, one would expect to find recorded somewhere, either in writing or in non-standard varieties of Castilian, an intermediate stage of development exhibiting a disyllabic hiatal allomorph as depicted in bold in the following hypothetical diachronic equation: *-ae* > ****-aa** > *-á*. The same may be said for third conjugation imperatives which, after the loss of intervocalic /d/, would have left a vocalic sequence such as *-íe*. According to Penny, *-íe* also underwent assimilation to *-í*. But where is the concrete evidence for the intermediate stage of a diachronic equation such as *-íe* > ****-íi** > *-í*? Such cases of progressive assimilation before the contraction of two like vowels into one can be found in the evolution of a closely related language, namely, Old Portuguese, e.g., MONACHUM > *moago* > *moogo* > *mogo*; SOLAM > *soa* > *soo* > *só*; MOLAM > *moa* > *moo* > *mo*; NUDUM > *nuo* > *nuu* > *nú*; PELAGUM > *peago* > *peego* > *pego*; *ame(n)açar* > *ameaçar* > *ameeçar*; *incre(d)u(l)o* > *encreeo*. The fact remains that the vocalic sequence **-ae* would have suffered a loss of hiatus to *-ai*, not assimilation to *-á*, while **-íe* would have undergone apocope of final /-e/, evolving directly to *-í*, most likely to avoid merger with the Old Spanish imperfect in /-ie/ (hence, a morphologically motivated change). It is only the second conjugation imperatives such as *poné*, *comé*, etc., whose desinence could have evolved with loss of /-d-/ prior to loss of /-e/. The resulting vocalic sequence would have been /ée/, which, as seen in preceding discussions, would have evolved directly to /é/ (not /éi̯/) in Castilian, e.g., PONETE > *ponede* > **ponee* > *poné*. Thus it is unlikely that dialectal variants such as *facei* and *tenei* continue any sort of phonological development. Rather, all dialectal forms such as those cited above by Menéndez Pidal and García de Diego were most likely derived from the present indicative, i.e., pres.

ind. *dais, facéis, salís* minus /-s/ → imperative *dai, facéi, salí*, by analogy with the same pattern found in the original second person singular as shown in (31), thus constituting a morphological change:

(31)	pres.ind.	(*tú*)	*cantas*	:	(*vos*)	*cantáis*
	imper.		*canta*	:		X = *cantái*
	pres.ind.	(*tú*)	*comes*	:	(*vos*)	*coméis*
	imper.		*come*	:		X = *coméi*
	pres.ind.	(*tú*)	*vives*	:	(*vos*)	*vivís*
	imper.		*vive*	:		X = *viví*

Given the insuperable obstacles in deriving the *voseo* imperatives from forms which lost /-d-/ before /-e/, it makes infinitely more sense to suggest that forms such as *amad, poned, venid* evolved via loss of final /d/ to *amá, poné, vení*. After all, the loss of final /d/ is commonly found in lexical items outside of the verbal paradigm in many varieties of modern Spanish, e.g., *ciudá, salú, usté, verdá*, etc.[12] The loss of word-final /d/, however, should not be thought of as a post-medieval development. Menéndez Pidal (1941: 101) documents the loss of /-d/ as early as the 13th century: "desde el siglo XIII se hallan ejemplos escritos de *heredá, merçé*." Perhaps it is for this reason that, despite the apparent dialectal evidence for the loss of /-d-/ before /-e/ in some varieties of Ibero-Romance, Menéndez Pidal believed that the imperatives in *-á, -é*, and *-í* resulted from the loss of /-d/ of *-ad, -ed*, and *-id*: "Vos, -TE > -d, la -d antiguamente podía escribirse *-t: andat, sabet*. También se pierde en la pronunciación y esa pérdida estuvo de moda entre nuestros clásicos: *andá, hazé, subí*" (1941: 281).

The only other phonetic environment which could have given rise to the dental-deleted imperatives is found in the grammatical category of the reflexive verb, after the reduction of the enclitic reflexive pronoun, where the /d/ could have been lost in intervocalic position, e.g., *sentadvos > sentad(v)os > sentados > senta(d)os > sentaos* (compare the loss of /-d-/ of the past participle in modern Spanish in the phonetically identical environment, e.g., *hablado* → [a-βlá-o] ~ [a-βláu̯]). It is not inconceivable that the loss of /d/ began with reflexive verbs,

---

12. Lipski (1994: 46) recognizes the "sever reduction" of final /d/ (along with /s/ and /r/) as one of the 'Andalusian' phonetic traits which are concentrated in the Caribbean, the Pacific coast of South America, and the River Plate.

and later spread to non-reflexives since the former can often function non-reflexively, e.g., *poned(v)os el abrigo* 'Put on your coat!'> *pone(d)os el abrigo* > *poneos el abrigo* → *poné la mesa* 'Set the table!'.

Textual evidence shows that the loss of /d/ in reflexive imperatives began before the very period in which we find the first heavy concentration of non-reflexive imperatives without final /d/. For example, in the *Cancionero general* (Valencia, 1511) which contains writings from authors who flourished from ca. 1395–1520 (De Souza 1964: 37), one finds 51 occurrences of reflexives without /d/ by 15 different authors (-*aos* 44, -*eos* 2, -*íos* 5) vs. only 4 examples (four different authors) in which /d/ is retained (-*advos* 1, -*edvos* 1, -*idvos* 1, plus one *ydos* 1). Of the 51 reflexives without /d/, 11 occur in the writings of seven different authors who flourished from the early- to mid-15th century. Of the other 40 examples, 25 appear in the works of two authors from the mid- to late-15th century, while the remaining 15 were produced by six different authors who wrote during the late-15th and early-16th centuries. (Of the four examples which retain /d/, 3 occur from the early- to mid-15th century, the other in the late-15th- to early-16th century). The appearance of the non-reflexive impera-tives, on the other hand, was slightly later. One finds that of 26 authors who employed non-reflexive imperatives without /-d/, 20 wrote between the late-15th and early-16th centuries, 4 from the mid- to late-15th century, and only 3 from the early- to mid-15th century. Regarding the actual forms, one finds 555 occurrences of imperatives with retention of final /-d/ (though many of these function as plurals) vs. 64 occurrences without /-d/,[13] of which 55 were pro-duced by authors whose writings straddled the late-15th and early-16th centuries. The remaining 9 examples include 6 in writings from the mid- to late-15th century, and only 3 from the early- to mid-15th century. But while this proposal resolves the difficulties discussed above in deriving the singular imperative from the phonetic environment found in hypothetical forms like **cantae*, it does not explain how the newly formed dental-deleted allomorph would have eventually come to function only as a singular, while the reduced pronoun *os* (< *vos*) did not.

I would like to suggest that the loss of final /d/ from the Old Spanish

---

13. This does not include imperatives which involve an enclitic *-os*, i.e., *acordaos*, since the loss of /d/ in this case is intervocalic, not word-final, e.g., *acordadvos* > *acordad(v)os acordados* > *acorda(d)os* > *acordaos*. Furthermore, such are the forms which belong to the modern paradigm in the plural and alternate with forms retaining final /-d/, i.e., *¡acordadme!* vs. *¡acordaos!*

imperatives was not a straightforward phonological change. Lloyd (1987) introduces a morphological factor into the picture. Though he subscribes to the view that the *voseo* imperatives are direct descendents of the Old Spanish imperatives with loss of final /-d/, he believes that the "need to distinguish between *tú* and *vos* (and at the same time between singular and plural) probably helped maintain the final *-d* of the plural imperative in peninsular Spanish" (1987: 359). Thus, according to Lloyd, the loss of final /-d/ is the expected change, while the retention of it is due to morphological factors.

While I do not disagree with Lloyd's view regarding the retention of /-d/ in Peninsular Spanish, I believe it tells only part of the story. It remains to be explained why final /-d/ would be totally deleted in the *voseo* imperatives of some varieties of New World Spanish which generally retain final /-d/. For example, one finds no report of loss of final /-d/ in the Spanish of Guatemala or Honduras (Lipski 1994: 265–66, 270–72), indeed "intervocalic /d/ is resistant to elision" in Guatemala, yet the "use of *vos* and accompanying verb forms is the rule in Guatemalan Spanish" (Lipski 1994: 265–66) and "Honduran Spanish uses *vos* exclusively instead of *tú*, with the same verbal morphology found in the other Central American countries" (Lipski 1994: 272). And the imperatives in these two countries are of the type "*tomá, comé, viví*" (Páez Urdaneta 1981: 79–80). It also remains to be explained why the loss of /-d/ in the *voseo* imperative was so relatively late (i.e., late-15th- to early-16th centuries), when its loss in lexical items outside of the verbal paradigm is documented as early as the 13th century (Menéndez Pidal 1941: 101). Finally, in order to strengthen Lloyd's proposal regarding the reason for the retention of /-d/ in the plural, I would like to explain precisely how /-d/ came to be associated with the plural, since, in theory, there is no reason why it could not have been lost in the plural but retained in the singular, and still distinguish between these two grammatical categories.

Though the loss of final /d/ has been seen as a fairly regular or expected development, the shedding of this final consonant in the imperative was likely accelerated by its use as a singular. It is well known that throughout the Middle Ages *vos* and its verb forms functioned as both singular and plural. Though it began as a polite form of address, it eventually descended to the level of its modern function, i.e., a very intimate, informal form of address, in some regions even more familiar than *tú*. Somewhere along the continuum of its descent, perhaps toward the end of the Middle Ages (Lapesa 1970), it became functionally and semantically equivalent to *tú*. With regard to the reduction of the non-imperative forms (i.e., *-ades*, *-edes*, *-ides*, *-odes*) Dworkin (1988a: 151–52) writes:

> *tú* and *vós* were becoming functionally equivalent for some speakers in the late Middle Ages. In speaking to a single individual, *tú fablas* apparently came to be synonymous with *vós fablades*, especially as *vós* gradually lost its former prestige and status. It does not seem unreasonable to suggest that some speakers, in the interest of paradigmatic economy, might have attempted to level (albeit partially) the 2nd person verbal suffixes by bringing the ending associated with *vós* more closely into line with the desinence connected with *tú*, e.g., by altering *fablades* to *fabláis* and *fablás*. It may be no accident that the earliest examples of the reduction of -V*des* coincide chronologically with the reduction of social status suffered by *vós* when used as a singular pronoun.

In a similar fashion, when addressing an individual with an imperative, *¡(vos) fablad!* would have become synonymous with *¡(tú) fabla!* The reduction to *¡(vos) fablá!* would bring the form more into line with *¡(tú) fabla!* Testimony to the vacillation between presence and absence of /-d/ in the imperative is found in Nebrija (1492:126): "algunas vezes hazemos cortamiento de aquella *d*, diziendo *ama lee oi*."

The scenario described above by Dworkin would have led to a paradigm such as that in (32), if only for a relatively brief moment in the history of Spanish (parentheses indicate vacillation between presence and absence of /d/):

(32)		SINGULAR	PLURAL
	Indicative	*fablas*	*fablades*
		fabla(d)es	
		fabláis/fablás	
	Imperative	*fabla(d)*	*fablad*

It is at this point in time that /d/ would begin to be associated more with the plural. (The loss of /-d-/ in the suffix *-ades*, for example, began during the first decades of the 15th century).

But by the late-15th century, the verbal suffixes *-ades*, *-edes*, *-ides*, *-odes* had, for the most part, shed their dental consonant in both singular and plural (see Chapter 4 for full details). This does not mean, however, that /-d/ in the plural imperative was doomed. Outside of the verbal paradigm, one can cite another grammatical category which would link the /d/ of the imperative to the plural, namely nouns ending in /-d/. Common nouns such as *ciudad*, *heredad*, *merçed, verdad*, etc., which could be realized phonetically in the singular as [tsju-δá], [e-re-δá], [mer-tsé], [βer-δá] could only be realized phonetically in the plural as [tsju-δá-δes], [e-re-δá-δes], [mer-tsé-δes], [βer-δá-δes]. Thus speakers who consistently deleted word-final /d/ may have reanalyzed /-des/ as the plural morpheme, e.g., sg. /verdá/ + /-des/ → pl. /verda+des/. Note that this nominal plural morpheme is identical to that of the verbal system in second person suffixes *-ades*, *-edes*, *-ides*, *-odes*, i.e., thematic vowel + /-des/. Finally, the retention of /-d/ in the plural imperative was likely supported by the same retention in proparoxytonic forms, i.e., imp.ind. *amávades, poníades, veníades*; imp.subj. *amássedes, pusiéssedes, viniéssedes*; pluperf.ind. *amárades, pusierades, vinierades*; fut.subj. *amáredes, pusiéredes, viniéredes*, which did not totally shed their /-d-/ until the middle of the 17th century (Dworkin 1988a: 144).

This association of /d/ with the plural would have elevated the phonetic realization of this phoneme to morphemic status in the imperative as shown in (33):

(33)   Morpheme   Allomorphs   Morphemes
                              [−á]   >   /-á/ [singular]
        /-ád/ [2nd pers. sg. or pl.]

                              [−áδ]   >   /-ád/ [plural]

Once this morphemicization of /-d/ occurred, the dental would have to be totally deleted from the imperative as shown in (34) when used as a singular (again, parentheses denote vacillation of presence and absence of /-d/):

(34)   SINGULAR PLURAL   SINGULAR PLURAL
        Imp. *fabla(d) fablad* >   *fablá   fablad*

Thus what may have begun as a phonetic vacillation between presence and absence of /-d/ in the imperative when used as a singular (initiated by the morphological reason suggested by Dworkin), resulted in a full-fledged categorical deletion of the dental in the singular, once it had become a plural morpheme. The formation of the *voseo* imperatives, therefore, constitutes a morphological, not a phonological change, as previous scholarship has assumed. The data from the *Cancionero general* suggest that the period of phonetic vacillation with sporadic deletion of /-d/ began in the early-15th century, and that the morphemicization of /-d/ and subsequent deletion in the singular occurred between the end of the 15th and beginning of the 16th century, when one finds a sudden increase of dental-deleted forms. Because of this sudden increase of dental-deleted forms, it is unlikely that the process was simply a case of analogy with the original singulars as depicted below in (35), and suggested in (31) for some of the Peninsular dialectal forms such as *cantái, coméi, viví*:

(35)　pres.ind.　(*tú*)　　*cantas*　　:　(*vos*)　　*cantás*

　　　imper.　　　　*canta*　　:　　　　　X = *cantá*

Such a process as shown in (35) would have resulted in a more gradual appearance of forms over a longer period of time. The sudden burst of forms which appeared at the turn of the 16th century clearly points toward morphemicization followed by rapid deletion, though this morphologically motivated deletion of /-d/ in the singular imperative may have received support from the existing pattern of the original second person singular between indicative and imperative, which, to the speakers of the time, may have been perceived synchronically as a rule involving deletion of final /s/, e.g., /fablás/ 'You speak' → /fablá/ 'Speak!', like /fáblas/ 'You speak' → /fábla/ 'Speak!'

The present diachronic morphological analysis accounts for (a) the retention of /-d/ in the plural imperative, (b) the relatively late appearance of the dental-deleted imperatives *vis-à-vis* early (non-verbal) attestations of deletion of word-final /d/ (13th century), and (c) the total absence of /-d/ in the *voseo* imperative in varieties of Spanish which generally retain word-final /-d/. A straightforward phonological analysis, on the other hand, cannot account for any of these facts.

CHAPTER 4

The Morphological Spread of Sound Change

The Reduction of Old Spanish
-ades, -edes, -ides, -odes

Another morphological change in the history of Spanish which had been traditionally viewed as a case of sound change, before Dworkin's two-part study (1988a & 1988b), is the reduction of the Old Spanish second person verbal suffixes *-ades, -edes, -ides*, (and *-odes*), e.g., *amades* 'you love', *comedes* 'you eat', *vivides* 'you live', and *sodes* 'you are', all of which shed their intervocalic /-d-/, yielding in modern Spanish forms such as *amáis, coméis, vivís*, and *sois* (as well as *amás, comés*, and *sos* [singular only]). Dworkin (1988a: 144) writes: "Scholars have paid no attention to the nature of the process at work in the loss of the *-d-* of the verbal suffix *-Vdes* because it has been implicitly viewed as a straightforward sound change." According to Dworkin, Hispanists had concerned themselves primarily with the longer retention of /-d-/ in unstressed suffixes such as pluperf.ind. *amárades, comiérades, viviérades*, imp.subj. *amássedes, comiéssedes, viviéssedes*, etc. which did not shed their /-d-/ until the middle of the 17th century. Previous scholarship was either content simply to document and describe the lag between the reduction of stressed and unstressed suffixes in /-des/, or attempted to explain the persistence of /-d-/ in such forms in terms of phonological phenomena only. Dworkin further points out that during the same period in which /-d-/ was being shed from the stressed verbal suffixes (i.e., 15th century), it remained unaffected, not only in the unstressed suffixes, but in all other cases as well, i.e., nouns, adjectives, past participles: "in the late Middle Ages when *-Vdes* was losing its medial consonant, all other instances of [ð] remained intact."[1] This observation led Dworkin to question whether the reduction of the verbal suffixes did not in fact involve a morphological change (1988a:150):

> [D]oes the reduction of -V*des* involve a phonological or morphological change? ... It may not be insignificant that the earliest instances of the loss of -*d*- < -T- in Spanish occur within the system of verbal suffixes. A few Romanists have operated with the notion that some sound changes can, in theory, be produced by morphological conditions. A pattern or alternation limited at the outset to a specific morphological subclass (say, the verbal paradigm) may, in the long run diffuse by analogy, under the right circumstances, to nouns and adjectives.

Dworkin (1988a: 151) concludes that the high frequency of these suffixes, due to their use not only as plurals, but also as singular forms of address in the Middle Ages, made them more susceptible to reduction. Moreover, as seen in Chapter 3, their use as singulars may have further contributed to their reduction, as they would have thus been brought more into line with the original second person singular, *tú*, e.g., *vos fablades* > *vos fabláis/fablás* vis à vis *tú fablas* (Dworkin 1988a: 152). If this is true, then what we have here is a phonological change that was actuated by morphological, or morphosyntactic factors.[2] The further spread of this change to participles, adjectives, and nouns would, according to Dworkin, constitute a case of lexical diffusion. Dworkin (1988a: 150, 151) offers a nice summary of the lexical diffusion hypothesis and explains how it applies to the problem at hand:

> Students of language change have held two views on how a sound change can alter the pertinent lexical items of a language. One camp has long maintained that all forms whose structure exposes them to a given change are affected simultaneously [i.e., the neogrammarian view]. Another group of scholars claims that a sound change works its way through the lexicon item by item. This view,

---

1. It is not until the 16th century that one finds the loss of /-d-/, for example, in the participial suffixes -*ado*, -*ido* (Boyd-Bowman 1975: 2; Lapesa 1983:§93₄).

2. Some might argue that this change should be labeled a "morphophonological" change, since it is a phonological change that has occurred under specific morphological conditions. Blaylock (1986), by the way, refers to the loss of /-d-/ in the unstressed second person plural suffixes as a morphophonological change. In any case, Dworkin has successfully demonstrated that the loss of /-d-/ in these suffixes is not simply a case of straightforward sound change, but involves the interaction of phonological and morphological processes, as is clearly stated in the title of his article (1988a).

promoted and championed by William S.-Y. Wang [1969] and his followers on the basis of their studies of change in Chinese, is known as the lexical diffusion hypothesis. Conceivably a given change may be blocked by a competing process before it has had a chance to alter all morphemes subject to its effects. Thus many forms traditionally labeled as exceptions may represent a residue of items to which the sound change at issue had failed to spread ...

The foregoing observations on the inception and spread of a sound change may now throw some light on the processes underlying the reduction of -V*des*. If a sound change does work its way through the lexicon item by item, it must originate either in an individual leader word or in a particular subset of morphemes. It seems reasonable to contend that in many varieties of late Medieval Hispano-Romance there began a sound change deleting intervocalic [ð]. The verbal suffix -V*des* may have constituted a compact subset upon which this incipient change first acted. Several linguists have demonstrated that changes involving deletion of a segment usually affect first the most frequent morphemes. In Medieval Spanish the second person plural of the verb was used not only to address more than one person, but also as the formal form of address to a single individual. Thus in the spoken language the verbal suffix -V*des* must have occurred with considerable frequency. From this verb ending the change deleting [ð] could have spread in some social and regional dialects to the participial suffixes -*ado* and -*ido* (formations which straddle the border between verbs and adjectives) and later, from the verb system, item by item, to adjectives and nouns.[3]

---

3. Hock (1991: 649–50) similarly describes the lexical diffusion hypothesis, thus:

In 1969, Wang proposed the hypothesis that the mechanism of sound change may be lexical diffusion, a notion related to, but distinct from, Labov's variable rules. Under this hypothesis sound change application in many cases is specified vis-à-vis individual lexical items.

Phonetic change evidently takes time to be completed. But phonetically (or phonologically), change must be abrupt, in that a given segment either is phoneme X or phoneme Y. Under these circumstances, the only way that change can take time is by being lexically gradual, through the gradual diffusion of the change from one lexical item to another. Thus, at first only a small section of the lexicon is affected by the change X > Y. Along the way, as the change diffuses, there may be some fluctuation between X and Y. Eventually, however, Y will win out — provided the change runs its full course.

For strengths and weaknesses of the lexical diffusion hypothesis, see Hock (1991: 650–52). For applications of this hypothesis to problems in Romance more recent than Dworkin (1988a & 1988b), see Harris-Northall (1990), and Del Valle (1996).

Dworkin pursues the idea of lexical diffusion in his follow-up piece published the same year (1988b).[4] In that study, Dworkin attempts to determine whether the loss of /-d-/ can be pinpointed to one of the four second person verbal suffixes. After a meticulous examination of relevant texts, Dworkin concludes that "the suffix *-edes* may have been the first to undergo reduction" (1988b: 232). Alluding to the factor of frequency and its role in the reduction of morphemes discussed in the companion piece (1988a), though not mentioned again here, Dworkin points out that *-edes* was highly frequent as it carried out the function of a second person suffix in (a) the present indicative for *-er* verbs, (b) the present subjunctive for *-ar* verbs, and (c) the future indicative of all three conjugation classes (1988b: 232). He also stresses that the two earliest examples involve the future (*andarés, yrés* in the late-14th century *Libro de buen amor*) and asks: "Is this a clue that the reduction of stressed *-Vdes* originated in the future ending ...?" With regard to the diffusion of the change, Dworkin (1988b: 232) concludes: "Spanish is a language with a strong predilection for morphological regularity, especially in verb endings ... Once *-edes* had lost its medial consonant, it would not have taken long for *-ades* and *-ides* to follow suit."

The purpose of the present chapter is two-fold: (a) To adduce more textual evidence in an attempt to confirm or refute that the suffix *-edes*, perhaps in its role as future morpheme, was the starting point of the change; and (b) To show exactly how *-ades*, *-ides*, and *-odes* "followed suit", if indeed they did, and if indeed *-edes* was the starting point of the change.

The *Dança general de la muerte* provides some insight into the time frame during which the reduction of *-ades*, *-edes*, *-ides*, and *-odes* took place. This work exists in two versions: a manuscript, whose original date of composition is ca. 1392 (Sola-Solé 1981: 13–14),[5] and an edition of 1520. We are therefore provided with an opportunity to compare two stages of the language, roughly 130 years apart, as it is found in one literary work. In the manuscript, one finds the following reduced forms: *abés* (twice), *abrés, darés, podrés, tenés* (twice), *yrés, esteys, vayaes*, and *soes* (three times).[6] The 1520 edition offers *avréys, cantaréys* (twice), *daréys* (twice), *diréys, seréys* (4 times), *yréys, avéys, podéis, podéys* (twice), *tenéys, traéys, curéys, estáys, soys* (4 times), and *bivís*. One notes here

---

4. Although this follow-up piece carries the same publication date as Dworkin (1988a), it actually appeared first.

5. The date of the manuscript is said to be ca. 1480.

6. Dworkin (1988b) omits the forms *podrés* and *tenés* cited here.

that during the 130-year period separating the two versions of the *Dança*, the reduction of -V*des*, once apparently limited to -*edes* (e.g., fut. *darés*, pres. ind. *tenés*, pres. subj. *estéys*), and other second-conjugation suffixes (e.g., pres. ind. *sodes* > *soes*, pres. subj. *vayades* > *vayaes*), has diffused to grammatical categories not affected in the manuscript, i.e., the present indicative of the first and third conjugations (e.g., *estáys* and *bivís*).[7] It would therefore be beneficial to examine textual evidence during this 130-year period to gain further insight into the diffusion of this change.

The *Cancionero general* (Valencia 1511) is an excellent corpus of data to examine in an attempt to trace the reduction of -*ades*, -*edes*, -*ides*, and -*odes*. It contains the writings of 102 different authors spanning seven generations, from 1395–1520, the very period of time that separates the two versions of the *Dança*. Moreover, the lyric poetry of the *Cancionero general* may approximate more closely the every-day spoken register of the time, though one concedes here that no sample of written language ever truly represents colloquial speech habits. Dworkin (1988b: 231) points out that Juan de Mena (one of the 102 authors whose writings appear in the *Cancionero general*) opted for non-reduced forms in his "stately" *Laberinto de Fortuna*, but that he employed forms without /-d-/ in his lyric poetry, a fact which may indicate that, until their general acceptance, the reduced forms "may have carried for some speakers and writers a certain stigma or association with lower class speech or less serious and noble registers, genres and styles." Dworkin's reference to "lower class speech" may be better expressed as "colloquial speech", since many speakers are capable of producing both colloquial and more formal registers of speech, regardless of the social class to which they belong (though it is generally true that less educated speakers are less likely to be able to produce more formal registers). It is a long-standing belief that many linguistic changes begin in the more colloquial registers of speech, as Pulgram (1963: 40) so eloquently expresses:

> The vast majority of linguistic changes has its inception in the popular, colloquial rather than in the learned, classical, written, by nature and purpose conservative form of language. That is to say, since change initially, before it becomes the new standard, implies a deviation from the norm, from the old standard, it follows that in human societies, structured as they have been and

---

7. Other differences between the forms of the earlier and later versions of the *Dança* include the reduction of hiatus (e.g., -*aes* > -*áys* and -*oes* > -*oys*), and an increase in diphthongal -*eys*, formerly monophthongal -*és*.

are (and not, perhaps, as they will be or ought to be), the less educated and socially less favored majority is more prone to originate and propagate, consciously or unconsciously, deviations from the minority's unknown or incompletely known social norms — cherished perhaps by the minority for no other reason than in order to distance and distinguish itself from the mass.

Thus the diffusion of the change under study here is more likely to show up first in a register of writing which exhibits a more colloquial or popular style of speech, namely the poetry of the *Cancionero general*.

Evidence from the only two writers of the first generation (1395–1425) supports Dworkin's suspicion that the reduction of /-Vdes/ began with *-edes*, and specifically, when functioning as the second-person future morpheme. In the writings of Castilian-born Hernán Pérez de Guzmán, one finds that three out of four reduced forms involve the future, the other *aver*: *gozarés*, *serés*, *verés*, and *avés*. Similarly, in the writings of Pérez de Guzmán's Andalusian contemporary, Juan A. de Baena, one finds five occurrences of reduced *-edes* in future functions: *avréys*, *hallarés*, *podrés*, and *veré(y)s* (twice). Neither author uses the full-formed forerunner *-edes* in the future.

The only author classified as second generation (to 1440), the Marqués de Santillana, employed both reduced and non-reduced allomorphs of /-edes/ in the future: *estaréys*, *hallarés*, *seré(y)s* (twice), vs. *faredes*, *veredes*. These occurrences of reduced *-Vdes* are particularly significant given the conservative nature of this author's writing. Dworkin (1988b: 228): "The MSS which preserve the poetry and prose of the Marqués de Santillana display an overwhelming preference for *-Vdes*."

Authors classified as third generation (to 1455), were greatly in favor of the reduced allomorph for future functions. In the writings of Lope de Estúñiga, one finds only reduced *darés*, *dirés*, *harés*, *ternés* (3 times), and Gómez Manrique penned only *daréys*, *hallaréys*, *podréys*, *preguntarés*, *seréys*, *venceréys*. Antón Montoro likewise employed only reduced suffixes in the future, e.g., *avrés* (2), *diré(y)s* (2), *gastaréys*, *guardarés*, *harés*, *pesaréys*, *ternéys*. Others who only used the short future form include Juan Agraz (*morirés*), Bachiller de la Torre (*veréys*), and Juan Rodríguez del Padrón (*alcançaréys*, *hallaréys*). Only one author of this generation, Juan de Mena, was found to use the longer future suffix *-edes*, yet even in this case the shorter *-é(y)s* predominates: *avredes*, *seredes*, *veredes* vs. *acertarés*, *avréys*, *diréys*, *fallaréys*, *hallaréys*, *temeréys*.

The *Cancionero general* contains writings of several authors who cannot be classified specifically by generation though they can be identified as having flourished during the reign of Juan II (1406–1454), a time-frame which corresponds roughly to the first three generations (1395–1455). These writers used the short future suffix exclusively: Barba — *dexarés, passarés, veré(y)s* (2); Conde de Paredes — *bolveréys, daréys, dexarés, partiréys, veréys*; Francisco Vaca — *dirés, hallaré(y)s* (3), *sabrés*; Gonzalo Dávila — *andarés*; Juan Maestre el Trepador — *querréys*.

The total occurrences of the reduced future allomorph in the *Cancionero general* from 1395–1455 outnumber those of non-reduced *-edes* by a wide margin, i.e., *-é(y)s* 59 (92.2%) vs. *-edes* 5 (7.8%). Moreover, thirteen of fifteen authors used *-é(y)s* exclusively, while only two occasionally opted for *-edes*. Furthermore, no example of *-edes* as a future morpheme occurs in the *Cancionero general* after 1455. In light of these facts, it is fairly safe to conclude that (a) *-é(y)s* was the preferred future allomorph during the first half of the 15th century, though writers certainly had recourse to futures in *-edes* if, as Dworkin (1988b: 224) points out, meter required a trisyllabic form; and (b) the reduction of *-edes* > *-é(y)s* in the future indicative was pretty much a *fait accompli* by the middle of the 15th century.

The reduction of *-edes* in other functions lagged slightly behind its reduction as a future morpheme. Examples of non-reduced *-edes* in the present indicative can be found to 1455, as one might expect, in the writings of those authors who also occasionally opted for *-edes* in the future indicative, e.g., the Marqués de Santillana — *avedes, corredes, hazedes, merescedes, padecedes, queredes* (3), *sabedes, temedes, vedes*; and Juan de Mena — *avedes, fazedes, vedes* (3). However, such forms are also found in the poetry of those authors who strictly limited themselves to reduced *-é(y)s* as a future morpheme. For example, Gómez Manrique, Antón de Montoro and Francisco Vaca each offer an example of non-reduced *vedes*. Moreover, *-edes* is also found alongside reduced *-é(y)s* as a present subjunctive allomorph of *-ar* verbs in the writings of many authors, again, even those who eschewed *-edes* as a future morpheme. For example, the Conde de Paredes wrote both non-reduced *busquedes* and reduced *ahogués*, Juan de Mena employed *dedes, dexedes*, and *libredes* along with *miréys, penséys, perdonéys*, and *quitéys*, and the Marqués de Santillana used *-edes* exclusively in this grammatical category, e.g., *avisedes, dudedes* (twice), *pensedes*, and *receledes*.

Unlike future *-edes*, present indicative and present subjunctive *-edes* persisted throughout the second half of the 15th century, and perhaps even until the beginning of the 16th century, if only in a limited capacity, according to the data gleaned from the *Cancionero general*. Two lexical items of similar structural make-up, namely pres. ind. *vedes*, and pres. subj. *dedes*, seem to have been especially resistant to the *-edes* > *-é(y)s* change. The following authors from the 4th and 5th generations (to 1485) were found to have used, and in some cases preferred, these two forms: Guevara, Castillo, and Diego de San Pedro each used *vedes* (to the exclusion of *vé(y)s*), Jorge Manrique employed *dedes* (to the exclusion of *dé(y)s*), while Álvarez Gato vacillated between both *dedes* and *déys* (2), as well as between *vedes* and *veys*.[8] Only one writer of this period, Costana, used a reduced form, *deys*, to the exclusion of a non-reduced form.

One notes the beginning of a decline in the use of non-reduced *vedes* and *dedes* in the writings of authors who flourished during the reign of the Reyes Católicos (1479–1517). Other than one occurrence of *vedes* in the work of Perálvarez de Ayllón and another in that of Coruña, *véys* is the prevalent form, appearing twice in the writing of the Duque de Medina Sidonia, and one time each in the works of Francisco León, Soria, Suárez, and Vázquez de Palencia. While *deys* occurs once in the poetry of Conde de Feria and once again in that of the Duque de Medina Sidonia, no instance of *dedes* is found in the work of any other writer of this category. Likewise, *dedes* is totally absent from the writings of authors of the 6th and 7th generations (to 1520), while *deys* appears in the writings of Gerónimo de Pinar, Comendador Román, Tapia (4 times), Garcisánchez Badajoz, Luis de Vivero, Nicolás Núñez, Quirós. Two Castilian writers, Cartagena and Diego López de Haro, vacillate between *vedes* (twice each) and *veys* (three times each), while Valencian writers Francisco Fenollete and Bachiller Ximena exhibit similar vacillation between *vedes* and *veys* (twice). On the other hand, *veys* appears to the exclusion of *vedes* in the writings of Gerónimo de Pinar, Puertocarrero, Tapia (5), Garcisánchez Badajoz, the Vizconde de Vivero, Gerónimo de Artés (2), Nicolás Núñez, and Quirós (8). Thus only four of 14 writers of this category ever wrote a non-reduced form of *-edes* in the *Cancionero general*.

The foregoing analysis of data clearly brings the lexical diffusion hypothesis to

---

8. It should be noted that other than the verbs *dedes* and *vedes*, *-é(y)s* occurs to the exclusion of *-edes* during this period. The following authors offer the following forms with reduced present subjunctive *-é(y)s*: Guevara — *olvidéys, dubdéys, deys, estéys, lloréys, mandéys, matéys* (2), *membréys, miréys*; Juan Álvarez Gato — *mandés, deys* (2), *desamés* (2), *quexéys, desdeñés, toméys* (3), *dexéys, gustéys, troquéys*; Jorge Manrique — *matéys, culpéys, sanéys*; Diego de San Pedro — *negués*; Hernán Mexía — *escapéys, mandéys*; Costana — *estéys*; Castillo — *movéys*.

life. If the writings gathered together in the *Cancionero general* mirror in any way the linguistic reality of the various periods which this *cancionero* comprises, one may conclude with a reasonable degree of certainty that the reduction of *-edes* > *-é(y)s* was complete first in the grammatical category of future indicative, i.e., by the middle of the 15th century (and perhaps earlier), while in the present indicative and subjunctive *-edes* continued to maintain some degree of vitality. It was not until shortly after 1485 that *-edes* ceased to be used altogether in the present subjunctive, and in the present indicative, not until sometime after 1520. It would be worth investigating at some future date the reasons for the apparent longevity of the structurally similar *vedes* and *dedes*.

The lag in the completion of *-edes* > *-é(y)s* may indicate a similar lag in the start of the change in the respective grammatical categories. Given the considerable time-gap between the completion of the reduction of *-edes* in the future on the one hand (mid-15th century or earlier), and in the present indicative and subjunctive on the other (late 15th- early-16th centuries), together with the fact that many of the earliest examples of *-és* appear in the grammatical category of the future indicative, it appears that the loss of /-d-/ in the verbal suffix *-edes* indeed began in the future, as Dworkin (1988b) tentatively concludes.

One may wonder why the reduction of the second person plural verbal suffixes began in the future rather than in some other grammatical category. Perhaps the structure of the monosyllabic future suffix of the original second person singular, i.e., /-ás/, spurred on the reduction of *-edes* to *-és* (perhaps further aided by the vocalic quality of the first person singular suffix, /-é/), e.g., *vos cantaredes* > *vos cantarés* via leveling pressure from *tú cantarás*, supported by *yo cantaré*. A clue that such leveling may have been at work can be seen in an example from the *Cancionero general*, in which Francisco Vaca (flour. ca. 1406–1454) in one instance confused the verbal endings of *tú* and *vos*, writing *vos cantarás* instead of *vos cantarés*. The common factor of stress shared by fut.ind. /-ás/ and /-édes/ may explain why the verbal endings of *tú* would have first influenced the reduction of *-edes* in the future, whereas atonic /-as/ and /-es/ would have less effect on tonic *-ades*, *-ides*, *-odes*, and non-future *-edes* during the same period. However, while leveling by the original second person singular may have been a factor in the general reduction of *-ades*, *-edes*, *-ides*, and *-odes* as suggested by Dworkin (1988a: 152), leveling by future /-ás/ cannot be the only reason why *-edes* first reduced in the future, since the earliest examples of future *-és* do not solely involve the use of *vos* as a singular, e.g.,"temedes vos que todas yrés por esa vía" (*Libro de buen amor* MS S v. 1451d).

Some may wish to view the reduction of *-edes* > *-és* as simply a natural part of this morpheme's development during the grammaticalization process, that is, when it passed from a free lexical item to a bound grammatical morpheme. When any element becomes a dependent grammatical morpheme, there is a general tendency for that element to undergo phonetic attrition.[9] Compare the reduction of the object pronouns from Latin to Spanish during their grammaticalization process, i.e. ILLUM, ILLOS, ILLAM, ILLAM, ILLI, etc. > *lo, los, la, las, le,* etc.[10] During this period in particular, witness the final reduction of clitic *vos* > *os* in the imperative, e.g., *acordadvos* > *acordad(v)os* > *acorda(d)os* > *acordaos*. From Latin to Spanish, inflected forms of HABERE underwent extreme morphological reduction during the grammaticalization process of the future (cf. HABEO > *-é*, HABES > *-ás*, HABET > *-á*, etc.).[11] Thus the reduction of the future morpheme *-edes* may have simply been a continuation of its earlier reduction from *avedes* > *-edes*. During the 15th century, though the future suffix is generally bound, one can still find instances in which it is free, e.g., *vello es* (= *verlo és*), Cartagena, *bolveros eys* (= *os bolveréys*), Nicolás Nuñes (*Cancionero General*), thus indicating that the grammaticalization process was still underway.

While grammaticalization might have played a role in the reduction of future *-edes*, I believe that the primary factor responsible for its initial reduction was the high frequency with which this suffix occurred, together with its relation to *avedes*, also of considerably high frequency. With regard to the correlation between frequency and linguistic change within the verbal paradigm, Penny (1991: 101) writes: "The more frequent a set of forms ... the more likely it is to show the disruptive effects of phonological change." A sample taken from the *Estoria de Espanna I*, for example, shows that *-edes* indeed occurred more frequently than *-ades*, *-ides*, or *-odes*, and that its role as a future morpheme was particularly predominant, due, no doubt, to the fact that it served all three conjugations. One finds the second person plural suffixes in descending order of frequency as follows (with the suffix followed by the number of occurrences): *-edes* 98, *-ades* 25, *-odes* 7, *-ides* 5. Of the 98 occurrences of *-edes*, 39 are

---

9. Other changes that a given element will undergo when passing from free to bound morphemic status include semantic bleaching, obligatory appearance, taking on a fixed position, and inseparability from its host.

10. For details regarding the grammaticalization of the clitic pronoun, see Rini (1990) and (1995a).

11. For the reduction of HABEO > *(h)e*, see Rini (1995b).

synthetic futures. Of the remaining 59 forms in -edes, 30 are instances of avedes (the remaining forms include 21 other verbs in the present indicative, and 8 present subjunctive forms). Thus the categories of future indicative and auxiliary aver make up 70% of all suffixes in -edes.[12] During the Middle Ages, the form avedes, in fact, occurred more frequently than any other present indicative second person plural form. For example, in a sample of common verbs selected at random from Royal and non-Royal Scriptorium Alfonsine texts, avedes occurs 319 times, followed by sodes 187, sabedes 117, queredes 89, dezides 70, fazedes 61, tenedes 56, estades 30 (fablades and ponedes occur only twice and once respectively). The high rate of occurrence of avedes, often in its role as auxiliary, no doubt led to the creation of a reduced allomorph avés. In light of the forego-ing data, it is not surprising that the earliest reduced forms of -edes adduced by Dworkin (1988b) are in fact futures (in the late-14th century Libro de buen amor) and the auxiliary avés in compound tenses (in the early-15th century Libro rimado de palacio), shown in (1):

(1)   *Libro de buen amor*
        "*andarés* en amor de grand dura sobejo" (MSS S & G v. 1332d)
        "temedes vos que todas *yrés* por esa vía" (MS S v. 1451d)

        Libro rimado de palacio
        "Solamente por mi onra pues en esto me *avés* puesto" (MS N, v. 327a)
        "lo que nos *avés* mandado o aquí non estaredes" (MS N, v. 449d)

Likewise, the *Dança general de la muerte* exhibits the reduction of -edes to -és when it functioned as a future morpheme or as the suffix of aver, as shown in (2):

---

12. Similarly, in the *Estoria de Espanna II* one finds -edes 494, -ades 177, -odes 49, -ides 38. The breakdown of the 494 occurrences of -edes is as follows: present indicative 234 (with the most frequent verbs being avedes 58, sabedes 46, queredes 31, tenedes 18, devedes 16, fazedes 15); future 140 (most frequent verb being avredes 16), present subjunctive 113 (most frequent verb being dedes 20). In the non-Royal Scriptorium Alfonsine *General estoria V* (Escorial: Monasterio R.I.10), copied during the 15th century (i.e., the period during which the intense reduction of -edes took place), one finds -edes (111 = 34 fut.ind., 57 pres.ind., 20 pres.subj.), -ades (58 = 30 pres.ind., 28 pres.subj.), -odes (20), and -ides (17).

(2)   Lo que de él leuastes, *abrés* a pagar. (LIX, 7)
çurrón nin talegua non *podrés* traer, (LXXVII, 7)
allí *darés* cuenta de vuestros traspasos. (LXVII, 7)
quitadlo de vos, e *yrés* mas liuiano. (XLV, 4)
en su santo reyno, do *abés* a venir; (LXI, 4)
pagad los cohechos, que *abés* leuado, (LXVII, 2)

In addition, I have found that the *Historia Troyana*, translated from Latin to Aragonese by Juan Fernández de Heredia between 1380–1396, offers the example of reduced *-edes* as a future morpheme of *tener* in (3), flanked by two examples of futures with non-reduced suffixes:

(3)   Padre mucho amado uos guardaredes aquesta ordenança car uos
ternés conuusco mill caualleros combatientes con todos los peones
desta ciudat et estaredes çerca (*Historia Troyana*, ADMYTE vol. 0).

If the high rate of occurrence of the future suffix *-edes* itself was not enough to lead to its reduction to *-és*, then the allomorphs *avedes* ~ *avés* would surely provide the model for the creation of a set of future allomorphs in *-edes* ~ *-és*. Speakers were clearly aware of the connection between the future suffix *-edes* and the auxiliary *avedes* (i.e., that the former was a reduced allomorph of the latter), as one finds coexisting variants during the Middle Ages such as *cantar la avedes* ~ *cantar la edes* ~ *la cantaredes* ~ *avedes de cantarla*. After high frequency *avedes* reduced to *avés* in compound tenses, it would not be long before reduced *avés* spread to the future, i.e., *avedes puesto* > *avés puesto* → *cantarla (av)edes* > *cantarla (av)és*.

But although high frequency likely actuated the reduction of *-edes* in the future and in auxiliary *avedes*, it is highly unlikely that frequency was the only factor involved in the entire reduction of *-ades*, *-edes*, *-ides*, and *-odes*. If frequency had been the only factor, how does one explain, for example, the late retention of /-d-/ in verbs of relatively high frequency such as *vedes* and *dedes* (late-15th and early-16th centuries)? It therefore remains to be determined how the loss of /-d-/ diffused beyond the grammatical categories of future and present perfect indicative.

The early textual evidence suggests that the reduction of *-edes* > *-és* diffused via allomorphs *avedes* ~ *avés*, first to *tener*, which was closely associated with *aver* on both semantic and syntactic grounds, yielding the new set of allomorphs *tenedes* ~ *tenés*. One of the earliest examples of *tenés*, shown in (4), occurs with a past participle, in the *Libro rimado de palacio*, straddling auxiliary and stative functions, thus clearly demonstrating the link between *aver* and *tener*:

(4)   'que yo quite vuestra mula que aquí *tenés* empeñada' (MS N, v.459d)

Other early examples, shown in (5), appear in the manuscript version of the *Dança general de la muerte* in non-auxiliary roles:

(5)   non *tenés* manera de andar a dançar, (LXIX, 3)
       ya non *tenés* tienpo de saltar paredes, (LXXI, 2)

Evidence from the earlier history of Spanish also supports the contention that *tenés* was created on the basis of *avés*. As seen in Chapter 2, the Old Spanish preterite *tove*, which would have never evolved via straightforward phonological processes from Latin TENUI, was without question remodeled on OSp. *ove*, which had developed through regular phonetic changes from Latin HABUI.

The auxiliary role of *aver* would also serve as a link through which the reduction of *-edes* > *-és* could diffuse to other auxiliary verbs (e.g., *deber*, *poder*, etc.), and other verbs which sometimes appeared with infinitives (e.g., *querer*, *saber*). It is therefore not surprising that Dworkin (1988b) finds the example of *querés* in the *Libro rimado de palacio* shown in (6):

(6)   "Viene a mí un judío e dize: '¿*Querés* aver...'" (MS N, v. 473b)

I have found an early example of *podés*, shown in (7), in the *Gran Conquista de Ultramar*, written in 1295, but copied sometime between 1300–1400:

(7)   Et quando fueron antel dixieron le Sennor uos *podés* entrar enla cipdad sin contienda ca el Emperador se fue dend con toda su yent pora la montanna (*Gran Conquista de Ultramar*, ADMYTE vol. 0).

I have also found the auxiliaries *avés* (5), *podés* (8), *querés* (11), *tenés* (1), alongside futures *podrés* (2), *vernés*, *yrés* (3) in the *Cuento de Tristán de Leonis* (ADMYTE vol. 0), written in Castilian in 1410 ca. ad quem.

An early example of *querés* also appears in the *Cancionero general* in the writings of Juan de Baena (first generation, 1395–1425), as do two examples of *sabé(y)s*. One continues to find such forms in the poems of writers from the second and third generations (to 1455) as well as those who flourished during the Reign of Juan II (1406–1454). Examples include: Marqués de Santillana — *querés* (twice); Lope de Estúñiga — *podéys*, *devés*; Gómez Manrique — *devé(y)s*

(10), *podés, queréys* (3), *sabéys* (4), *tené(y)s* (7); Bachiller de la Torre — *tenéys*; Juan de Mena — *aveys, devéys, podéys* (4), *sabéys* (3), *tené(y)s* (5); Antón de Montoro — *avé(y)s* (2), *devéys, queré(y)s* (2), *sabéys* (2); Juan Rodríguez del Padrón — *queréys*; Barba — *tenéys*; Conde de Paredes — *avéys, devéys, podéys, queréys* (2), *sabéys* (2); Gonzalo Dávila — *avés, podéys*; Francisco Vaca — *avé(y)s* (4), *devé(y)s* (3), *tenéys* (2).

Once sets of allomorphs such as *avedes ~ avés, tenedes ~ tenés, podedes ~ podés, queredes ~ querés, devedes ~ devés, sabedes ~ sabés* were established, the reduction of *-edes* > *-és* would then diffuse further to all other verbs of the second conjugation, as well as to verbs of the 1st conjugation in the present subjunctive (e.g., *amedes* > *amé(y)s*). As one might expect, examples from these grammatical categories in the *Cancionero general* increase in number and verb type in the indicative after the first generation of writers, and in the subjunctive after the second generation of writers. Examples include: (to 1425) Juan de Baena — ind. *conocés*, subj. *maravillés*; (to 1455) Marqués de Santillana — *leés, merescéys, posséys, valéys*; Lope de Estúñiga — *desconoscés, merescés* (12), *valés*; Gómez Manrique — subj. *dexéys* (2), *dubdéys, fiés, hallés, miréys, toméys, tornéys*; Juan de Mena — ind. *fazéys, hazéys* (2), *merescéys, valé(y)s* (2), subj. *miréys, penséys, perdonéys, quitéys*; Antón de Montoro — ind. *hazés* (2), *ponés, traéys*, subj. *cismés*; Conde de Paredes — subj. *ahogués*; Juan Maestre el Trepador — ind. *socorréys*, subj. *caguéys*; Francisco Vaca — ind. *hazé(y)s* (2), subj. *emendéys, miréys*.

Another channel through which the reduction *-edes* > *-és* may have diffused is that which connects the future and present indicative. These two tenses are closely associated with one another in that (a) they share imperfect aspect, (b) the present can express future actions, and (c) the future can express wonder or probability in the present. It is not inconceivable, therefore, that after *-edes* began to reduce to *-és* in the future, the latter allomorph would then spread to the present tense as depicted in (8):

(8)		fut. ind.		pres. ind.
	variant 1:	*sabredes*	:	*sabedes*
	variant 2:	*sabrés*	:	X = *sabés*

The spread of *-és* from the future to the present would lead imbalanced future and present indicative pairs such as *sabrés ~ sabedes* to a more balanced configuration with reduced suffixes for each member, i.e., *sabrés ~ sabés*. Such a pattern would receive support from that which had already been established in the paradigm of *aver*, i.e., *avrés ~ avés*.

I would now like to address the question of how the loss of /-d-/, a change initially limited to the suffix *-edes*, diffused to *-ades*, *-ides*, and *-odes*. Let us first consider the reduction of *-ades* > *-áis*.

There are various ways in which *-ades* may have begun to shed its dental consonant. First, one might simply assume that when *-edes* shed its dental consonant, *-ades*, *-ides*, and *-odes*, belonging to the same grammatical category, would likewise, almost automatically, shed theirs. However, the contention that there was some type of reciprocal morphological influence between the first and second conjugation allomorphs presents a serious obstacle.

Rarely in the history of Spanish have 2nd and 3rd conj. verbal suffixes become more like 1st conj. verbal suffixes, or vice versa.[13] First conjugation suffixes, in fact, have generally remained distinct from those of the 2nd and 3rd conj., with the exception of the future and conditional, which are comprised of the infinitive plus an inflected form (present and imperfect tenses respectively) of HABERE. Compare in (9), for example, the 1st vs. 2nd and 3rd conjugation paradigms from just two verb tenses, the imperfect indicative and preterite:

(9)   Imperfect indicative:

1st conj.		vs.	2nd and 3rd conj.	
-aba	*-ábamos*		*-ía*	*-íamos*
-abas	*-abais*		*-ías*	*-íais*
-aba	*-aban*		*-ía*	*-ían*

Preterite:

1st conj.		vs.	2nd and 3rd conj.	
-é	*-amos*		*-í*	*-imos*
-aste	*-asteis*		*-iste*	*-isteis*
-ó	*-aron*		*-ió*	*-ieron*

---

13. This is not to say that at a very early stage, i.e., Latin, such influence did not occur between conjugation classes. Craddock (1983), for example, suggests that the irregular "strong" preterites such as UENIT extracted an unstressed ending /-ut/ from Hispano-Romance preterites such as /kantáut/, /impléut/, and /partíut/, yielding */venut/, the forerunner of OSp. *veno* and Ptg. *veio*. Craddock's hypothesis, however convincing, still stands even if one eliminates first conjugation /kantáut/ from his analysis.

So the question remains: Why would the reduction of *-edes* > *-és* in the second conjugation have caused *-ades* of the first conjugation to become *-aes* (and later *-áis*)?

Another possibility is that when reduced *avés* exerted its pressure on *tenedes* to spawn *tenés*, and then on other auxiliaries, most of which belonged to the second conjugation, one first-conjugation verb which also functioned as an auxiliary was also affected, namely *estar*. In this scenario, one would expect to find *estaes* (or *estáys*) among the earliest examples of reduced auxiliaries. However, the first example of *estáys* cited by Dworkin (1988b) appears in the lone extant manuscript of *El corbacho* (1438), copied in 1466. Likewise, the first example of *estáys* that I have been able to find appears in the *Cancionero general* in the writings of Juan de Mena (3rd generation, 1425–1455).

Yet another possible link between the reduction of *-edes* and *-ades* is the future-to-present indicative conduit described above. For example, future allomorphs such as *cantaredes ~ cantarés* may have spurred on present indicative sets like *cantades ~ cantáis*. In this scenario, the earliest examples of reduced *-ades* would involve any first conjugation present indicative verb. A look at the textual evidence presented below will show, however, that the reduction of *-ades* > *-aes* → > *-áys*) did not begin in the present indicative.

I would like to suggest here that *-ades* first reduced to *-aes*, not under the influence of the *-edes* > *-és* change in the second conjugation, rather, because of the same change in the *first* conjugation. One must keep in mind that *-ades* and *-edes* served in the indicative as first and second conjugation morphemes respectively, but that in the subjunctive these morphemes were reversed, as shown in (10):

(10)   *vos fablades* 'you speak'   vs.   *vos fabledes* 'that you may speak'
         vos queredes 'you want'   vs.   *vos querades* 'that you may want'

Such being the case, *-ades* could have been affected by the set of allomorphs *-edes ~ -és* within the same conjugation class, and even within the same verbal paradigm, creating a new pair of allomorphs via analogy, as depicted in (11):

(11)   2nd conjugation
         ind. *avedes*   :   subj. *ayades*
              avés   :   X = *ayaes*

I have made a similar claim in a separate study regarding the vocalic formation of *-éis*, suggesting that monophthongal *-és* expanded to diphthongal *-éis*, though through morphological contamination by subjunctive -*áis*, e.g., *querés* (ind.) x *queráis* (subj.) > innovative *queréis* ~ older *querés*.[14] In that study, I support this claim with textual evidence from the *Cancionero general*, in which one finds that when an author vacillated between forms in -*és* and -*éis*, he also often employed a subjunctive form in -*áis* of the same verb. I reproduce in (12) the same list of authors and forms:

(12)	AUTHOR	VACILLATIONS	SUBJ. FORM
	Alvarez Gato	*querés* ~ *queréys*	*queráys*
		tenés ~ *tenéys*	*tengáys*
	Manrique, Gómez	*devés* ~ *devéys*	*deuáys*
	Manrique, Jorge	*querés* ~ *queréys*	*queráys*
	Pinar (Gerónimo)	*querés* ~ *queréys*	*queráys*
	Puertocarrero	*querés* ~ *queréys*	*queráys*
	Quirós	*hazés* ~ *hazéys*	*hagáys*
		podés ~ *podéys*	*podáys*
		querés ~ *queréys*	*queráys*
		tenés ~ *tenéys*	*tengáys*
		verés ~ *veréys*	*veáys*
	Santillana	*serés* ~ *seréys*	*seáys*
	Soria	*querés* ~ *queréys*	*queráys*
		sabés ~ *sabéys*	*sepáys*
		tenés ~ *tenéys*	*tengáys*
	Tapia	*querés* ~ *queréys*	*queráys*
		tenés ~ *tenéys*	*tengáys*
	Ximénez	*querés* ~ *queréys*	*queráys*

Likewise, in the case of -*ades* > -*aes* (> -*áis*), textual evidence supports the suggestion that this reduction first occurred within the same conjugation class as -*edes* > -*és*, as one finds that the earliest examples of reduced -*ades* indeed involve subjunctive forms of the second conjugation. Dworkin (1988b: 226) has noted that in Heredian manuscripts which date from the final decade of the 14th century, the most frequent example of reduced forms is pres. subj. *queraes* (16 occurrences), and that in the *Crónica de Morea*, among reduced *avés*, *podéys*, *querés*, and *soes* one finds pres. subj. *fagaes*, *queraes*, and *seaes*. In the

---

14. For full details, see Rini (1996).

Cancionero general, the earliest example of reduced *-ades* that I have been able to find is pres. subj. *ayays*, which appears in the poetry of Juan de Baena (first generation, 1395–1425). In the writings of the Marqués de Santillana (second generation, 1410–1440) one finds subj. *hagays*, *seays*. Evidence that this change may have diffused within the same paradigm is supported by the fact that the earliest reduced subjunctive forms involve second-conjugation verbs which also exhibit reductions in the indicative: cf. *querés* ~ *queraes*, *soes* ~*seaes* in the *Crónica de Morea*, *avréys* ~ *ayays* from Juan de Baena, and *seréys* ~ *soys* ~ *seáys* from the Marqués de Santillana.

Once the second-conjugation subjunctive allomorphs *-ades* ~ *-áys* had been established in a number of verbs, they would easily be adopted by verbs of the first conjugation indicative, which, before this point, had only employed *-ades*. That is, because of allomorphic sets such as *querades* ~ *queráys*, verbs such as *amades* would acquire *amáys*, as depicted in (13):

(13)   2nd conjugation subjunctive   1st conjugation indicative
        querades   :   *amades*
        queráys   :   X = *amáys*

At the same time, the reduction of *-ades* > *-áys* in the first conjugation indicative would be further aided by reduced forms of the same conjugation in the subjunctive, as in (14):

(14)   2nd conjugation
        subj.   *amedes*   :   ind. *amades*
              amé(y)s   :   X = *amáys*

Thus one frequently finds in the *Cancionero general* pairs such as *penséys* ~ *pensáys* (Juan de Mena), *deys* ~ *days* (5), *matéys* (2) ~ *matáys* (2), *mandéys* ~ *mandáys* (Guevara), *deys* (2) ~ *days* (4), *(des)amés* (2) ~ *amáys* (Juan Álvarez Gato), *matéys* ~ *matáys* (Jorge Manrique), *juzguéys* ~ *juzgáys*, *mostréys* ~ *mostráys* (Cartagena). Although the first two examples of first conjugation forms in *-áys* are found in the writings of the Marqués de Santillana (*desseáys*, *fatigáys*), the first significant concentration of such forms does not surface until the third generation (1425–1455), the very point in time when one notes a significant increase in reduced *-edes* in the present subjunctive (e.g., *amedes* > *amé(y)s*). Examples include: Gómez Manrique — *buscáys*, *desseáys* (2), *diciplináys*, *emendáys*, *lleváys*, *mostráys*, *quedáys*, *reynáys*, *rezáys* (vs. *clamades*, *fincades*, *mirades*); Juan de Mena — *buscáys*, *days*, *engañáys* (3), *estáys* (2), *matáys, mostráys* (2), *penáys, pensáys, robáys, usáys* (vs. *dades, hallades* (2), *tentades*); Antón de Montoro — *andáys, halláys, juráys, miráys, mostráys* (2), *serenáys*; Juan Rodríguez del Padrón — *miráys*. Authors who flourished during the reign of Juan II (1406–1454) offer the following examples of *-áys* (with no occurrence of *-ades*): Barba — *miráys, soltáys, tractáys*; Conde de Paredes — *lleváys, negáys, sacáys, usáys*; Gonzalo Dávila — *calláys, esperáys, halláys, prestáys*; Juan Maestre el Trepador — *mandáys*; Francisco Vaca — *alcançáys, juzgáys, miráys*.

Since the suffix *-ades* also functioned as a third conjugation subjunctive morpheme, e.g., *digades* (← *dezir*) one would think that its reduction would have been swept up with the same change in the second conjugation, i.e., *digades* > *digáys* like *tengades* > *tengáys*. Although examples of reduced *-ades* in the *-ir* conjugation are not abundant given the comparatively low frequency of this conjugation class, Dworkin (1988b: 226) indeed cites an early example of pres. subj. *vayaes* in the manuscript copy of the *Dança general de la muerte*. However, speakers must have made some psychological distinction between second and third conjugation *-ades*, since further textual evidence reveals that the reduction of *-ades* > *-áys* diffused to a significant number of verbs in the second conjugation well before spreading to an equally significant number of third-conjugation verbs. It could hardly be a coincidence that authors of the third generations of the *Cancionero general* (1425–1455) consistently wrote *-áys* for second conjugation subjunctives, but *-ades* for subjunctives of the third conjugation; witness Gómez de Manrique — *digades, murades* vs. *deváys, leáys, seáys, temáys*; and Juan de Mena — *comprimades, digades, presumades, sigades* vs. *padezcáys, podáys, queráys, sepáys*. Even the author who in general most frequently conserved forms with /-d-/, the Marqués de Santillana, vacillated between forms with and without /-d-/ in the second conjugation subjunctive, but retained /-d-/ in the third conjugation, e.g., *hagáys, seáys* vs. *entendades, querades*, but only *digades*. It is not until the fourth generation onward (i.e., post 1455) that one finds *-áys* as a third conjugation subjunctive suffix to the total exclusion of *-ades*; witness Álvarez Gato — *digáys*; Carasa — *biváys*; Cartagena — *consumáys* (2), *digáys* (2), *oyáys*; Dávila — *muráys*; Fenollete — *consintáys*; Fernández de Heredia — *sintáys*; D. L. de Haro — *digáys* (2); Mexía — *digáys, sintáys*; Núñez — *vengáys*; N. Núñez — *pidáys*; Pinar — *sintáys*; Proaza — *sigáys*; Puertocarrero — *biváys, consintáys, finjáys* (2), *huyáys, muráys, pidáys, sirváys*; Quirós — *muráys*; Soria — *muráys*; Suárez — *sufráys*; Torrellas — *presumáys*; Ximénez — *digáys*. One therefore concludes that the reduction of third conjugation

-ades was indeed incorporated into the reduction of second conjugation *-ades*, but not without somewhat of a time lag. This lag in the diffusion of *-ades* > *-áys* between the second and third conjugations in 15th-century Castile is not unlike the present-day reduction of /-ádo/ > [-áo] ~ [-áu̯], which probably began in the past participle, diffused to adjectives, but has not yet spread to all nouns, e.g., *lado* 'side' → [láo] vs. *hado* 'fairy' [áðo], not *[áo]. One may therefore connect the loss of /-d-/ in *-ir* subjunctives with the initial loss of /-d-/ in the second conjugation present indicative, as part of a long chain reaction, as shown in (15):

(15)	2nd conjugation			3rd conjugation		
pres.ind.	pres.subj.		pres. subj.		
avédes	:	*ayades*	:	*vayades*	:	*digades*
avés	:	X = *ayáis*	:	X = *vayáis*	:	X = *digáis*, etc.

The reduction of *-ides* > *-ís*, unlike the developments described above, where the loss of /-d-/ diffused from indicative to subjunctive (and vice-versa), does not appear to be connected to the loss of /-d-/ in the second conjugation subjunctives. The only way to link the loss of /-d-/ in *-ides* to the chain of events described thus far would be to suggest that after third-conjugation subjunctive *-ades* reduced to *-áys* (e.g., *digades* > *digaes* > *digáys*), the newly reduced subjunctive forms influenced their indicative counterparts to do the same, as depicted in (16):

(16) | 3rd conjugation | | |
|---|---|---|
| pres.subj. | pres. ind. | |
| *digades* | : | *dezides* |
| *digáys* | : | X = **dezíes* > *dezís* |

For this hypothesis to stand, however, one would have to show that the loss of /-d-/ in the subjunctive was somewhat anterior to that of the indicative. But textual evidence reveals that the reduction of *-ides* predates the reduction of subjunctive *-ades*. As noted above, although the earliest example of reduced *-ades* in the third-conjugation present subjunctive is *vayaes* in the *Dança general de la muerte*, widespread diffusion in this grammatical category did not occur until the second half of the 15th century according to the data gleaned from the *Cancionero general*. Conversely, attestations of the *-ides* > *-ís* change are already found in the writings of authors who wrote in the first half of the 15th century (1406–1455). Examples include: Gómez de Manrique — *descendís, dezís, escrevís, regís, venís*; Juan de Mena — *dezís* (3); Antón de Montoro — *dezís, henchís, pedís*; Rodrigo de Ávalos — *herís*; Gonzalo Dávila — *arrepentís,* *morís*; Pedro Torrellas — *dezís*; Francisco Vaca — *dezís*. Moreover, the *Cancionero general* contains only three examples of *-ides*, all of which appear in the writings of the most conservative author, the Marqués de Santillana — *concluydes*, *dezides*, *plañides*.[15] It is even more significant that an author such as Juan de Mena, who still employed non-reduced /-Vdes/ in many instances (e.g., *avedes*, *avredes*, *comprimades*, *dades*, *dedes*, *dexedes*, *digades*, *fazedes*, *hallades*, *libredes*, *presumades*, *seredes*, *sigades*, *tentades*, *vedes*, *veredes*), would have written *dezís* three times in the *Cancionero general*, but never *dezides*. De Souza (1964: 13) therefore concludes that the three lone forms in *-ides* "[p]robablemente deban ser consideradas, ya en esa época, formas muy arcaicas, pero prestigiosas."

Data from ADMYTE (vol. 0) offer even more support that *-ides* > *-ís* preceded 3rd conj. subj. *-ades* > *-áys*, as one finds the former development to be more widely diffused. For example, although forms with /-d-/ predominate by a wide margin in this volume, *dezís* occurs 24 times (18%) vs. *dezides* 110 (82%), while *digáys* occurs only 6 times (6.74%) vs. *digades* 83 (93.26%).[16] In the texts in which *dezís* appears, *dezides* occurs only 15 times (i.e., *dezís* 61.5% vs. *dezides* 38.5%), while the subjunctive shows an almost completely opposed ratio of the reduced vs. non-reduced suffix: *digades* 15 (75%) vs. *digáys* 5 (25%). One therefore concludes that the more advanced state of the *-ides* > *-ís* change in these texts indicates an earlier inception of that change.

Just how *-ides* reduced to *-ís* is a question which, to date, has not been satisfactorily answered, and for which one finds no consensus in the recent literature. Penny (1991: 138), for example, proposes that *-ides* first suffered the loss of /-d-/ yielding *-íes*, and that "almost immediately the resulting hiatus was resolved to monosyllabic pronunciation ... via assimilation." Lloyd too believes the process began with a phonological change, i.e., the loss of /-d-/, but that "[t]he model offered by the ending *-és* probably stimulated the further reduction of ... *-íes* to *-ís*" (1987: 359).[17] Lloyd also points out that the further reduction of *-íes* (< *-ides*) was motivated by the potential merger with the suffix /-ie/

15. But even these must have been conservative forms for the Marqués de Santillana, who on other occasions used forms in *-ís*. Cuervo (1954), for example, cites *venís* by the Marqués de Santillana, as well as the following data: *decís*, *salís* in the *Cancionero de Baena*, 15 forms in *-ís* by Gómez Manrique, more than 30 in *-ís* by Antón de Montoro, and 8 in *-ís* in Eneida (1436).

16. One of the 6 examples of *digáys* exhibits hiatus, i.e., written *digaes*.

17. Cuervo (1893:120) was the first to explain *-ís* as having resulted from analogy with *-és*.

(phonetically [-jé] or [-íe]) of the imperfect indicative: "The form *-ís* in the peninsula was undoubtedly determined originally by the pressure from the imperfect form *-iés* which was still alive in the fourteenth and fifteenth centuries" (1987: 359). Fontanella de Weinberg (1976: 250) had stated that *-ides* could have resulted in *-ís* from a straightforward phonological process, but that analogy with *-és* may have been a factor: "Todos estos resultados [i.e., *-áis/-ás*, *-éis/-és*, *-ois/-ós*, *-ís*] son explicables por evolución fonética, pero es posible que en la simplificación … de *-íes* > *-ís* haya incidido por analogía la contracción de *-ees* > *-és*." Lathrop (1996: 156) offers a unique explanation, claiming that the reduction of *-ides* was initiated by a morphological process, namely, analogy with *-áis*: "OSp. *-ides* would have given *-íes*, *-iés* with loss of *-d-*. But in this case, since *-ades* gave *-áis*, *-ides* followed suit yielding *-íis* which simplified to *-ís*."

Each of these explanations is problematic. Penny's claim that **-íes* would have resulted in *-ís* via assimilation of unstressed /e/ to stressed /í/ presupposes an intermediate stage of ***-íis*. No such form is attested, however. This obstacle also renders Lathrop's analogical explanation unlikely. Moreover, attestations of verbs in *-ís* predate any in *-áys*, so that the former could not possibly have resulted from analogy with the latter. The view that seeks analogy with *-és* (< *-edes*) is more plausible, since the second and third conjugations are closely associated with one another in that they share many verbal suffixes. But how does one explain why *-ides*, if reduced by analogy with *-és*, did not itself result in *-és* (i.e., *-ides* > **-íes* X *-és* > *-és*)? The opposite development indeed occurred to some extent, where *-és*, by analogy with third conjugation *-ís*, resulted in a second conjugation *-ís*.[18] De Souza (1964: 9 n. 22) cites one such example from the 15th century, *descendís* for *descendés*, written by Gómez Manrique in the *Cancionero general*, and such forms can be found in some varieties of modern Ecuatorian, Peruvian and Chilean Spanish (Páez Urdaneta 1981: 97, 98, 109). Finally, any view that claims that *-ides* first reduced to **-íes* is also weakened by the fact that no attestation of such a form appears anywhere. On the contrary, one finds a direct substitution of forms in *-ides* with those in *-ís*.

It seems more likely that as the suffix *-ides* began to undergo extreme weakening of its interdental fricative, the potential merger with imperfect indicative /-ie/, pointed out by Lloyd (1987: 359), would have been a factor significant enough to thwart the total loss of this consonant. There may have also

---

18. For a good discussion of this topic, see Fontanella de Weinberg (1976).

been a phonological constraint against the loss of /-d-/ before the stressed high front vowel /í/. Compare the typologically similar loss of /-d-/ in Modern Spanish, which is widely diffused geographically and sociolinguistically in the case of the 1st conjugation past participle /-ádo/ → [-áo] ~ [-áu̯], but which tends not to occur in the case of 2nd and 3rd conjugation participle, i.e., /-ído/ → [-íðo] ~ [-íᵟo], but rarely [-ío]. Thus /-ídes/ was probably often realized phonetically as [-íðes] and [-íᵟes], but rarely, if ever, *[-íes]. Even if one concedes that *[-íes] might have been uttered by some speakers, it surely did not oust realizations with the dental fricative, and therefore never led to any phonologization of *[-íes] > **/-íes/. This explains the total lack of attestations in *-íes.

I, therefore, like Lathrop, am inclined to believe that the formation of -ís resulted from a straightforward morphological development, though not from analogy with -áis. Also, like Lloyd, I believe that the suffix -és was involved in this morphological change, but I do not see how it could have operated alone. Rather, it seems more likely that extra-paradigmatic leveling between the second and third conjugation paradigms would have led to the replacement of -ides by -ís, with other forms such as the 1st person plural playing roles of equal importance to that of second person -és. For example, before the reduction of any suffix in /-Vdes/, one found second and third conjugation paradigms in Old Spanish, as shown in (17), with common suffixes in bold:

(17) | Second Conjugation | | Third Conjugation | |
|---|---|---|---|
| *fazer* | | *dezir* | |
| *fago* | *fazemos* | *digo* | *dezimos* |
| *fazes* | *fazedes* | *dizes* | *dezides* |
| *faze* | *fazen* | *dize* | *dizen* |

Once the second conjugation acquired a reduced allomorph by the processes described above, the third conjugation would have felt a void, as indicated in (18) by X:

(18) | Second Conjugation | | Third Conjugation | |
|---|---|---|---|
| *fazer* | | *dezir* | |
| *fago* | *fazemos* | *digo* | *dezimos* |
| *fazes* | *fazedes ~ fazés* | *dizes* | *dezides ~ X* |
| *faze* | *fazen* | *dize* | *dizen* |

Of particular importance was the pattern long-established by the relationship between the 1st and 2nd person plural forms of each paradigm, i.e., *fazemos* ~

fazedes vis à vis *dezimos ~ dezides*, such that shortly after speakers had taken on the newly reduced variant in the second conjugation, the creation of a new variant in the third conjugation was inevitable, as shown in (19):

(19)   *fazemos*   *dezimos*   *dezimos*
                    (—leveling→)   >
        fazés   *dezides*   *dezís*

It therefore comes as no surprise that one finds in the prose *Tratado sobre el título de duque*, for example, among mostly non-reduced forms in /-Vdes/, examples of second conjugation *avés* and third conjugation *venís* (Dworkin 1988b: 229).

Other morphological factors within the 3rd conjugation itself which may have aided as leveling forces are: (a) the imperative suffix *-id*, which, like the present indicative suffix, functioned in the present and near future tenses; and (b) the infinitival morpheme *-ir*. Thus one now had symmetrical morphological patterns between the two verb classes involving oxitonic forms, i.e., *fazer ~ fazed ~ fazés* vis à vis *dezir ~ dezid ~ dezís*. One therefore concludes that the genesis of *-ís* did not result directly from the diffusion process per se, since there was really never any "loss" of /-d-/ in OSp. *-ides*. Nevertheless, the suffix *-ís* owes its existence to the suffix *-és* and the intimate relationship between the second and third conjugations. Finally, one notes here that the replacement of *-ides* by *-ís* was accomplished rather quickly once the latter arrived on the scene, and that *-ides* was completely extinguished by the end of the 15th century. The *Cancionero de Baena* (ca. 1425) contains one instance of *dezís* vs. 12 of *dezides*, and the *Corbacho* (1438) shows a mixture of forms in *-ides* and *-ís*, e.g., *dezís* 2 vs. *dezides* 0, *dormís* 0 vs. *dormides* 1, *venís* 2 vs. *venides* 0. The *Cancionero Castellano de Paris* (copied 1444) offers only *dezís* (1), but the *Cancionero de Salvá* (ca. 1460) contains *dezís* 1 vs. *dezides* 2. Shortly thereafter, there is a total reversal in the preference for one form over the other: *dezís* 3 vs. *dezides* 1 in the *Crónica Troyana*; *dezís* 1 vs. *dezides* 0 in the *Cancionero de París* (ca. 1470); *dezís* 3 vs. *dezides* 0 in the *Meditationes Vitae Christi* (ca. 1493); *dezís* 1 vs. *dezides* 0 in *De las mujeres ilustres en Romance* (1494); *dezís* 2 vs. *dezides* 0 in the *Cancionero Castellano y Catalán* (1480?, copied 1490–1500); *dezís* 3 vs. *dezides* 0 in the *Historia de las Amazonas* (1550). Two very well known works, Nebrija (1492) and the anonymous *Lazarillo de Tormes*, show only forms in *-ís*.

It now remains to be explained whether or not the reduction of *sodes > soes > sois* was at all linked to the diffusion of the loss of /-d-/ in the suffixes *-ades* and *-edes*. One possibility is that the initial reduction of *sodes* > *soes* was motivated by the loss of /-d-/ in pres. subj. *seades* > *seaes* (> *seáys*), which itself would have been swept up in the general reduction in the second conjugation (originally motivated by the second conjugation indicative reduction of *-edes* > *-és*). This hypothesis requires that attestations of *seaes* (or *seáys*) occur before those in *soes*. Another possibility is that the loss of /-d-/ from *sodes* was due to the high frequency with which this form occurred, without any pressure from subjunctive *seáys*. As shown above, in a sample of common verbs selected at random from Royal and non-Royal Scriptorium Alfonsine texts, *sodes* was the next most common verb (187 occurrences) after *avedes* (319 occurrences). Moreover, *sodes* occurs in the Alfonsine corpus more than twice as frequently as other common verbs, cf., *queredes* 89, *dezides* 70, *fazedes* 61, *tenedes* 56. This hypothesis requires that examples of *soes/soys* appear in the available texts before examples of *seaes/seáys*.

The textual evidence in Dworkin (1988b), which shows the earliest examples of *soes* and *seaes* (forms representing the first stage of development from *sodes* and *seades* and therefore disyllabic and trisyllabic respectively), is inconclusive, though *soes* does occur more frequently than *seaes*. Dworkin (1988b: 226–227) cites the occurrence of both *soes* and *seaes* from the late-14th century *Crónica de Morea*, as well as one occurrence of *soes* in the *Libro rimado de palacio* (copied in the early-15th century), and three of *soes* in the *Dança general de la muerte*. Evidence from the *Cancionero general* is less helpful, as one finds no examples of early, disyllabic *soes* or trisyllabic *seaes* (or of earlier *sodes* and *seades*). The earliest attestations of monosyllabic *soys* and disyllabic *seáys* appear at the same time, i.e., in the writings of the Marqués de Santillana (flour. 1410–1440), though these forms do tell that reduction of hiatus, i.e., *soes* > *soys*, *seaes* > *seáys*, occurred before the second half of the 15th century.

My own further investigation of other texts, however, has turned up evidence which suggests that *soes* is earlier than *seaes*. The *Crónica de Veinte Reyes*, composed sometime between 1252 and 1350, and copied sometime between 1300–1400, offers the following example of *soes* in (20), but only *seades* in the subjunctive:

(20)   "Buenos caualleros *soes*. Pensad de vos anparar quanto pudieredes ca en mj non tenedes ayuda ninguna." (ADMYTE vol. 0).

The *Sumas de la Historia Troyana*, written in Castilian between 1300 and 1350, but copied anywhere between 1340–1420, contains the following example of *soes* in (21), but no examples of *seaes* or *seáys*:

(21)   & yo uos pido por cortesia que vos me digades quien es ella que tanto es loada de vos Señor dixo melyagans vos seades bien venjdo & amj pareçe agora que vos oystes mj dolor & non me plaze punto dello pero bien creo que vos **soes** cauallero andante ansi bien commo yo ... (ADMYTE vol. 0).

Manuscript P of the *Libro del Cauallero Çifar* (Olsen 1984), which dates from the late-14th or early-15th century, offers two occurrences of *soes*, 11 of *soys*, (vs. 43 of *sodes*), while the subjunctive shows only *seades* (19).[19]

The *Cuento de Tristán de Leonis*, copied 1390 *a quo*–1410 *ad quem*, shows a slightly more advanced stage of development in the subjunctive than the aforementioned texts, with one occurrence of *seáys* vs. 29 of *seades*. Yet, the indicative forms in this text appear to be even further advanced: *soys* 31 (40%), *soes* 7 (9%) vs. *sodes* 40 (51%). Similarly, the *Cancionero de Salvá* (compiled 1459 *a quo*) contains *soys* 4, *sodes* 1 vs. *seáys* 1, *seaes* 1, and *seades* 1. Likewise, the *Cancionero Castellano de París* offers *soys* 6, *sodes* 1 vs. *seáys* 1, *seades* 1. The *Crónica Troyana* exhibits exclusive use of *soys* in the indicative (16 occurrences) vs. *seáys* 1, *seades* 1, while the *Cancionero de Baena* (compiled ca. 1430–1435, copied ca. 1445–1470) offers *soys* 9 (39.1%), *soes* 1 (4.4%), *sodes* 13 (56.5%), and exclusive use of subjunctive *seades* 7.

Conversely, I have only found two texts in ADMYTE (vol. 0) which show the opposite trend, i.e., a higher number of reductions of *seades* than of *sodes*. The *Biblia Latina* (translated from Latin to Castilian ca. 1250 ad quem, copied 1300–1400) contains *seáys* 1, *seades* 14 vs. *sodes* 29, and the *Libro de las Doñas* has *soys* 2 (16.66%), *soes* 1 (8.33%), *sodes* 9 (75%) vs. *seáys* 1 (12.5%), *seaes* 3 (37.5%), *seades* 4 (50%)

A comparison of all forms of *so(d)es* and *sea(d)es* with and without /-d-/ as they occur in ADMYTE (vol. 0) also proves revealing. The table in (22) includes all occurrences of *sodes, soes, soys* vs. *seades, seaes, seáys*:

---

19. The date of composition of the *Çifar* is believed to be 1300 *a quo*–1361 *ad quem* (Olsen 1984:XII).

(22)   Occurrence of *sodes/soes/soys*; *seades/seaes/seáys*
        (ADMYTE vol. 0):

sodes	203 (56.5%)	*seades*	77 (72.64%)
soes	16 (4.5%)	*seaes*	6 (5.66%)
soys	140 (39%)	*seáys*	23 (21.7%)
total	359		106

In the texts which exhibit all 16 occurrences of *soes*, one actually finds a rise in
the rate of occurrence of non-reduced subjunctive forms, i.e., from 72.64%
overall > 90% in these texts, as shown in (23) in bold:

(23)   Occurrence of *seades/seaes/seáys*; *sodes/soys* in texts which contain
        soes:

soes	**16 (10%)**	*seaes*	3	(6%)
sodes	97 (61%)	**seades**	**45**	**(90%)**
soys	46 (29%)	*seáys*	2	(4%)

Even when examining only those texts which contain all occurrences of *seaes*
and *seáys*, i.e., texts which show the most advanced state of *seades* > *seáys*, one
finds that the development of *sodes* is still more advanced than that of *seades*,
shown in (24):

(24)   Occurrence of *sodes/soes/soys*, *seades* in texts which contain *seaes/*
        seáys:

seáys	25 (28.1%)	*soys*	115 (53.7%)
seaes	10 (11.2%)	*soes*	9 (4.2%)
seades	**54 (60.7%)**	**sodes**	**90 (42.1%)**
total	89		168

The textual evidence gathered for this study from the *Libro del Cauallero Çifar*
and ADMYTE (vol. 0) does not support the hypothesis which proposes that the
reduction of *seades* > *seaes* (> *seáys*) influenced the reduction of *sodes* > *soes*
(> *soys*). If reduced *seáys* had influenced *sodes* to reduce to *soys*, one would
expect to find a higher rate of occurrence of *seáys* vis à vis *seades* than *soys* vis
à vis *sodes*. One therefore concludes that the reduction of *sodes* > *soys* cannot
have been part of the overall diffusion process initiated by the reduction of
avedes and *-edes* in the future indicative. Rather, the high frequency of *sodes*
appears to have been enough to initiate independently the loss of /-d-/ in this

form, though in a parallel fashion to, and only shortly after, the loss of this consonant in fut. ind. *-edes* and pres. ind. *avedes*. Nevertheless, a separate morphological factor may have expedited the process of *sodes* > *soes* > *soys*.

Recall that in his first of the two-part study, Dworkin (1988a) proposed that the use of /-Vdes/ in general in the singular may have contributed to the reduction of such forms, as they would have thus been brought more into line with the original second person singular. Dworkin (1988a:152) gives the example of *fablades* > *fabláis* ~ *fablás* vis à vis *(tú) fablas*. It may not be insignificant that most of the earliest examples of reduced *sodes*, i.e., *soes*, function as singulars. For example, of the four early occurrences of *soes* adduced by Dworkin (1988b), three function as singular forms of address — one in the *Libro rimados de palacio* shown in (25):

(25)   "faremos, diz, cuenta, que *soes* buen escudero" (MS N, v. 468a)

and two more in the *Dança general de la muerte* shown in (26):

(26)   "Venit a mi dança, pues *soes* mortal" (MS, XXV, 7)
"syn dubda tened, que *soes* escripto" (MS, LIII, 3)[20]

The two sole examples of *soes* which I have found in the *Libro del Cauallero Çifar*, shown in (27), address an individual:

(27)   Cauallero, dixo el sseñor de la hueste, *soes* vos el que trayades las armas del sseñor deste logar el dia que yo fuj ferido?
Señora, pues que vos *soes* ençinta, a siete dias avredes fruto.

And of the 16 occurrences of *soes* found in ADMYTE (vol. 0), 13 function as singular forms of address (1 in the *Sumas de la Historia Troyana*, 1 in the *Cancionero de Baena*, 7 in the *Cuento de Tristán de Leonis*, and 4 in the *Cancionero de París*).

In addition to the aforementioned instances of singular *soes*, the *Çifar* contains 11 examples of monosyllabic *soys*, all of which function as singular forms of address. Likewise, the *Cancionero de Baena* offers one example of *soes* and 9 of *soys*, and all 10 are singulars. In the *Cancionero de París*, which contains 4 examples of *soes* as a singular vs. one *soes* as a plural, one finds 4 examples of monosyllabic *soys*, three of which address an individual. Similarly,

---

20. The one example of *soes* as a plural is as follows: "que en el mundo *soes* de qualquiera estado." (MS, VIII, 2).

in the *Cuento de Tristán de Leonis*, 30 of 31 occurrences of *soys* function as singulars.[21]

In the case of the reduction of *sodes* > *soes* > *soys*, one cannot argue, to be sure, that *soes* and *soys* were brought more in line with *eres*, unlike Dworkin's suggestion regarding *fablades* > *fabláis/fablás* vis à vis (*tú*) *fablas*. Nevertheless, there was a morphological factor in the singular, heretofore undiscovered, which may have promoted the initial reduction of *sodes* > *soes*.

High frequency, no doubt, led /sódes/, which was in the Middle Ages already realized phonetically as [sóðes], to acquire a variant with a very weak interdental fricative, i.e., [só$^\delta$es]. This probably occurred in both the singular and plural, as depicted in (28):

(28)   <u>SINGULAR</u>   <u>PLURAL</u>
       /sódes/ → [sóðes] ~ [só$^\delta$es]   /sódes/ → [sóðes] ~ [só$^\delta$es]

As the variant [so$^\delta$es] became increasingly more frequent, the paradigm of the verb *se(e)r* was realized phonetically as in (29):

(29)   [seér] ~ [sér]
       [só]   [só-mos]
       [só-$^\delta$es] ([éres])   [só-$^\delta$es]
       [es]   [són]

It is at this point that singular [só-$^\delta$es] may have been reanalyzed and restructured on the basis of the first person singular, i.e., /sódes/ → [só-$^\delta$es] + (leveling from 1st sg. /só/) > /só + es/ → [só-es]. The morpheme /-es/ was already accustomed to suffixation with stems ending in stressed vowels in the singular, cf., (*tú*) *crees, lees, vees, caes, traes*, including those ending in stress /ó/, e.g., pres. subj. *loes, loe, loen* (from *loar* 'to praise'). Thus if leveling by *yo so*, speakers reduced *vos sodes* [só-$^\delta$es] to *vos soes* [só-es], then one may conclude that the

21. In many of the texts which exhibit only *soys* and *sodes* (i.e., no instance of *soes*), the former functions more often as a singular form of address: e.g., in the *Breve Confesionario*, one finds only one instance of *soys*, which functions as a singular; in the *Cancionero de Salvá*, *soys* occurs three times as a singular vs. once as a plural. In the *Crónica Troyana*, one finds sg. *soys* 10 times vs. pl. *soys* 6; in the *Meditatione Vitae Christi*, sg. *soys* 6 vs. pl. *soys* 4; in the *Pierres y Magalona*, sg. *soys* 17 vs. pl. *soys* once. Conversely one finds sg. *soys* once vs. pl. *soys* 3 in the *Esopete Historiado I* (and sg. 0 vs. pl. 4 in the *E.H. II*); in the *Historia de las Amazonas*, sg. *soys* 1 vs. pl. *soys* 8; in the *Cancionero Castellano de París*, sg. *soys* once vs. pl. 6; in *De las mujeres ilustres en Romance*, sg. *soys* once vs. pl. *soys* once.

deletion of [$^{\delta}$] in this case resulted from purely morphological conditions.

The early history of this paradigm offers further support for the foregoing proposal. The forerunner of *sodes*, i.e., *SUTIS, was restructured on the basis of the 1st and 3rd persons plural, as shown in (30):

(30)   Development of Present Indicative Plural of Latin ESSE

SUMUS	>	SU-MUS	>	*somos*
		↓		
ESTIS (ES- replaced by SU-)	>	*SU-TIS	>	*sodes*
		↑		
SUNT	>	SU-NT	>	*son*

The appeal to morphological influence between the first and second persons singular explains why a much greater number of the earliest examples of *soes* occur in the singular, not the plural. If frequency alone had been responsible for the reduction of *sodes > soes*, one would expect it to have occurred first in the plural, where *sodes* was the only form to express 'you (pl.) are', whereas in the singular, the duty was shared by *eres*.

The plural *sodes* then acquired *soes* as a plural allomorph via diffusion from the singular, as depicted in (31):

(31)
SINGULAR	PLURAL	PLURAL
/sódes/ ~ /sóes/–(diffusion)→	/sódes/ ~ X >	/sódes/ ~ /sóes/

The further reduction of *soes > soys* took place sometime between the end of the 14th- and beginning of the 15th centuries. As seen above, the *Libro del Cauallero Çifar* (copied either in the late-14th or early 15th century) shows *soes* (2) and *soys* (11) as singulars in free variation, though clearly with a preference for the latter. Likewise, the *Cuento de Tristán de Leonis* (ca. 1410) contains *soes* (4) and *soys* (30) as singulars. And the data from the *Dança general de la muerte* show quite clearly that *soes* had become obsolete sometime during the 15th century — all three instances of *soes* in the manuscript are replaced by *soys* in the 1520 edition, shown in (32):

(32)   Manuscript (composed ca. 1392, copied ca. 1480)
"que en el mundo *soes* de qualquiera estado" (VIII, 2)
"Venit a mi dança, pues *soes* mortal" (XXV, 7)
"syn dubda tened, que *soes* escripto" (LIII, 3)

1520 Edition (Sevilla)
"que en el mundo *soys* de cualquier estado" (8, 2)
"venid a mi dança, pues que *soys* mortal:" (30, 7)
"sin duda tened, que *soys* escrito" (62, 3)

This change appears to involve a simple loss of hiatus, a fairly common phonological process throughout the entire history of Spanish, so there does not seem to be any reason to seek morphological factors here. However, one might ask why *soes* reduced to *soys* in the singular when other verbs exhibiting /-Ves/ in this grammatical category did not, e.g., *caes* > *cais, *traes* > *trais, pres. subj. *loes* > *lois, etc. (The same question may be asked regarding the reduction of -*aes* > -*áys*). It should be noted here that the 1st sg. allomorph of OSp. *so*, i.e., *soy*, was becoming quite frequent during this period. Gago (1997) reveals that, although the change of *so* > *soy* began in the 14th century (and perhaps earlier), there was a significant increase in the use of *soy* in the written language during the first half of the 15th century:

> En la primera mitad del siglo XV los resultados son similares a los de siglos anteriores en los verbos *dar*, *estar* e *ir*, con un elevado porcentaje de formas etimológicas (*do* 100%, *esto* 95%, *vo* 100%). El verbo *ser* es el único que presenta una situación marcadamente diferente, pues las forms modernas [i.e., *soy*] alcanzan ya un 25,5% — produciéndose una reducción simultánea en el porcentaje de formas etimológicas ... Entre los años 1450 y 1480 la situación cambia de forma notable, *ser* presenta un 37,8% de formas modernas [i.e., *soy*].

One might consider the possibility that the loss of hiatus from *soes* > *soys* may have been due, not only to the high frequency and natural tendency to reduce two vowels in hiatus to one diphthong, but also to the great increase in the use of 1st sg. *soy* during the same century, whereby *soys* (allomorph of *soes*), would be reanalyzed synchronically as *soy* 'I am' + /-s/ → *soys* 'you are', not unlike imp.ind. *era* 'I was' + /-s/ → *eras* 'you were'. Perhaps *soys* then influenced -*aes* to reduce to -*áys*.

With regard to the relative chronology of -*odes* > -*ois* and -*ides* > -*ís*, in light of the textual evidence gathered for the present study, the acceptance into the written language of the reduction of -*odes* was clearly anterior to that of -*ides*. For example, in the *Cuento de Tristán de Leonis*, the reduced allomorphs of /sodes/ make up almost half of the total occurrences of that verb form, i.e., *soes* 7 (9%) and *soys* 31 (39.7%) vs. *sodes* 40 (51.3%), but -*ides* remains intact: e.g., 50 occurrences of *dezides* vs. zero of *dezís*. Similarly, the *Libro del*

Cauallero Çifar offers a number of reduced allomorphs of /sodes/, i.e., *soes* 2 (3.6%), *soys* 11 (19.6%) vs. *sodes* 43 (76.8%), yet only non-reduced forms in *-ides*: e.g., *dezides* 31, *venides* 4, *resçebides* 3, *dormides* 2, *(r)reydes* 2, *partides* 1. One therefore presumes that the earlier acceptance into the written language implies an earlier inception of the change in the spoken language.

In light of the data gathered for the present study, the relative chronology of the reductions of *-ades*, *-edes*, *-ides*, and *-odes*, in terms of when these changes began, may be established as follows:

1. ind. *-edes* > *-és* (later *-éys*)
2. *-odes* > *-oes* (later *-ois*)
3. 2nd-conj. subj. *-ades* > *-aes* (later *-áys*) and subj. *-edes* > *-és* (later *-éys*)
4. *-ides* > *-ís*
5. ind. *-ades* > *-áys* and 3rd-conj. subj. *-ades* > *-áys*

Though a given change may have begun before another, this does not necessarily mean that this change was completed first. For example, it is clear that *-edes* > *-és* began before *-ides* > *-ís*, yet forms in *-edes* (in particular *vedes* and *dedes*) persisted well beyond those in *-ides*.

It has been determined here that the reduction of the Old Spanish verbal suffixes in /-Vdes/ indeed constitutes a case of morphological change as Dworkin (1988a & 1988b) has claimed. It has also been determined here, however, that although the loss of /-d-/ from *-ades* and *-edes* constitutes a case of lexical diffusion from one of these morphemes to the other (as does indeed the spread of the loss of /-d-/ in each of these four suffixes from one lexical item to another), the suffixes *-ides* and *-odes* underwent morphological reductions independent of the diffusion process set in motion by the reduction of *-edes* to *-és* in the future indicative and auxiliary *aver*.

The present analysis also has implications for general linguistic theory of the nature of linguistic change. With regard to Labovian vs. diffusionist approaches to the spread of linguistic change, Hock (1991: 650) writes:

> In the 1969 version of the [lexical diffusion] hypothesis, the vehicle through which lexical diffusion takes place is tentatively defined as the quasi-analogical generalization process which Sturtevant had proposed. At this point, then, the difference between lexical diffusion and Labov's sociolinguistic approach is relatively minor. In both views, the variability between old and new phonetic realizations of given forms can give rise to the extension of the new pronunciation to other linguistic forms. *The difference lies mainly in the degree or speed of*

the generalization, which is relatively fast and sweeping for Labov (cf., e.g., the
change on Martha's Vineyard), but relatively slow and in terms of individual
lexical items for Wang ... That is, the difference would roughly correspond to
the one between rule-governed analogical change on one hand and the more
'traditional' types of analogy on the other (such as four-part analogy and
leveling). In addition, however, there is the difference that Labov invokes a
sociolinguistic factor as the starting point for change, but Wang does not.

The present analysis of well-documented data, i.e., verb forms with both non-
reduced and reduced variants of *-ades* and *-edes* which could be precisely dated
(and in most cases, generation by generation) over a period of roughly one
hundred and thirty years, supports the slower, almost item by item, analogical
spread of sound change as proposed by Wang (1969). This is not to say,
however, that once a given portion of Medieval Spanish society had come to
prefer, for example, the reduced variable *-és* over the longer variable *-edes* in
some grammatical contexts, e.g., from indicative function in *-er* verbs to
subjunctive function of *-ar* verbs, that it did not then spread quickly to many
verbs in that category, as would be indicated by a high concentration of reduced
forms suddenly appearing in a given generation (e.g. pres.ind. *-ays* in the 3rd
generation). It has been clearly demonstrated here, however, that the initial
spread of *-és* was indeed gradual, both grammatically (i.e., from future functions
to auxiliaries to non-auxiliaries, or from indicative to subjunctive functions), and
lexically (e.g., among auxiliaries, from *aver* to *tener* to *poder* etc.), and that in
some grammatical categories the complete adoption (i.e., in every lexical
morpheme), was extremely slow, as demonstrated by the long retention of *-edes*
in pres.ind. *vedes* and pres.subj. *dedes*.

As regards the potential for the Labovian or diffusionist approaches to
explain the *cause* of linguistic change, Hock (1991: 650–51, 652) writes:

> Later formulations of lexical diffusionist doctrine redefine the differences
> between the two approaches and in so doing, sharpen them. Lexical diffusion
> is now claimed to be not the result of change, but its very mechanism. And
> conversely, variability or variation now is considered the result of change, not
> its mechanism or cause.
>
> This later theoretical development must be considered unfortunate. For
> denying the motivational force of variability, the theory has deprived itself of
> the ability to explain how lexical diffusion might take place at all: If in fact
> sound change were to affect each lexical item individually, without at least
> temporarily being accompanied by variability between the old and new
> pronunciations, there would be no reason at all for the change to repeat itself

in other linguistic forms ... Only variability between old and new pronunciations can motivate generalization of a given change to other, new forms ...

The best evidence for relatively slow, lexically gradual, generalizations
of processes which the neogrammarians would consider sound changes comes
from non-lexical diffusionist sources, above all from the work of Labov and
his associates. For instance, Labov has noted that the New York change of [æ]
to [eə] etc. is being implemented in a much less sweeping manner than other
changes in progress.

The evidence of such changes clearly shows that in many cases, sound
change may be much more 'diffusionist' in its nature than originally envisaged
by Labov and his school. However, as noted earlier, the motivation or vehicle
for these 'diffusionist' changes must be the same as that for the more rule-
governed, sweeping generalizations, namely the variable coexistence of old and
new pronunciations in given forms.

While I agree with Hock with respect to variability or variation as a mechanism
of, or motivational force behind, the spread of sound change, I would not go so
far as to say that variation is the *cause* of the change. Nor would I say, thus
concurring with Hock, that lexical diffusion in and of itself is a *cause* of change.
I would say, in agreement with Hock, that lexical diffusion is indeed the result
of change, not the cause, but in opposition to his view, that lexical diffusion is
also a mechanism of change (i.e., a means through which change advances). I
would therefore disagree with Hock's implication that variability or variation is
a mechanism of linguistic change. Variation is a state, indeed a necessary player
in the game, without which no diffusion would occur, but it is not the mechanism of change. And although variation is necessary for, and leads to, further
diffusion of sound change, variation cannot be identified as the original or sole
cause of change, since something had to have led to the variation in the first
place. In the case study of the present chapter, for example, at one point there
was no variation of -*edes* (i.e., in the 13th century). Thus, "variation" could not
have caused the "variation" of -*edes* ~ -*és*. In this particular case, high frequency
of occurrence of the morpheme -*edes* was likely the *cause* of its original reduction
to -*és* (perhaps in conjunction with leveling factors from other future morphemes,
e.g., 1st pers.sg. -*é*, 1st pers.pl. -*emos*). Hence, pressures from within the linguistic
system, i.e., structural causes, appear to have led to the original variation, which in
turn led to the diffusion of the change. We might therefore conclude that
"variability or variation" approaches account for "why" sound change spreads,
while the "lexical diffusion" approach accounts for "how" linguistic change
spreads, while neither really explains the "cause" of a given linguistic change.

CHAPTER 5

Hidden Morphological Factors in Apparent Syntactic Change

It is not entirely new to suggest that morphological factors play a role in syntactic change. To take just one example from the history of the Spanish pronominal system, Echenique Elizondo (1981: 115) suggested that leveling gave rise to *leísmo*, a syntactic change in which the third person singular indirect object pronoun *le* came to function as a direct object. At the same time, she believed that the lack of a substitution in the plural of *los* by *les* was due to similar leveling forces in the plural by the first and second person forms which exhibited /o/:

> [S]i atendemos a razones *estructurales*, observamos que la extensión de *le* al acusativo encontraba su apoyo en las formas simétricas *me* y *te*, comunes ambas al dativo y al acusativo de singular de la primera y segunda personas. Consecuencia de ello fue que el leísmo cundiera más en singular que en plural … Además, la forma *los* se veía reforzada, seguramente, por su semejanza con *nos*, *vos*, y *os* [my emphasis].

This idea may be depicted as follows in (1) (the feminine forms are irrelevant here and have therefore been placed in parentheses):

(1) Etymological D.O. Pronominal System   Early *leísta* System

me	*nos*		*me*	*nos*
te	*vos*		*te*	*vos*
↓				
lo	*los*	>	*le*	*los*
(la)	*(las)*		*(la)*	*(las)*

I do not believe there is any doubt that such leveling was involved in this change. Thus a morphological change (leveling) caused the syntactic change (the extension of the function of *le* from dative to accusative).

But might some of the changes in the history of Spanish which on the surface appear to be of a purely syntactic nature actually turn out to be the result of morphological factors when we examine them more closely? In a separate study, I have suggested that the apparently straightforward syntactic change of *vos* 'you pl.' > *vos otros* 'you others' > *vosotros* 'you pl.' would not have occurred had it not been for the structural similarity between the rising form *vosotros/-as* and its possessive counterpart *vuestro/-a* 'your(s)' and in particular, *vuestros/-as* (cf. the morphological similarities between, for example, *mí* and *mío*, *mía*, *míos*, *mías*, or *tú* and *tu*, *tuyo*, *tuya*, *tuyos*, *tuyas*). Innovative *vosotros* was taken to be in allomorphic status with, e.g., *vuestros* (e.g., /vosotr-/ ~ /vuestr-/), despite the fact that there was no etymological connection between the segment /-tros/ of one form and the other. Had it not been for this morphological coincidence, I believe that the informal plural of Spanish would now be *vos todos*, a syntagm which is well attested in Old Spanish, yet virtually unknown to modern philologists, and an exact parallel to the Southern American English *y'all*.[1]

In what follows, I would like to treat two cases of Spanish historical grammar that have traditionally been viewed as straightforward syntactic changes: (a) The evolution of OSp. *a y* > ModSp. *hay* 'there is/are'; and (b) The shift of Latin fut. ERIS 'you will be' > Old and modern Spanish pres.ind. *eres* 'you are'.

The -*y* of Spanish *hay*[2]

If there is a consensus about any development in the history of Spanish, it is that ModSp. *hay* derives from OSp. *a* plus the Old Spanish adverb *y* 'there'.[3] Compare the following commentaries regarding the provenience of *hay* (sometimes in

---

1. See Rini (1999) for a full discussion of Old Spanish *vos todos*.

2. The present analysis of Sp. *hay* is a revised version of a paper (Rini 1998b) presented at the *Primer Coloquio de Lingüística Hispánica* (Miami University, October 4–5, 1997), which subsequently appeared in *Perspectives on Spanish Linguistics, volume 3, Proceedings of the First Hispanic Linguistics Coloquium* (eds. Gutiérrez-Rexach, Javier and José del Valle).

3. In this section I shall represent inflected forms of OSp. *aver* without the etymological *h-*, e.g., *a*, *avié*, *ovo*, *oviesse*, etc., and reserve the use of it for modern Spanish only, despite the fact that in some medieval texts, one finds, for example, *ha*, *haya*, etc. It should be noted here, however, that forms with and without *h-* were sought for this study and thus make up the database analyzed in this chapter.

conjunction with discussions about the development of *doy, estoy, soy, and voy*) from just a few standard works of Spanish historical grammar:

> Menéndez Pidal (1941: 303): "*ha*, y unido al adverbio *i*, resulta el *hay* impersonal."

> Hanssen (1913: 101): "El verbo impersonal haber tiene *hay* (*ha* + *y*) en lugar de *ha*."

> García de Diego (1951: 205): "Verbos que desarrollan una *y* después de la desinencia regular en la 1.a pers. de sing. del pres. de ind. *doy, soy, voy, estoy*, y en la 3.a de sing. *hay* junto a *ha*."

> Lloyd (1987: 357): "In Spanish we have the example of *hay* 'there is' < *ha y* < HABET IBI (literally 'it has there')."

> Penny (1991: 162): "It has been speculated that the added element is the Old Spanish adverb *y* 'there', a notion which is probably correct in the case of the contemporary expansion of *ha* (< HABET) > *hay* 'there is/are', but which is less likely to be true in the case of the verbs under consideration here [*doy, estoy, soy, voy*]."

This consensus actually dates back to the 19th century, when even Friedrich Diez (1844:906) and Wilhelm Meyer-Lübke (1890:306), who disagreed on many points of historical Romance grammar, were in agreement on this one, drawing a parallel to the French construction *il y a* 'there is/are'. This comparison with French has been repeated most recently by Lloyd (1987: 357): "The creation of the fused form *(h)ay* must be parallel to the similar French construction *il y a*, in which the adverb is atonic." One might add here that Catalan similarly offers *hi ha*. It therefore comes as no surprise that, in light of the Western Romance constructions shown in (2), Spanish philologists, and Romance scholars in general, find nothing to disagree about on this point of Spanish historical grammar:

(2) | Old Spanish | ModSp. | French | Catalan |
| --- | --- | --- | --- |
| *a y* | *hay* | *il y a* | *hi ha* |

But as transparent as this development appears for Spanish, the French and Catalan evidence raises a couple of questions when one considers it carefully. First, one might ask why the agglutination of this adverb only occurred in the present tense in Spanish, when the French and Catalan constructions have counterparts in the imperfect indicative. That is, if ModSp. *hay* truly parallels the French and Catalan constructions, why do we not find in Spanish, imperfect **habíay* 'there was/were', like the French and Catalan counterparts shown in (3)?:

(3)   <u>Spanish</u>   <u>French</u>   <u>Catalan</u>
          *habíay   il y avait   hi havia

One might try to account for the absence of an imperfect *habíay in Spanish by
suggesting that the adverb y, which would have been a semivocalic offglide,
dissimilated completely from the similar tonic vowel of the verbal desinence, as
shown in (4a). Compare in (4b) the total dissimilation of the atonic from the
tonic vowel in Lat. AUGUSTUM > Sp. agosto:

(4)   a.   OSp. avía y > *avíay [aβíai̯] > *avía(y) [aβía(i̯)] > había
        b.   Lat. AUGUSTUM > *A(U)GUSTU > *AGUSTU > Sp. agosto

Another possible explanation for the lack of *habíay in Modern Spanish is that
adverbial y may have become agglutinated to a tonic vowel only, thus a y > hay,
but not avía y > *havíay, since the final vowel of imperfect avía was atonic.
However, in the 13th century, the predominant desinence of the imperfect was
/-jé/, in which the /e/ bore the stress. Thus unlike ModSp. había, OSp. avié
exhibited no such tonic /í/ from which any dissimilation of adverbial y could
occur, but indeed exhibited a tonic vowel which preceded adverbial y, such that
analytic avié y should have suffered agglutination to *aviéy, if in fact a y
suffered agglutination to hay. Yet, to the best of my knowledge, no occurrence
of a synthetic *aviéy appears anywhere, despite the existence of analytic avié y
(81 examples of the analytic structure appear in ADMYTE). In an article which
otherwise explains very thoroughly and convincingly why longer hay eventually
ousted shorter ha, García (1991:26) suggests that agglutination of y occurred
only in the present tense because of the much higher frequency of the existential
use of aver in this tense: "The reinterpretation of aver + y took place, however,
only in the Present Indicative — far and away the most frequent tense for the
existential use of the verb, especially in spoken language." But again, French and
Catalan exhibit morphological reflexes of the same adverb in the imperfect,
despite the fact that the existential use of Fr. avoir and Cat. haver must be higher
in the present tense in these languages as well.

    Another complication brought to the fore by the French and Catalan
evidence is that of word order. One might ask why modern Spanish did not
inherit from Old Spanish, forms with preverbal agglutination of adverbial y, as
depicted in (5):

(5)   Why not Sp.*y ha, *y había?
        cf. Fr. il y a, il y avait; Cat. hi ha, hi havia

By no means am I suggesting that the Spanish construction should have evolved with a preverbal *y* simply because the French and Catalan constructions did. Rather, a close look at the history of Spanish itself, even without regard for what happened in other Romance languages, still leaves one wondering why Spanish ended up with *hay*, and not *y ha and *y había. García (1991: 26) believes that postverbal position was the logical place for agglutination of *y* in Spanish: "But though in Old Spanish *y* occurred before as well as after *ha*, the syntagm could be reinterpreted as a single word only where post-position allowed the deictic to be (mis)taken for a suffix: in pre-position, *y* is likely to have received greater stress, which would have helped it retain its syntactic autonomy." But there are two good reasons why one should expect preverbal positioning of *y* in modern Spanish.

First, one might expect the adverb to have followed the lead of the Old Spanish atonic pronouns, which, as is well known, underwent cliticization (i.e., they passed from free to bound morphemes) in pre-lexeme position with inflected verbs (and, contrary to what García says about preverbal positioning of *y*, the atonic pronouns, after cliticization, do not receive greater stress, nor retain their syntactic autonomy). Thus, like the change from *dixieron le* > *le dijeron*, why not OSp. *(h)a y* > *y ha? In a separate study, I have argued that a morphological factor prohibited the clitics from becoming bound morphemes in post-verbal lexeme position. I also suggested that the free subject nominal may have been one of the many factors which caused the clitic pronoun to move to preverbal position in subordinate clauses (*cuedaron que **les** enbiava **su cuñada** alguna cosa de comer, por que **se** tardava **la yantar** (Estoria de Espanna)*) and that similarly, the fixed presence of the bound subject morpheme in post-verbal lexeme position blocked the morphological binding of the clitic in this position in declarative main clauses, thus keeping the two important verbal inflexions, object and subject, far enough away from each other, perhaps for maximum communicative efficiency. As long as the clitic pronoun functioned as an independent lexical item, it was free to occur in postverbal position (just like nominal objects in Old and modern Spanish, e.g., OSp. *vieron a Iohan* → OSp. *vieron a él* or *vieron lo*), or in preverbal position for some desired effect, perhaps because of discourse factors (as suggested by Barry 1987), or for communicative purposes (as suggested by Nieuwenhuijsen 1995). But once the clitic was to take a *permanent* position as a bound morpheme in the objective conjugation, there must have been some reservation on the part of speakers (either consciously or unconsciously) about positioning these two important grammatical morphemes right next to each other.

This is not to say, however, that two important grammatical morphemes cannot occur together, but there must have been some desire to keep these two particular elements apart. Perhaps it is because of the fact that free subject and object morphemes are often divided by the verb. The bound morphemes may have simply followed the pattern of the free morphemes, though in an inverse manner (i.e., free-morpheme order is (S)-V-O, while bound-morpheme order is O-V-S). It is very likely, otherwise, that the clitic would have become a bound, grammatical morpheme in post-verbal lexeme position in these structures had this position not already been taken, as it had been for millennia, by the subject morpheme. Speakers were clearly aware that this slot had been reserved for the subject morpheme. This is observable in the fact that Latin HABEO, HABES, etc., after centuries of fluctuation between pre- and post-infinitival position, finally took the post-verbal lexeme position upon passing from free lexical morphemes to bound subject morphemes (e.g., *é (de/a) cantar ~ cantar é > cantaré*, not **écantar*).

Evidence to support this hypothesis can be found in the case of the grammaticalization of the clitic and the infinitive: where there was a subject morpheme of /Ø/, the clitic was not blocked from taking the basic V-O position. Further evidence to support this hypothesis may be adduced from the informal affirmative commands, where here too, the subject morpheme is /Ø/. Compare in (6) the morphological structure of the second person singular affirmative indicative and imperative:

(6)   Affirmative Indicative: Lex. Morph. + Theme Vowel + Subj. Morph.
        Cantas 'You (sg.) sing':   /kant/   /a/   /s/

        Affirmative Imperative: Lex. Morph. + Theme Vowel + Subj. Morph.
        ¡Canta! 'Sing (sg.)!'   /kant/   /a/   /Ø/

Consequently, the clitic was allowed to take permanently the basic V-O position in affirmative imperatives, since there was no subject morpheme to block it from this position, e.g., /kántaØ/ + /la/ (= *la canción*) (/kántala/ vs. /kántas/ + /la/ (= *la canción*) → /lakántas/.

In the case of a few verbs (*decir* 'to say, tell', *hacer* 'to make, do', *poner* 'to put', *salir* 'to leave', *ser* 'to be', *tener* 'to have', *ir* 'to go', and *venir* 'to come'), both the subject morpheme and the theme vowel are suppressed in the imperative, as shown in (7):

(7)   Aff. Imp.:   Lex. Morph. + Theme Vowel + Subj. Morph.

¡di!	/di/	/Ø/	/Ø/
¡haz!	/az/	/Ø/	/Ø/
¡pon!	/pon/	/Ø/	/Ø/
¡sal!	/sal/	/Ø/	/Ø/
¡sé!	/se/	/Ø/	/Ø/
¡ten!	/ten/	/Ø/	/Ø/
¡ve!	/be/	/Ø/	/Ø/
¡ven!	/ben/	/Ø/	/Ø/

As one might expect, the permanent postposing of the clitic is therefore not blocked, e.g., *¡Dímelo!* 'Tell me!', *¡Póntelo!* 'Put it on!', etc.

Conversely, as in the case of the present indicative, the subject morpheme (as well as the theme vowel) is present in all negative commands, as shown in (8):

(8)   Neg. Imp.:   Lex. Morph. + Theme Vowel + Subj. Morph.

¡No cantes!	/no/ + /kant/	/e/	/s/
¡No digas!	/no/ + /dig/	/a/	/s/
¡No hagas!	/no/ + /ag/	/a/	/s/
¡No pongas!	/no/ + /pong/	/a/	/s/
¡No salgas!	/no/ + /salg/	/a/	/s/
¡No seas!	/no/ + /se/	/a/	/s/
¡No tengas!	/no/ + /teng/	/a/	/s/
¡No vayas!	/no/ + /bay/	/a/	/s/
¡No vengas!	/no/ + /beng/	/a/	/s/

The clitic must therefore occur in preverbal position, e.g., /no/ + /kántes/ + /la/ (= *la canción*) → /nolakántes/, /no/ + /dígas/ + /lo/ → /nolodígas/, etc.

Some might suggest that evidence from the formal commands, especially the plurals, invalidates the above hypothesis since, in the affirmative, the subject morpheme is clearly present, yet the clitic is postposed, *cántela* 'Sing (sg.) it!', *cántenla* 'Sing (pl.) it!'. However, it is entirely possible that the pattern found in the formal imperatives (both singular and plural) simply mirrors through syntactic analogy that which was originally formed in the second person singular for the reasons stated above, i.e., *cántenla ~ no la canten* by analogy with *cántala ~ no la cantes*. After all, the formal imperatives come much later in the history of Spanish than do the informal, which continue uninterrupted from the Latin forms in the singular. Furthermore, because of the force of these direct commands, the informal are more commonly used than the formal. Other more "polite" constructions are often used in place of the formal commands (*Favor de cantarla*, *¿Me la canta Ud.?*, etc.). The informal plural imperatives too possess a subject morpheme of sorts, though not identical to that of the present indicative (cf. OSp. *Cantad* 'Sing (pl.)!', opposing OSp. *Cantades* 'You (pl.) sing.'), yet postpose the clitic, e.g., *¡Cantadla!* But again, this pattern probably follows that of the singular informal imperative because of the frequent use in Old Spanish of this plural form as a singular: That is, plural *¡Cantadla!* ~ *¡No la cantedes!* following the pattern of singular *¡Cantadla!* ~ *¡No la cantedes!* which is syntactically analogical with original singular *Cántala* ~ *No la cantes*.

It may seem that if the foregoing analysis of familiar imperatives is accurate, the clitic should have become bound in postverbal position with third person singular present indicative verbs, which, like affirmative familiar imperatives, lack an overt subject marker: That is, instead of *la mira* 'He is looking at her' why not **mírala* 'He is looking at her', like *mírala* 'Look at her'. However, syntagmatic analogy with, for example, *la miro*, *la miras*, *la miramos*, *la miráis* and *la miran*, all of which exhibit phonetic realizations of the subject morpheme, appears to have prohibited postverbal binding of the clitic in the third person singular.[4] Likewise, *y* should have become bound in preverbal position. After all, when pronominalization occurs with the impersonal form of *haber*, preverbal position is the rule, e.g., *¿Hay muchas casas bonitas por ahí? Sí, **las** hay*; *¿Había muchas personas en la playa? Sí, **las** había*.

The second, and more important reasons why one should expect preverbal positioning of *y* in modern Spanish is that the order *y + a* was more common in Old Spanish than the order *a + y*, though, as will be seen below, this order dominated in the present tense only. Gago (1997: 85, n.16) reports that in a search of various 13th-century texts (*Estoria de Espanna I*, *General estoria I*, *General estoria IV*, *Libro de las leyes*, *Fuero de Burgos*, and *Fuero juzgo*) the order *y a* was found to occur 76% of the time, as shown in (9):

(9)   Pre- vs. Postverbal Analytic *y* in 13th-c. texts (Gago 1997)

Order	total	percentage
y a	109	76%
a y	34	24%

---

4. For a full discussion of the nature and position of the object pronoun in both Old and modern Spanish, see Rini (1995).

In my own research, I have found that the order *y a* was even more prevalent in ADMYTE (vols. 0 & 1), occurring 96% of the time, as shown in (10):

(10) Pre- vs. Postverbal Analytic *y* in ADMYTE (vols. 0 & 1)

Order	total	percentage
y a	624	96%
a y	26	4%

It could be argued that the low number of occurrences of analytic *a y* is due to the fact that by the 13th century, this analytic structure had already begun to undergo agglutination, and thus, many previously analytic instances of *a y* make up the large number of occurrences of synthetic *(h)ay* (there are 4,056 occurrences of this form in ADMYTE vols. 0 & 1). If we include with analytic *a y* the 4,056 examples of synthetic *ay*, assuming the latter continues the former, we then get a ratio as follows in (11):

(11) Pre- vs. Postverbal Analytic & Synthetic *y* in ADMYTE

Order	total	percentage
y a	624	13%
a y/ay	4082	87%

This ratio of pre- vs. postverbal *y* is more what one would expect to find in the Middle Ages to explain the eventual agglutination of *y* in post-lexeme position. However, the ratio of pre- and postverbal analytic *y* with impersonal *aver* is much closer in the case of tenses and moods other than the present, with the exception of the pluperfect indicative (which may be due to the small sample available). In one case, preverbal positioning of *y* is actually more frequent than postverbal positioning. Observe the data in (12) gleaned from ADMYTE:

(12) Pre- vs. Postverbal Analytic *y* in ADMYTE (vols. 0 & 1)

Tense/mood	Forms	total	percentage
imp.ind.	*y avía/ié*	49	35%
	avía/ié y	91	65%
pres.subj.	*y aya*	13	39%
	aya y	20	61%
imp.subj.	*y oviesse*	21	42%
	oviesse y	29	58%
fut.ind.	*y avrá*	5	50%
	avrá y	5	50%

fut.subj.	*y oviere*	25	69%
	oviere y	11	31%
plup.ind.	*y oviera*	0	0%
	oviera y	4	100%
pret.perf.	*y ovo*	35	25%
	ovo y	104	75%
cond.	*y avría/ié*	3	33%
	avría/ié y	6	67%

The average ratio found in tenses and moods other than the present indicative is *y* + Verb 36% vs. Verb + *y* 64%. In accordance with this average regarding non-present indicative forms, one finds that, on the one hand, the number of occurrences of analytic *a y* actually found in ADMYTE is too low. On the other hand, the number of occurrences of Verb + *y* is clearly inflated when one includes all examples of *ay* with *a y*. This means that some, but certainly not all, examples of synthetic *ay* probably continue earlier analytic *a y*, if one expects the ratio of the present indicative to be in line with that of the other tenses and moods, granting that there is nothing in particular about the present indicative that would have called for a preponderance of the Verb + *y* order. To be exact, though speaking completely hypothetically, only *1,083 of the 4,056 occurrences of *ay* would truly represent cases in which *a y* had already fused to *ay*, as shown below in (13a). We are left with *2,973 examples of synthetic *ay* (i.e., 4,056 total — *1,083 included with *a y* = *2,973) which are unaccounted for, as shown in (13b):

(13)	a.		*a y*	26	
		+	*ay*	*1,083	
			a y/ay	*1,109	64%
		vs.	*y a*	624	36%
	b.			4,056	*ay*
			− *1,083	*ay*	< *a y*
			*2,973	*ay*	< ?

Even if one dismisses the foregoing discussion as pure fantasy, the fact remains that the element *y* occurred after *a*, either bound or free, with an astronomically higher number of examples than it did after any other inflected form of *aver* (i.e., 4,082 vs. 91, 20, 29, 5, 11, 4, 104, 6). This imbalance of forms suggests that either there was some other source from which *hay* arose, or that some other factor guided the adverbial *y* to post-lexeme position against the developing trend of pre-lexeme affixation of clitics with inflected verb forms.

Old Spanish had a form related to *ay*, also of relatively high frequency, and which carried out the same function as *ay*, though in a different mood: the present subjunctive *aya*. This form, like the other inflected forms of impersonal *aver*, originally functioned in Old Spanish as an impersonal expression of general existence, not only with, but also more frequently without adverbial *y*, as it still does, along with *hubo* and *había*, in modern Spanish, e.g., *Espero que haya suficiente vino para la fiesta*; *Hubo un terremoto en Sudamérica ayer*; *Había gente de todas partes en el congreso*. Also, as seen above in (12), adverbial *y* occurred either before or after *aya* at about the same ratio as it did with respect to inflected forms of other tenses. Thus Old Spanish expressed general existence in the present tense with any of the structures shown in (14):

(14) | Indicative | Subjunctive |
|---|---|
| *a* | *aya* |
| *y a* | *y aya* |
| *a y* | *aya y* |

I would like to suggest here that subj. *aya* had a built-in pseudo-allomorph of adverbial *y* — that speakers of Old Spanish may have associated the palatal of this form with the adverbial *y* in present indicative analytic constructions like *y a* and *a y* from which, through reanalysis and subsequent restructuring, they would derive the synthesized allomorph of the present indicative, as shown in (15):

(15)   Pres.subj. *aya*,
morphologically /ay-a/ —(restructuring)→ pres.ind. /ay/

It should not be difficult to imagine how speakers who uttered phrases with an existential subjunctive *aya* could easily abbreviate this subjunctive form to produce indicative *ay* as demonstrated below in (16) with the following example from the *Estoria de Espanna I*:

(16)   *E quando cuedas tu auer fecha cibdat que semeie a carthago en que* **aya** *tal torre ...* —(restructuring)→

*como en otra cibdat que semeia a carthago en que **ay** *una torre que...*

It would not be long before adverbial *y* would cease to be used with subj. *aya*, since, in the mind of the speakers, this form contained the necessary element as an interfix. Perhaps this is why there is a relatively low number of examples of *aya* with either pre- or postposed adverbial *y* — the adverb occurs less with *aya* than with any other inflected form of impersonal *aver*, despite the fact that *aya* itself occurs frequently (i.e., the adverb occurs in only 33 of 2,337 occurrences of *aya* in ADMYTE.[5] In descending order of frequency, counting both pre- and postverbal position, adverbial *y* occurs with the 3rd person forms shown in (17) at the rate indicated in parentheses:

(17)   Rate of Occurrence of Pre- and Postverbal Analytic *y*

Form	Percentage
ovo	(4.8%)
avía/-ié	(4.3%)
oviere	(4%)
avría/-ié	(3.1%)
avrá	(1.9%)
oviera	(1.8%)
aya	(1.4%)

If it is true that subjunctive *aya* is one source of *hay*, then it also follows that structures such as *y aya* and *aya y* should have been restructured to *y ay* and *ay y*, as depicted below in (18):

(18)   Pres.subj. *y aya, aya y,*
morphosyntactically /y+ay-a/, /ay-a+y/ —(restructuring)→
pres.ind. /y+ay/, /ay+y/

Conversely, if the traditional hypothesis is correct, one should find no attestation of such structures. That is, if synthetic *hay* is a continuation of analytic *a y*, then syntagms such as *y ay* and *ay y* would presuppose the existence of redundant **y *a y* and **a *y y*, which are not attested anywhere and no doubt never existed. The examples in (19 a, b) are therefore highly significant and revealing:

---

5. Granted, many of these 2,337 occurrences of *aya* function in place of *tenga*, as *aver* shared the duties now expressed in modern Spanish only by *tener*. Nevertheless, *aya* was still quite frequent in its role as subjunctive of impersonal *a, a y, y a*. The same would be true in the case of other tenses and moods of *aver* in the 3rd person.

(19)   a.   <u>Examples of *ay y*</u>:

    & *este como quier que de las otras generationes de las mezclas de las animalias estrannas unas con otras non* **ay y** *njnguna que despues faga otra generation que serie ya tercera si por signo o marauilla no contesce* (*General estoria I*, 1272–1275).

    Et daquel Jnfant Theseo que fue muy buen uaron & de muchos et muy grandes fechos que fizo Egeo esse Rey de Athenas uos contaremos adelant en sos logares de muchas & grandes razones que **ay y** *dellos* (*General estoria II*, 14th century).

    Otrosi a de auer unos diez omnes de pasada el encon fasta en par de la huerta en unos portiellos que **ay y** (*Libro de la montería*, written 1342–1355, copied ca. 1350).

    Car nos pobres somos escuantra ti & uencidos asi como nuestros padres los nuestros dias como sonbra son sobre tierra & no **ay y** *tardança ninguna* (*Biblia latina*, translated 1250, copied 1300–1400).

    & *aquel que presentare sea mayor & aya la cura & los otros que fuesen ordenados atitulo della no* **ay y** *derecho ni demanda por razon que fueron ordenados para ella* (*Siete partidas*, Alfonso X, copied 1491).

    & *ay ende mucha miel & leche & mayormente enla ysla delas cabras que es asi llamada por la grand abundancia de cabras que* **ay y** *ende son las cabras de grand uirtud* (*De propietatibus rerum, Propiedades de las cosas*, 1494).

    & *la complesion suya es vencida & es fecha semejante al vencedor della: & non* **ay y** *ninguna parte que pueda sensiblemente contrallar ala parte alternante…* (*Prognóstica, las prognósticas*, 1495).

    aposentamiento para las auersidades **ay y** (*Tratado de Amores de Arnalte y Lucenda*, written 1491, copied 1546).

b. <u>Examples of *y ay*</u>

*Et **y ay** muy bellas fuentes* (*Viaje de Juan de Mandauilla*, translated ca. 1357–1390, copied 1357–1500).

*Mas muchos **y ay** que eneste nuestro tiempo fazen lo contrallo...* (*Castigos y documentos para bien vivir III*, written 1293, copied 1440–1460).

*Mas aquesto sera que en la parte apostemada non aya calor njn uermejor ca seria mas ynflada Ca mjentra **y ay** mala conplision caliente alguna de aquellas non es conuenjente* (*Cirugía rimada*, written 1412, copied 1493).

One might attempt to argue that synthetic *hay* from *a y* was able to occur with an additional adverbial *y* in these examples because the original *y* had become bound and had lost its adverbial meaning during the agglutination process. This would be a reasonable explanation for such constructions if they were found during a period after the alleged agglutination process was complete. The foregoing examples occur, however, before such a process would have been completed, i.e., when one still finds the idea of 'there is/are' expressed by analytic *a y* and *y a* (as well as by unaccompanied *a*). It therefore makes more sense to conclude that *y ay* and *ay y* are indeed reanalyses and subsequent restructurings, employed in the indicative, of subjunctive *y aya* and *aya y*.

The eleven examples shown in (19) are the only examples of their kind found in both the Alfonsine corpus and ADMYTE (vols. 0 & 1). These structures probably existed for only a short time and are therefore not abundantly attested because the bound -*y* of restructured *ay* would have been associated with the free morpheme *y* in the still extant analytic syntagms *y a*, and, especially, *a y*. Thus short-lived *y ay* and *ay y* would eventually give way completely to *ay*. This development would subsequently have two profound effects on the entire system: (a) The form *ay* would encourage any remaining analytic structures of the type *a y* to become synthetic, i.e., *a y > ay*; and (b) The dropping of analytic *y* in the present tense (i.e., *y ay* and *ay y >* simply *ay*), where it had been more abundant than in any other tense or mood, would encourage its wholesale abandonment in all other third singular forms of impersonal *aver*, as well as in any other syntagm in which it had previously existed, such as the following examples with the verb *ser*: *sera y, eran y, fuere y, seremos i, fue i, fu y, hi era, y sera, hi seran* (Pottier 1968: 212).[6]

The present analysis explains why Spanish, unlike French and Catalan, has no remnant of adverbial *y* in the imperfect indicative (or in any other verbal construction), and also why the element *-y* of ModSp. *hay* wound up as a verbal suffix instead of a verbal prefix. The traditional analysis, which seeks the origin of the *-y* of ModSp. *hay* in the Old Spanish adverb *y* alone, fails to explain both of these facts. I therefore conclude that the parallel which has been drawn between ModSp. *hay* and Fr. *il y a* is only minimally accurate, despite the fact that the parallel between OSp. *y a ~ y avié* and ModFr. *il y a ~ il y avait* is exact. But even if one is reluctant to accept the main idea put forth here, i.e., that speakers of Old Spanish derived *ay* from *aya* through reanalysis and subsequent restructuring, I believe it is difficult to deny that subjunctive *aya*, at the very least, provided the model upon which speakers modified their analytic structures *y a* and *a y* to a new, synthetic *ay*.

The Origin of Spanish *eres*

Spanish *(tú) eres* 'you are' has posed since the mid-nineteenth century perhaps one of the most formidable challenges for specialists of Spanish historical grammar. There was, at one point, Latin (TU) ES, and then suddenly, *(tú) eres* (first documented in the *Auto de los reyes magos*, ca. 1200). Since laborious combing of textual evidence was not likely to produce intermediate stages of development between ES and *eres* (one finds only *(tú) ies*, the diphthongized reflex of ES, in the *Glosas Emilianenses*), philologists have had to limit themselves to thought experiments and pure ingenuity in their attempts to account for the origin of this form. Nineteenth-century brainstorming produced three different theories, which may be summarized, in modern linguistic terminology, as follows (the originator of each theory appears in parentheses):

---

6. The implication of this analysis for the proposed agglutination of adverbial *y* to OSp. *do, esto, so,* and *vo* (> ModSp. *doy, estoy, soy,* and *voy*) is that no such agglutination occurred in the case of these verbs either. For an explanation of how these verbs acquired their final *-y*, see Rini (1994–5).

(a) In order to avoid homonymy with third person EST, which was in the process of shedding its final consonant (i.e., EST > ES(T) > *es*), Latin second person (TU) ES acquired an additional suffix of the second conjugation, i.e., ES + -ES > *ESES. Dissimilatory rhotacism of intervocalic /s/ would thus yield *eres* (Büchmann 1853).

(b) The ambiguity of ES and ES(T) was resolved by the replacement of present indicative (TU) ES with Latin future indicative ERIS 'you will be'. Regular phonetic evolution of originally future ERIS would yield *eres* (Delius 1868).

(c) Homonymy with third person ES(T) was avoided by the direct replacement of second person ES with ERES (> *eres*), an analogical creation based on the imperfect indicative root morpheme, i.e., ER- (< ERAS), plus the regular second conjugation suffix -ES (Diez 1844).

Of these three theories, the most widely accepted is that which derives *eres* from the Latin future ERIS. However, it is probably safe to say that none of these theories has ever gained complete acceptance by the scholarly community concerned at any point in time over the last one hundred and forty-five years.[7] Even some of those who have adopted this view have not done so without some reservation. For example, Menéndez Pidal (1941: 302) wrote: "[E]l castellano tomó *extrañamente* el futuro *eris* [my emphasis]." And Bourciez (1956: 438) remarked that Castilian *eres* "offre un *remarquable* transfert du futur au présent [my emphasis]."

In the last two decades there has probably been less agreement than ever before about the origin of *eres*. Lathrop (1980: 40–41 n. 11) accepted the ERIS > *eres* etymology, though one detects some reservation in his comment: "The second person singular of the future of *esse* 'to be' was *eris*; this form *is supposed to have given* the Spanish *eres*. *If this is true*, as it appears to be, *eres* is the only vestige in Spanish of the ancient future tense [my emphasis]." Alvar and Pottier (1983), on the other hand, state with total conviction: "Tú *eres* procede de eris." Urrutia and Álvarez (1983: 243) likewise proclaim: "Para evitar la homomorfia entre la segunda y tercera persona del singular se ha tomado para aquélla la forma de futuro ERIS > *eres*." In stark contrast with these two comments, however, in the same year Montgomery (1983) launched an attack on

---

7. For the most thorough review of the literature on the origin of *eres*, at least through 1983, see Griffin (1994).

the *eres* < ERIS theory. He objected to ERIS for the following reasons (1983: 449): (a) It would be an isolated, irregular vestige of a tense which otherwise disappeared completely; (b) The shift from future to present lacks parallels in the spoken (modern?) language; (c) A change involving a single form, independent of the verbal system as a whole has no precedent in Spanish or Romance; and most importantly, (d) The chronology of the merger of (TU) ES and ES(T) on the one hand, and the disappearance of the future tense on the other would not possibly allow for a substitution of ES by ERIS. With regard to this last objection, Montgomery (1983: 450) wrote in his critique of Menéndez Pidal:

> To put it briefly, the "daño causado por la fonética" which was to level TU ES and ILLE EST, providing the motivation for a new second-person form, dates from the eleventh or twelfth century. Even allowing for some imprecision in these dates resulting from the slowness of linguistic change, the ancient ERIS had ceased to exist long before it might have been pressed into the new use which has been claimed for it.

Montgomery then proceeded to combine the other two theories (apparently unaware that they had been originated in the 19th century), proposing, in effect, a case of morphologically conditioned sound change in which imperfect *eras* served as the impetus for the dissimilatory rhotacism of **eses* (< ES + -ES) > *eres*.

Several years later, Lloyd (1987: 299) cited Montgomery's article, and appears to have been somewhat convinced by the arguments therein:

> The form that takes the place of second person *es* is *eres* which appears to be the reflex of the Latin future form ERIS ... The question remains, however, of whether any forms of the Latin future could have persisted in speech long enough for this form to have replaced the older one ... One plausible conclusion might be that perhaps *eres* is an analogical form based on the stem *er-* from the imperfect tense forms, *era, -s*, etc.

Penny (1991: 162), on the other hand, makes no reference to Montgomery's proposal, and instead embraces the ERIS > *eres* theory, however cautiously:

> With the simplification of word-final -ST > -S ... the 2nd and 3rd sing. forms became identical and in the Latin of Cantabria *it seems* that this ambiguity was resolved by the introduction into the 2nd pers. of originally future ERIS. [my emphasis]

In a somewhat delayed reaction to Montgomery's 1983 piece, Griffin (1994: 470) states forcefully that "the arguments against deriving *eres* from the Latin future *eris* are invalid" and that, with respect to the other proposals, "most are clearly impossible." Griffin (1994: 471) first rejects categorically any theory which would depend on the rhotacism of intervocalic /s/ since: (a) rhotacism involves a voiced, not voiceless sibilant; (b) rhotacism, though more common in Spanish than some realize, does not occur in intervocalic position (but only before a voiced consonant); (c) rhotacism of intervocalic /s/ is a phenomenon of pre-Classical Latin, not of Romance. Griffin, therefore, concludes that, even though Latin fut. ERIS itself, for example, is the product of rhotacism (i.e., *ESIS > ERIS): "there is simply no way to arrive at *eres* by this route" (1994: 471–72).

Griffin then states that the view that *eres* is the result of analogy with ERAS is actually "less satisfactory" than that which depends on rhotacism of intervocalic /s/, on the grounds that analogy, by definition, occurs when one of two already similar forms becomes more like the other, and that second person singular ES and imperfect root morpheme ER- have nothing in common except that they are both forms of the verb 'to be'. He further states that ER- and ES are in fact "strongly opposed to each other with respect to tense, making analogy even less likely" and that "it is improbable that the *er-* of the imperfect *era*, occurring in no other tense of the verb *ser*, should lose the feature of tense in *era* and have the vowel of its ending changed to give it the look of the present of an *-er* verb" (1994: 471).

Griffin then attempts to lessen the chronological gap between the EST > *es* change and the loss of future ERIS, such that the latter might have remained long enough to replace second person ES. He first asserts that textual evidence such as the gloss from Silos *get* and Mozarabic *yed*, which appear to attest to the late retention of final /-t/ cannot be taken at face value. According to Griffin, such forms must have acquired an analogical /-t/ from its retention in other verbal suffixes (cf., early medieval *matod*). He arrives at this conclusion by observing that the loss of /s/ did not occur before a consonant, such that EST > *es* > *yes* > *ye* (cf. Ptg. and Leon. *e, ye*) > *yet* (with analogical *-t*), and not EST > *et* > *yet*. As regards the loss of the synthetic future, following a lead he picked up from Ford (1911) and Pottier (1977), Griffin (1994: 472) suggests that while it is true that in Iberia the future had been lost for centuries in its primary function, a secondary function of this morphological group, namely, the future of probability, persisted for some time — according to Griffin, long enough to witness the EST > *es* change. The function of the form ERIS (> *eres*), already as a type of present-tense form (i.e., probability or conjecture about a present-tense situation), would subsequently be expanded beyond this modal realm to the present tense indicative in general, thus repairing the ambiguity of (TU) ES and (ILLE) ES(T). Attempting to close the book on the case, Griffin (1994: 475) asserts: "In conclusion, it may be said with confidence that the Latin future *eris* is the only possible source of Spanish *eres*. It is the only etymology to which there are no valid objections."

Some of Griffin's arguments are valid, others are not. His argument against rhotacism is indeed a valid one. One must ask, however, whether it might be possible that a present-tense forerunner of *eres*, i.e., *ESIS, developed alongside the precursors of future and imperfect indicative ERIS, ERAS during the pre-Classical period. If Classical fut. ERIS and imp. ERAS resulted from *ESIS and *ESAS respectively (i.e., lexical morpheme ES- from infinitive ESSE plus future and imperfect indicative suffixes -IS and -AS), realized phonetically as *[eẓis] and *[eẓas], then it is also possible to postulate ES- plus present indicative -IS yielding a pre-classical present indicative *ESIS, realized *[eẓis], later rhotacized to *[eris]. Such a scenario, however possible in purely historical phonetic terms, may be quickly discarded, since no such present tense *ERIS has ever been attested alongside future and imperfect ERIS and ERAS. Moreover, it is doubtful that third person EST had shed its final /t/ already during the pre-classical era, thus eliminating any motive for the creation of a pre-classical present tense *ES-IS.

Griffin's claim that the Latin future tense forms employed to express probability in the present remained in this present-tense function long after they had been lost as true futures is certainly worthy of further consideration. Though Griffin does not support his claim with any evidence — indeed he limits himself to pure conjecture upon saying that ERIS "must have long been in popular use and it must have served in this capacity for some time before dropping out of use" (1994: 472) — he could well have substantiated his claim by observing synthetic and analytic future use in modern Spanish, as well as the cyclical nature of the evolution of the future itself throughout the history of Latin and Spanish.

The Latin future, synthetic in nature (e.g., AMABO 'I shall love'), was replaced by an analytic structure comprised of the infinitive and an inflected form of HABERE (e.g., AMARE HABEO), which itself was synthesized (e.g., OSp. *amar é* > Sp. *amaré*) and is beginning to be replaced by the analytic structure involving an inflected form of *ir + a +* infinitive (e.g., *voy a amar*). Presumably, the Latin synthetic future itself resulted from the synthesis of a previously analytic structure (e.g., *ama bho* > AMABO) such that the evolution of the future has been "a sequence in which analytic forms repeatedly become synthetic and are then replaced by new analytic forms" (Pulgram 1963: 37). The future of the verb 'to love', for example, in the history of Spanish may be summarized as follows in (20) (where > indicates evolution, :: indicates replacement):

(20)   Prehistoric Lat. *ama bho* > Lat. *amabo* :: *amare habeo* > OSp. *amar é* > Old and ModSp. *amaré* :: ModSp. *voy a amar*

Recent studies on the use of the future in modern Spanish have revealed that in some varieties of Spanish, the future tense is expressed most frequently with the analytic *ir + a +* infinitive construction, while the synthetic "future" forms are actually used more often as the so-called "future of probability". In the most recent article on the subject, Westmoreland (1994–95:217) states:

> From the above survey we may offer several general conclusions regarding American norms of usage. The *ir a* structure is at least twice as common as the synthetic form for expressing future time. Where it appears in oral speech, the simple [i.e., synthetic] form is generally relegated to expressing modal functions of probability, uncertainty or the hypothetical.

Thus, just as one might express in modern Spanish the idea "you will be/you are going to be/you're gonna be…" with the newer, innovative analytic *(tú) vas a ser*, but "you must be/you are probably…" with the older, synthetic *(tú) serás*, it is not inconceivable, indeed it is very likely, that, at some point in time, speakers of Latin expressed future-tense "you will be" with newer, analytic SE(D)ERE HABES, but present-tense "you must be/are probably…" with older, synthetic ERIS. Observe the following schema in (21) of the aforementioned parallel:

(21)   <u>Future Tense: Analytic Structure 'You will be Pedro's wife'</u>
        <u>Spanish</u>   <u>Latin</u>
        Tú vas a ser la mujer de Pedro   TU SE(D)ERE HABES UXOR
                                              PETRIS

        <u>Pres. Prob.: Synthetic Structure 'You must be Pedro's wife, right?'</u>
        <u>Spanish</u>   <u>Latin</u>
        Tú serás la mujer de Pedro, ¿verdad? NONNE ERIS UXOR
                                              PETRIS

Despite the plausibility of the foregoing scenario, Griffin fails to explain how the synthetic future of probability shifted to a purely present-tense function, no longer expressing probability. It is easy (and perhaps dangerous) to envisage a shift in the function of ERIS from probability to non-probability in the present, as in the following example: NONNE ERIS UXOR PETRIS 'You must be Pedro's wife, right?' > ERIS UXOR PETRIS 'Are you Pedro's wife?' > 'You are Pedro's wife'. But we are able to accept this only because ERIS resembles so closely the form we are all familiar with in modern Spanish; that is, we can easily associate ERIS UXOR PETRIS with *eres la mujer de Pedro* and make the semantic leap because of the morphological coincidence between ERIS and *eres*. Could we do the same, however, with *serás*?; that is, can anyone conceive of *serás* shifting into a purely present-tense function, as in *serás la mujer de Pedro* 'You must be Pedro's wife' > 'You are Pedro's wife'? Of course not. In fact, this is precisely one of the reasons why I have never been able to accept that future ERIS is the source of *eres*. How could it have come to be used in the present without expressing probability? It seems, following the parallel which I have drawn with the modern structures, that any examples of the "future of probability" that can shift from one tense to another, shift back to the future, not into the real present. For example, in a room full of colleagues waiting for the chairman to arrive to begin the meeting, the utterance *"Vendrá pronto"* can mean 'He is probably coming soon' or 'He might/must be coming soon' and even 'He will come soon'. But, if the chairman is in sight, walking down the corridor toward the meeting room, one would never utter *"Vendrá"* to mean 'He is coming', rather, only *"Viene"*. It is precisely because the synthetic future can still express a real future that it has a particular, modal sense, i.e., probability, when used in the present. Indeed, Westmoreland's statement that the *"ir a* structure is at least twice as common as the synthetic form for expressing future time" also means that synthetic structures can still be used as real futures, albeit less than half as frequently. It is in fact not uncommon for one form to be shifted from one tense to another to create a certain affect. Witness, *Si fuera rico*, its English parallel *If I were rich*, and its French counterpart *Si j'etais riche*, all used in the present to express a contrary to fact situation, yet *fuera*, *were*, and *étais* are not likely ever to become "real" present-tense forms. One must therefore conclude that the use of ERIS in the present tense to express probability could have only been achieved as long as it could still function as a real future as well, however seldom. This does not mean that the parallel drawn above between synthetic and analytic structures in Latin and Spanish is wrong, rather, it is just overly simplified. It is more likely that although probability in the present was expressed in spoken Latin by the synthetic future only, true future actions were likely expressed primarily by the analytic structure, but still occasionally by the synthetic structure as shown in (22) (as well as with the present indicative), just as in modern Spanish:

(22) Future Tense: Analytic Structure 'You will be Pedro's wife'

Spanish	Latin
Tú vas a ser la mujer de Pedro	TU SE(D)ERE HABES UXOR PETRIS
Tú serás la mujer de Pedro	ERIS UXOR PETRIS

Pres. Prob.: Synthetic Structure 'You must be Pedro's wife, right?'

Spanish	Latin
Tú serás la mujer de Pedro, ¿verdad?	NONNE ERIS UXOR PETRIS

Once the Latin synthetic future was totally ousted by the analytic structure, the synthetic form could not have survived for long (if at all) as a means of expressing probability in the present since the ability to do so was entirely dependent upon shifting the form from one function (i.e., future) to another (i.e., present). In fact, the same text in which *eres* is first attested (*Auto de los reyes magos*) already exhibits a synthesized realization of the originally analytic future (i.e., HABERE + HABET > *auer á* > *auerá*), shown in (23), employed to express probability in the present (*Auto*, lines 96–99):

(23) [Herodes]: *¿Quanto í á que la uiſtes*   'How long ago did you see it
          i que la percibiſtis?   and perceive it?'
      [Caspar]: *XIII dias á,*   'Thirteen days ago,
          *i mais non **auera**,*   and probably no more'

Thus it appears that the Latin synthetic future, even in its role as a future of probability, would have been long gone by the time *eres* came on the scene. It might be worth noting as well, that the two examples of *eres* in this text, shown in (24), cannot in any way be interpreted with probability, which could have otherwise linked this form to ERIS (*Auto*, lines 138–39):

(24) *¡Hamihala, cumo **eres** enartado!*   'Golly, how you are deceived!'
      *¿por que **eres** rabi clamado?*   'Why are you called a rabbi?'

I therefore disagree with Griffin's claim that ERIS is the only possible source of Spanish *eres*. On the contrary, ERIS as the etymon of *eres* has never looked more doubtful.

Having rejected both phonological change (i.e., rhotacism) and syntactic change (i.e., a shift from fut. ERIS > pres. *eres*) as theoretical approaches to the origin of *eres*, perhaps a return to, and further exploration of, the nature of morphological change may shed some light on this conundrum.

Some of Griffin's objections to Diez's original morphological view are valid, and some are not. Diez believed that it was perhaps better to accept *eres* as a somewhat altered form of the extant ERAS than as a continuation of the extinct ERIS. Although Diez appears to have been right to discard ERIS, Griffin is correct to reject the notion that speakers attempting to remedy the impending clash between (TU) ES and (ILLE) ES(T) would have opted for a root morpheme that occurred in no other tense than the imperfect indicative. After all, speakers had other options from which to choose and create an innovative replacement for original ES. The most logical choice would likely have been the attested *sees* (< SEDES), whose root morpheme /se-/ was also found in (a) the infinitive, /se-ér/; (b) the Old Spanish past participle /se-ído/ (which alternated with /sido/); (c) the imperative, /sé/ or /sé-y/; as well as (d) the imperfect indicative form descendent from SEDERE, not ESSE, i.e., /se-ía/ and /se-jé/. Alternatively, leveling from the first person SU-M (> OSp. *so*) in the singular produced *SU-S > *sos*, much as SU-MUS (and perhaps SU-NT) in the plural produced *SUTIS (> OSp. *sodes*). There is no reason why either *sees* or *sos* could not have sufficed as replacements for ES. These are no more anomalous than the ultimate choice, *eres*, as shown in (25):

(25)   *seer*   *seer*   *seer*

so	*somos*	*so*	*somos*	*so*	*somos*
sees	*sodes*	**sos**	*sodes*	**eres**	*sodes*
es	*son*	*es*	*son*	*es*	*son*

Montgomery's (1983:453) belief that the adoption of *sees* would necessarily have included that of first person *seo* (< SEDEO), thus producing an unacceptable paradigm with three different roots (i.e., *seo, es, son*), is unfounded, and his claim that "*sos* may have sounded rather like a plural, as it does today" is astounding, given that *sodes* and its later reductions, *soes* and *sois*, functioned as both singulars and plurals, and that non-diphthongal *sos* now functions solely as a singular in *voseante* regions of America. The fact remains, that the form which speakers ultimately chose bears a striking resemblance to imperfect indicative *eras* (< ERAS). Perhaps this form was indeed involved in the change, though not as Diez had imagined.

Griffin's claim that "the imperfect stem *er-* and the present second singular *es* have nothing in common other than the fact that both are forms of the verb *ser*" (1994: 471) was wrong-headed in that it completely ignored the fact that ERAS and ES were intimately connected through aspect, a point made very clear by Montgomery, and which appears to have been deliberately ignored by Griffin. Montgomery (1983: 453–54): "The imperfect was the most powerful available model for the new creation because of its strong aspectual affinity with the present: these are the two distinctively imperfective tenses of Spanish." This point by Montgomery is well taken. But if one is to claim that *eres* was indeed the result of a morphological change involving ERAS, one has to substantiate this claim by operating within some sort of framework of morphological change.

The two most systematic types of morphological change, as discussed in Chapter 1, are leveling and analogy. We have already seen that leveling would produce a form such as *sos* (< *SU-S). We have also discussed how analogy involves the extension or creation of a derived form from a base form that is either syntactically, semantically, or structurally related. For example, in the analogy in (26), the extension of the plural morpheme from one base form to another is due to the formal similarities between the two base forms:

(26) <u>book</u>   :   <u>foot</u>
      books   :   X = foots

We have seen in Chapter 2 similar clear-cut cases of analogy from the history of Spanish. For example, OSp. *tove*, not likely the result of a phonetic evolution of Lat. TENUI, has been accounted for through analogy with OSp. *ove* (clearly phonetically derived from Lat. HABUI) as in (27), where the analogy was made on both semantic and syntactic grounds (i.e., both verbs expressed 'to have' and both functioned as auxiliaries):

(27) <u>*aver*</u>   :   <u>*tener*</u>
      ove   :   X = *tove*

In the case of *eras* and *eres*, however, there are not two different base forms — they share the same infinitive, *seer* — so, as demonstrated in (28), *eres* cannot have resulted from analogy with *eras*:

(28) <u>*seer*</u>   :   Ø (cannot repeat base form 1, *seer*)
      eras   X = Ø

Nevertheless, a morphological process related to analogy can indeed be invoked to explain the creation of *eres* on the basis of *eras*, namely, backformation.

As discussed in Chapter 1, whereas in analogy the new form is the synchronically derived formation, in backformation, the new form becomes the base form, derived backward from the originally derived, longer form, as demonstrated again in (29):

(29)   operation   :   orientation
      operate   :   X = orientate (replacing 'orient')

It was also shown in Chapter 1 that backformation, though not a common process, is not completely unknown to the history of Spanish (cf. the examples in Chapter 1 like that of *el tiempos* ~ **la tempora* > (reanalysis) *el tiempos* ~ *los tiempos* > (backformation) *el tiempo*). I would therefore like to suggest that *eres* was not the result of some sort of morphological alteration, not of **ES-ES* via rhotacism as originally proposed by Büchmann (1853), nor of an altering of ERAS to *eres* as originally suggested by Diez (1844), but that *eres* may have entered into Spanish intact — however, not via future ERIS, as originally put forth by Delius, but rather, as a backformation of the Old Spanish future subjunctive *fueres* (morphologically analyzable as /fu-eres/) on the basis of the relationship between this form and pluperfect and imperfect indicative *fueras* and *eras*, as shown in (30):

(30)   *fueras*   :   *fueres*
      eras   :   X = *eres*

Such a backformation would not only have been based on the structural similarity between *fueras* and *fueres*, but also on the semantic and functional similarity between the two forms — both express actions one step removed, either further back or further forward in time from the respective imperfective functions of *eras* and the new present-tense *eres* respectively as shown in (31):

(31)   *fueras* 'you had been'   ←   *eras* 'you were'
                                eres 'you are'   →   *fueres*
                                                       'you may be'

The relationship of *fueras* and *eras* was closer than one might think; at times, almost appearing to be allomorphic, particularly when these forms were accompanied by a past participle, as shown in the passage in (32):

(32)   *Piensas te que por que non **eras cayda** enla mala obra de fornjcaçion con ese omne que por eso seas linpia del pecado por çierto ... E sepas que diuersas vegadas **fueras cayda** enla mala obra sinon que dios por la su graçia & merçed sin meritos tuyos te ha querido guardar (Libro de las Doñas, p. 84–85).*

It was this close connection between *fueras* and *eras* on the one hand, and *fueras* and *fueres* on the other, that may have led speakers to produce from *fueres* the backformed *eres* via analogy as shown above in (30).

Also, it is important to note that the function of *fueres* was at times more closely associated to the present tense than one may realize, especially given that the present indicative tense can (and could) express a future action. Observe the following passages in (33), in which *fueres* clearly expresses the idea 'you are [in the future/at some future date]':

(33)   *Si **fueres** mas poderosa ... te dare la cama (Esopete Historiado I, p. 68).*
        [If you **are** {in the future} more powerful ... I shall give you the bed]

        *e no temeras al dyablo enemigo si **fueres** armado de fe (Imitatio Christi).*
        [and you will not fear the devil if/as long as you **are** {in the future} armed with faith.]

        *& boluio se a ihesu christo & dixole: señor, miembrate de mi quando **fueres** enel tu rreyno (Meditationes Vitae Christi, p. 70)*
        [And he turned to Jesus Christ and said to him: Lord, remember me when you **are** {in the future/at some future date} in your kingdom.]

After the temporal conjunction *mientre* 'while', *fueres* actually seems to overlap with the present, meaning 'while you are {now and in the future}' as demonstrated with the passage in (34):

(34)   *Et si le desfallecier el seso, perdonagelo & non lo desprecies mientre **fueres** mancebo (Fuero Juzgo, p. 76.)*
        [And if he loses his mind, pardon him, and do not despise him while/as long as you **are** {now and in the future} a young man.]

The use of *siempre* also gives *fueres* the ability to express 'you are now and in the future' after *si*, as in (35):

(35)   *mira amigo de quanto peligro te puedes librar e de quan grande temor*
        *salir si **fueres** siempre receloso e suspechoso dela muerte* (*Imitatio*
        Christi, p. 37).
        [Look, friend, of how much danger you can deliver yourself from,
        and from such great fear escape if you are always {now and in the
        future} fearful of death.]

If the idea 'you are' was intended to mean only 'now', then pres.ind. *eres* was
employed, as is clearly demonstrated in (36):

(36)   *Sy agora **eres** fijo, el nuestro señor dios te fara que seas despues padre*
        (*Castigos y Documentos para bien vivir*, p. 125).

At times, the future subjunctive forms appear to be no more than allomorphs of
the present indicative after certain conjunctions. Observe the examples in (37),
in which *fueres* and *eres* seem to be allomorphs that have simply been assigned
different syntactic functions:

(37)   *Sy non **fueres** casto, encubre & faz senbalante que lo **eres*** (*Castigos*
        y Documentos para bien vivir, p. 125).

        *Sy agora **eres** fijo, el nuestro señor dios te fara que seas despues*
        *padre. E des que **fueres** padre, sabras que es amor de fijo commo*
        qujer que el Rey sea dado de amar (*Castigos y Documentos para bien*
        vivir, p. 125).

        *Sy **fueres** rico, diran que **eres** arrufado & sy **fueres** pobre, diran que*
        ***eres** de mal recabdo* (*Bocados de oro*, p. 76).

In light of these examples, it comes as no surprise that the Old Spanish future
subjunctive was eventually replaced by the present indicative.

        Finally, it should be pointed out that although the form *fueres* is virtually
non-existent in modern Spanish, it occurred in Old Spanish with roughly the
same frequency as the other two forms involved in the proposed backformation
process (i.e., *fueras* and *eras*). The number of occurrences found in ADMYTE
(vol. 0) of *fueras*, *eras*, and *fueres* are shown in parentheses in (38):

(38)   <u>fueras</u> (116)   :   <u>fueres</u> (98)
        eras (89)   :   X =

The form *fueres* was thus readily available to take part in the backformation
process.

I therefore conclude that there is absolutely no need to seek the origin of Sp. *eres* in an etymon such as fut. ERIS, which belonged to a set of inflected forms that otherwise vanished without a trace, and whose shift from future to present brings with it such drawbacks as those described here, when we have a perfectly good etymon from which to derive *eres*, i.e., FUERIS, which is not only known to have survived from Latin to Old Spanish, but whose function in Old Spanish was so close to that of the present tense that it was in fact eventually replaced by it. And although one may never be able to prove the validity of the present solution, it does at least account for the mysterious *eres* through a recognized, established model of documented morphological change (i.e., backformation). It could well be that there is a better solution to the problem at hand, but whether or not further exploration of this matter will produce such a solution remains to be seen.

Conclusion

My conclusion to this study will be very brief. Indeed, I do not wish to reiterate the many conclusions regarding specific developments that I have reached throughout this book, nor do I believe that they can be all synthesized into one all-encompassing statement. To be sure, I have not proposed here any new theory of morphological change, nor did I ever intend to do so. I have, however, attempted to show in this book that the role of morphology in the evolution of Spanish has been, and indeed still is, in need of further exploration and consideration. During the study of the individual topics contained herein, it was found that previous treatments had often either misapplied concepts of morphological change such as analogy and leveling, or ignored the possible role of morphological processes such as reanalysis and backformation, morphemicization, contamination and blending, as well as that of the morphemic boundary, and even the paradigm itself, in controlling sound change. I therefore hope to have demonstrated through these studies the need for further refinement of our understanding of the various morphological processes and the degree to which they have participated in the evolution and shaping of Spanish.

References

ADMYTE [computer file]. 1992-. *Archivo digital de manuscritos y textos españoles*. Madrid: Micronet.

Alarcos Llorach, Emilio. 1968. *Fonología española*. 4th ed. Madrid: Gredos.

Alvar, Manuel and Bernard Pottier. 1983. *Morfología histórica del español*. Madrid: Gredos.

Antilla, Raimo. 1989. *Historical and Comparative Linguistics*. Amsterdam: John Benjamins.

Ayerbe-Chaux, Reinaldo. 1986. *Text and Concordance of the* Obra completa de Juan Manuel. Madison: The Hispanic Seminary of Medieval Studies.

Barrutia, Ruchard and Armin Schwegler. 1994. *Fonética y fonología españolas*. 2nd ed. New York: Wiley & Sons, Inc.

Barry, Anita K. 1987. "Clitic Pronoun Position in Thirteenth-Century Spanish." *Hispanic Review* 55.213–220.

Beardsley, T. S., Jr., ed. 1975. *Studies in Honor of Lloyd A. Kasten*. Madison: The Hispanic Seminary of Medieval Studies.

Black, Robert G. 1985. *Text and Concordance of the* Cancionero Castellano. Madison: The Hispanic Seminary of Medieval Studies.

Blaylock, Curtis. 1986. "Notes on the Chronology of a Morphophonological Change in Golden-Age Spanish: The Loss of -D- in Proparoxytonic Forms of the Second Person Plural Verbs." *Hispanic Review* 54.279–285.

Bourciez, Edouard. 1956. *Elements de Linguistique Romane*. 4th ed. Paris: C. Klincksieck.

Boyd-Bowman, Peter. 1975. "A Sample of Sixteenth-Century 'Caribbean' Spanish Phonology." Milan et al. 1974.1–11.

Büchmann, G. 1853. "Die spanische Form 'eres', zweite Person des Präsens 'soy', ich bin." *ASNS* 12.231–232.

Corfis, Ivy A. 1985. *Text and Concordance of the* Cuento de Tristán de Leonis. Madison: The Hispanic Seminary of Medieval Studies.

Corfis, Ivy A. and Carlos Petit. 1990. *Text and Concordance of the* Ordenanzas Reales I-1338, Biblioteca Nacional, Madrid. Madison: The Hispanic Seminary of Medieval Studies.

Cornu, Jules. 1880. "Grey, ley et rey disyllabes dans Berceo, l'Apolonio et l'Alexandre." *Romania* 9.71–98.

Corominas, Joan. 1981. *Diccionario crítico etimológico castellano e hispánico*. Madrid: Gredos.

Craddock, Jerry R. 1983. "Descending Diphthongs and the Regular Preterite in Hispano-Romance." *Bulletin of Hispanic Studies* 60.1–14.

———. 1994. Review of Ralph Penny, *A History of the Spanish Language*. *La corónica* 23.86–90.

Crystal, David. 1985. *A Dictionary of Linguistics and Phonetics*. Cambridge: Basil Blackwell.

Cuervo, Rufino J. 1893. "Las segundas personas de plural en la conjugación castellana." *Romania* 22.71–86.

———. 1954. "Las segundas personas de plural en la conjugación castellana." *Obras*, vol. II. Bogotá: Caro y Cuervo, 138–166.

Dalbor, John B. 1980. *Spanish Pronunciation: Theory and Practice*. 2nd ed. New York: Holt, Rinehart and Winston, Inc.

Dangerfield, Michael L. 1986. *Text and Concordance of the* Claros varones de Castilla *and* Letras. Madison: The Hispanic Seminary of Medieval Studies.

De Gorog, Ralph and Lisa S. De Gorog. 1978. *Concordancias del "Arcipreste de Talavera"*. Madrid: Gredos.

Delius, N. 1868. Review of Friedrich Diez, *Grammatik der romanischen Sprachen, vol. 2." Jahrbuch für romanische und englische Literatur* 9.220–228.

Diez, Friedrich. 1844. *Grammatik der romanischen Sprachen*. Bonn: Weber.

Dworkin, Steven N. 1980. "Phonotactic Awkwardness as a Cause of Lexical Blends: The Genesis of Spanish *cola* 'tail'." *Hispanic Review* 48.231–237.

———. 1988a. "The Interaction of Phonological and Morphological Processes: The Evolution of the Old Spanish Second Person Plural Verb Endings." *Romance Philology* 42.144–155.

———. 1988b. "The Diffusion of a Morphological Change: The Reduction of the Old Spanish Verbal Suffixes *-ades*, *-edes*, and *-ides*." *Medioevo Romanzo* 13.223–236.

———. 1995. "Two Studies in Old Spanish Homonymics." *Hispanic Review* 63.527–542.

———. 1998. "Yakov Malkiel, 1914–1998." *La corónica* 27.249–262.

Echenique Elizondo, María Teresa. 1981. "El sistema referencial en español antiguo: Leísmo, laísmo y loísmo." *Revista de Filología Española* 61.113–157.

Fontanella de Weinberg, María B. 1976. "Analogía y confluencia paradigmática en formas verbales de voseo." *Boletín del Instituto Caro y Cuervo* 31.249–272.

Ford, Jeremiah D. M. 1911. *Old Spanish Readings*. Boston: Ginn.

García, Erica C. 1991. "Morphologization: A Case of Reversible Markedness?" *Probus* 3.23–54.

García de Diego, Vicente. 1951. *Gramática histórica española*. Madrid: Gredos.

Gago Jover, Francisco. 1997. "Nuevos datos sobre el origen de *soy, doy, voy, estoy*." *La corónica* 26.75–90.

Griffin, David A. 1994. "On the Origin of Spanish *eres*." *Hispanic Review* 62.469–476.

Gutiérrez-Rexach, Javier and José del Valle eds. 1998. *Perspectives on Spanish Linguistics, volume 3. Proceedings of the First Hispanic Linguistics Coloquium*. Columbus, Ohio: The Ohio State University.

Harris-Northall, Ray. 1990. "The Spread of Sound Change: Another Look at Syncope in Spanish." *Romance Philology* 44.137–161.

Hartman, Steven Lee. 1989. Review of Paul M. Lloyd, *From Latin to Spanish*. *Probus* 1.145–150.

Hanssen, Friedrich. 1903. *Metrische Studien zu Alfonso und Berceo*. Valparaiso.

———. 1913. *Gramática histórica de la lengua castellana*. Halle: Niemeyer.

Herrera, María Teresa. 1987. *The Text and Concordance of the* Tratado de patología general Biblioteca *Nacional, Madrid, 10.051*. Madison: The Hispanic Seminary of Medieval Studies.

Hock, Hans H. 1991. *Principles of Historical Linguistics*. Amsterdam: Mouton de Gruyter.

Jeffers, Robert J. and Ilse Lehiste. 1982. *Principles and Methods for Historical Linguistics*. Cambridge: MIT Press.

Joset, Jacques, ed. 1974. Arcipreste de Hita, *Libro de buen amor, 2 vols*. Madrid: Espasa-Calpe.

Kasten, Lloyd, John Nitti, and Wilhelmina Jonxis-Henkemans. 1997. *The Electronic Texts and Concordances of the Prose Works of Alfonso X, El Sabio*. Madison: The Hispanic Seminary of Medieval Studies.

Kurylowicz, Jerzy. 1947. "La nature des procès dits analogiques." *Acta Linguistica* 5.17–34.

Lapesa, Rafael. 1970. "Las formas verbales de segunda persona y los orígenes del *voseo.*" *Actas del tercer Congreso internacional de hispanistas*, 519–531.

———. 1983. *Historia de la lengua española.* Madrid: Gredos.

Lathrop, Thomas A. 1980. *The Evolution of Spanish.* Newark, Delaware: Juan de la Cuesta.

———. 1984. *Curso de gramática histórica española.* Barcelona: Ariel.

———. 1996. *The Evolution of Spanish.* 3rd ed. Newark, Delaware: Juan de la Cuesta.

Lazar, Moshé, ed. 1965. *La fazienda de ultra mar.* Salamanca: Gráficas Cervantes.

Lehmann, W. P. and Yakov Malkiel, eds. 1968. *Directions for Historical Linguistics: A Symposium.* Austin: Texas University Press.

Lipski, John M. 1994. *Latin American Spanish.* New York: Longman.

Lloyd, Paul M. 1987. *From Latin to Spanish.* Philadelphia: American Philosophical Society.

———. 1999. "Yakov Malkiel (1914–1998)." *Hispanic Review* 67.111–114.

Lozano López, Gracia. 1992. *Texto y concordancias del* Libro de las donas *Escorial ms. h.III.20.* Madison: The Hispanic Seminary of Medieval Studies.

Mackenzie, David and Ian Michael, eds. 1993. *Hispanic Linguistic Studies in Honour of F. W. Hodcroft.* Wales: Dolphin Book Co.

Malkiel, Yakov. 1945. "Old Spanish *nadi(e), otri(e).*" *Hispanic Review* 13.204–230.

———. 1951. "Lexical Polarization in Romance." *Language* 27.485–518.

———. 1959. "Toward a Reconsideration of the Old Spanish Imperfect in *-ía ~ -ié.*" *Hispanic Review* 26.435–481.

———. 1968. "The Inflectional Paradigm as an Occasional Determinant of Sound Change." Lehmann and Malkiel 1968. 23–64.

———. 1969a. "Sound Changes Rooted in Morphological Conditions: The Case of Old Spanish /sk/ Changing to /θk/." *Romance Philology* 23.188–200.

———. 1969b. "Morphological Analogy as a Stimulus for Sound Change." *Lingua e stile* 4.305–327.

———. 1970. "Le nivellement morphologique comme point de départ d'une 'loi phonétique': la monophthongaison occasionnelle de *ie* et *ue* en ancien espagnol." *Mélanges de langue et de littérature du Moyen Age et de la Renaissance offerts à Jean Frappier, 1.* Genève: Droz.

————. 1971. "Derivational Transparency as an Occasional Co-determinant of Sound Change: A New Causal Ingredient in the Distribution of -ç- and -z- in Ancient Hispano-Romance." *Romance Philology* 25.1–52.

————. 1975. "Old Spanish *bivo, bevir, vida*: A Preliminary Analysis." Beardsley 1975. 165–173.

————. 1976. "Multi-Conditioned Sound-Change and the Impact of Morphology on Phonology." *Language* 52.757–778.

————. 1980. "Points of Abutment of Morphology on Phonology: the Case of Archaic Spanish *esti(e)do* 'Stood'." *Romance Philology* 34.206–209.

————. 1981. "Drift, Slope, and Slant: Background of, and Variations upon, a Sapirian Theme." *Language* 67.535–570.

————. 1982. "Interplay of Sounds and Forms in the Shaping of Three Old Spanish Medial Consonant Clusters." *Hispanic Review* 50.247–266.

————. 1993. "Semantic Versus Formal Ingredients Distillable from Resistance to language Shift: The Case of Spanish *dormir, morir*." *Neophilologus* 77.395–402.

Manczak, Witold. 1958. "Tendences générales des changements analogiques." *Lingua* 7.295–352 and 387–420.

McMahon, April M. S. 1994. *Understanding Language Change*. Cambridge: University Press.

Menéndez Pidal, Ramón. 1904. *Manual elemental de gramática histórica española*. Madrid: Espasa-Calpe.

————. 1908. *Cantar de mio Cid. Texto, gramática y vocabulario*. Madrid: Espasa-Calpe.

————. 1941. *Manual de gramática histórica española*. 6th ed. Madrid: Espasa-Calpe.

————. 1950. *Orígenes del español*. 3rd ed. Madrid: Espasa-Calpe.

————. 1966. *Documentos lingüísticos de España I. Reino de Castilla*. Madrid: Consejo Superior de Investigaciones Científicas.

————. 1978. *Textos medievales españoles*. Madrid: Espasa-Calpe.

Meyer-Lübke, Wilhelm. 1890. *Grammaire des langues romanes*. Paris: Welter.

Mignani, Rigo, Mario A. Di Cesare, and George F. Jones. 1977. *A Concordance to Juan Ruiz Libro de buen amor*. Albany: State University of New York Press.

Milan, William G. et al., eds. *1974 Colloquium on Spanish and Portuguese Linguistics*. Washington: Georgetown University Press.

Montgomery, Thomas. 1983. *"(Tú) eres*: A Neologism." *Hispanic Review* 51.449–454.

Montoya Ramírez, Isabel. 1992. *Texto y concordancias de la* Defenssa de virtuossas mugeres *de Mosén Diego de Valera MS. 1341 de la Biblioteca Nacional.* Madison: The Hispanic Seminary of Medieval Studies.

Naylor, Eric W. 1983. *The Text and Concordances of the Escorial manuscript h.iii.10 of the* Arcipreste de Talavera *of Alfonso Martínez de Toledo.* Madison: The Hispanic Seminary of Medieval Studies.

Nieuwenhuijsen, Dorien. 1995. *"¿Colócolo o lo coloco?* The Position of the Clitic Pronoun in Old Spanish." *Neophilologus* 79.253–244.

Nebrixa, Antonio de. 1942 (1980). *Gramática de la lengua castellana*, ed. Antonio Quilis. Madrid: Nacional.

Olsen, Marilyn A. 1984. *Text and Concordance of the* Libro del Cauallero Çifar. Madison: The Hispanic Seminary of Medieval Studies.

O'Neill, John. 1987. *The Text and Concordance of Escorial Manuscript f.iv.1* Arte Cisoria *Enrique de Villena.* Madison: The Hispanic Seminary of Medieval Studies.

Páez Urdaneta, Iraset. 1981. *Historia y geografía hispanoamericana del voseo.* Caracas: La Case de Bello.

Penny, Ralph J. 1991. *A History of the Spanish Language.* Cambridge: Cambridge University Press.

———. 1993. "Neutralization of Voice in Spanish and the Outcome of the Old Spanish Sibilants: A Case of Phonological Change Rooted in Morphology." Mackenzie and Michael 1993. 75–88.

———. 1994. Review of Joel Rini, *Motives for Linguistic Change in the Formation of the Spanish Object Pronouns. Bulletin of Hispanic Studies* 71.381.

Pensado, Carmen. 1988. *"Soy, estoy, doy, voy* como solución de una dificultad fonotáctica." *Homenaje a Alfonso Zamora Vicente*, 207–218. Madrid: Castalia.

Pottier, Bernard. 1968. "Forma española *soy.*" *Lingüística moderna y filología española.* Madrid: Gredos, 211–213.

———. 1977. "La forma 'eres'." Estudios ofrecidos a Emilio Alarcos Llorach. Vol. 1. Oviedo: Universidad de Oviedo.

Pulgram, Ernst. 1963. "Synthetic and Analytic Morphological Constructs." *Weltoffene Romanistik: Festschrift für Alwin Kuhn*, ed. Guntram Plangg & Eberhard Tiefenthaler, 35–42. *(Innsbrucker Beitrage zur Kulturwissenshaft, 9/10).* Innsbruck: Sprachwissenshaftliches Institut der Leopold-Franzen-Universitat.

Rini, Joel. 1990. "Dating the Grammaticalization of the Spanish Clitic Pronoun." *Zeitschrift für romanische Philologie* 106.354–370.

———. 1991. "The Diffusion of /-ee-/ > /-e-/ in Ibero-Romance Infinitives: *creer, leer, veer, preveer, proveer, seer, poseer.*" *Neuphilologische Mitteilungen* 92.95–103.

———. 1992. *Motives for Linguistic Change in the Formation of the Spanish Object Pronouns.* Newark, Delaware: Juan de la Cuesta.

———. 1993. "On the Evolution of Spanish *cigüeña* and the Blending of Multiple Variants." *Hispanic Review* 61.519–529.

———. 1994–95 [actual appearance, 1999]. "The 'Clinching Factor' in the Addition of *-y* in Spanish *doy, estoy, soy, voy.*" *Journal of Hispanic Research* 4.1–12.

———. 1995a. "The Evolution of the Nature and Position of the Spanish Clitic Pronoun." *La corónica* 24.173–195.

———. 1995b. "Syntactic and Pragmatic Factors in the Morphological Reduction of Latin HABEO > Spanish *(h)e.*" *Neophilologus* 79.421–432.

———. 1996. "The Vocalic Formation of the Spanish Verbal Suffixes *-áis/-ás, -éis/-és, -ois/-os,* and *-ís*: A Case of Phonological or Morphological Change?" *Iberoromania* 44.1–16.

———. 1997a. "The Death of Old Spanish *beuir.*" *Studia Neophilologica* 69.95–107.

———. 1997b. "The Origin of Spanish *ser*: A Phonosyntactic Analysis." *Romance Philology* 50.295–307.

———. 1997c. "On the Etymology of Spanish *mismo.*" *La corónica* 26.141–156.

———. 1998a. "The Formation of Old Spanish *buey(s), bueyes, grey(s), greyes, ley(s), leyes, rey(s), reyes*: A Morphophonological Analysis." *Hispanic Review* 66.1–19.

———. 1998b. "The *-y* of Spanish *hay* Reexamined." Gutiérrez-Rexach and José del Valle 1998. 117–125.

———. 1999. "The Rise and Fall of Old Spanish 'Y'all': *vos todos* vs. *vos otros.*" *Essays in Hispanic Linguistics Dedicated to Paul M. Lloyd,* 209–21. Blake, Robert J., Diana L. Ranson, and Roger Wright, eds. Delaware: Juan de la Cuesta.

Rodríguez Bravo, Juan Luis and María del Mar Martínez Rodríguez. 1986. *Text and Concordances of Biblioteca Nacional Manuscript 9218 Historia del gran Tamerlán.* Madison: The Hispanic Seminary of Medieval Studies.

Smith, Colin. Ed. 1983. *Poema de mio Cid.* Madrid: Cátedra.

Sola-Solé, José María. Ed. 1981. *"La dança general de la muerte"*. *Edición crítica analítico-cuantitativa*. Barcelona: Puvill.

Souza, Roberto de. 1964. "Desinencias verbales correspondientes a la persona *vos/vosotros* en el cancionero general (Valencia, 1511)." *Filología* 10.1–95.

Spaulding, Robert K. 1943. *How Spanish Grew*. Berkeley: University of California Press.

Sturtevant, Edgar H. 1947. *An Introduction to Linguistic Science*. New Haven: Yale University Press.

Temprano, Juan Carlos. 1983. *Text and Concordance of the* Cancionero de las obras de Juan del Enzina. Madison: The Hispanic Seminary of Medieval Studies.

Urrutia Cárdenas, Hernán and Manuela Álvarez Álvarez. 1983. *Esquema de morfosintaxis histórica del español*. Bilbao: Universidad de Deusto.

Valle, José del. 1996. *El trueque s/x en español antiguo. Aproximaciones teóricas*. Tübingen: Beihefte zur Zeitschrift für romanische Philologie, band 278.

Waltman, Franklin M. 1972. *Concordance to* Poema de mio Cid. University Park: The Pennsylvania State University Press.

Wang, William S.-Y. 1969. "Competing Changes as Cause of Residue." *Language* 45.9–25.

Webster's. 1956. *Webster's New World Dictionary of the American Language*. Cleveland/New York: The World Publishing Company.

———. 1984. *Webster's Ninth New Collegiate Dictionary*. Massachusetts: Merriam-Webster Inc.

Westmoreland, Maurice. 1994–95 [actual appearance, 1998]. "Evolving Future Tense Preferences in American Spanish." *Journal of Hispanic Philology* 19.213–228.

Wright, Roger. 1992. "The Asterisk in Hispanic Historical Linguistics." *Journal of Hispanic Research* 1.1–16.

Index of Subjects

The *Current Issues in Linguistics Theory* series (edited by E. F. Konrad Koerner, University of Ottawa) is a theory-oriented series which welcomes contributions from scholars who have significant proposals to make towards the advancement of our understanding of language, its structure, functioning and development.

Current Issues in Linguistics Theory (CILT) has been established in order to provide a forum for the presentation and discussion of linguistic opinions of scholars who do not necessarily accept the prevailing mode of thought in linguistic science. It offers an alternative outlet for meaningful contributions to the current linguistic debate, and furnishes the diversity of opinion which a healthy discipline must have. In this series the following volumes have been published thus far or are scheduled for publication:

1. KOERNER, Konrad (ed.): *The Transformational-Generative Paradigm and Modern Linguistic Theory*. 1975.
2. WEIDERT, Alfons: *Componential Analysis of Lushai Phonology*. 1975.
3. MAHER, J. Peter: *Papers on Language Theory and History I: Creation and Tradition in Language. Foreword by Raimo Anttila*. 1979.
4. HOPPER, Paul J. (ed.): *Studies in Descriptive and Historical Linguistics. Festschrift for Winfred P. Lehmann*. 1977.
5. ITKONEN, Esa: *Grammatical Theory and Metascience: A critical investigation into the methodological and philosophical foundations of 'autonomous' linguistics*. 1978.
6. ANTTILA, Raimo: *Historical and Comparative Linguistics*. 1989.
7. MEISEL, Jürgen M. & Martin D. PAM (eds): *Linear Order and Generative Theory*. 1979.
8. WILBUR, Terence H.: *Prolegomena to a Grammar of Basque*. 1979.
9. HOLLIEN, Harry & Patricia (eds): *Current Issues in the Phonetic Sciences. Proceedings of the IPS-77 Congress, Miami Beach, Florida, 17-19 December 1977*. 1979.
10. PRIDEAUX, Gary D. (ed.): *Perspectives in Experimental Linguistics. Papers from the University of Alberta Conference on Experimental Linguistics, Edmonton, 13-14 Oct. 1978*. 1979.
11. BROGYANYI, Bela (ed.): *Studies in Diachronic, Synchronic, and Typological Linguistics: Festschrift for Oswald Szemérenyi on the Occasion of his 65th Birthday*. 1979.
12. FISIAK, Jacek (ed.): *Theoretical Issues in Contrastive Linguistics*. 1981. Out of print
13. MAHER, J. Peter, Allan R. BOMHARD & Konrad KOERNER (eds): *Papers from the Third International Conference on Historical Linguistics, Hamburg, August 22-26 1977*. 1982.
14. TRAUGOTT, Elizabeth C., Rebecca LaBRUM & Susan SHEPHERD (eds): *Papers from the Fourth International Conference on Historical Linguistics, Stanford, March 26-30 1979*. 1980.
15. ANDERSON, John (ed.): *Language Form and Linguistic Variation. Papers dedicated to Angus McIntosh*. 1982.
16. ARBEITMAN, Yoël L. & Allan R. BOMHARD (eds): *Bono Homini Donum: Essays in Historical Linguistics, in Memory of J.Alexander Kerns*. 1981.
17. LIEB, Hans-Heinrich: *Integrational Linguistics. 6 volumes. Vol. II-VI n.y.p.* 1984/93.
18. IZZO, Herbert J. (ed.): *Italic and Romance. Linguistic Studies in Honor of Ernst Pulgram*. 1980.
19. RAMAT, Paolo et al. (eds): *Linguistic Reconstruction and Indo-European Syntax. Proceedings of the Colloquium of the 'Indogermanischhe Gesellschaft'. University of Pavia, 6-7 September 1979*. 1980.
20. NORRICK, Neal R.: *Semiotic Principles in Semantic Theory*. 1981.
21. AHLQVIST, Anders (ed.): *Papers from the Fifth International Conference on Historical Linguistics, Galway, April 6-10 1981*. 1982.
22. UNTERMANN, Jürgen & Bela BROGYANYI (eds): *Das Germanische und die Rekonstruktion der Indogermanischen Grundsprache. Akten des Freiburger Kolloquiums der Indogermanischen Gesellschaft, Freiburg, 26-27 Februar 1981*. 1984.

23. DANIELSEN, Niels: *Papers in Theoretical Linguistics. Edited by Per Baerentzen.* 1992.
24. LEHMANN, Winfred P. & Yakov MALKIEL (eds): *Perspectives on Historical Linguistics. Papers from a conference held at the meeting of the Language Theory Division, Modern Language Assn., San Francisco, 27-30 December 1979.* 1982.
25. ANDERSEN, Paul Kent: *Word Order Typology and Comparative Constructions.* 1983.
26. BALDI, Philip (ed.): *Papers from the XIIth Linguistic Symposium on Romance Languages, Univ. Park, April 1-3, 1982.* 1984.
27. BOMHARD, Alan R.: *Toward Proto-Nostratic. A New Approach to the Comparison of Proto-Indo-European and Proto-Afroasiatic. Foreword by Paul J. Hopper.* 1984.
28. BYNON, James (ed.): *Current Progress in Afro-Asiatic Linguistics: Papers of the Third International Hamito-Semitic Congress, London, 1978.* 1984.
29. PAPROTTÉ, Wolf & René DIRVEN (eds): *The Ubiquity of Metaphor: Metaphor in language and thought.* 1985 (publ. 1986).
30. HALL, Robert A. Jr.: *Proto-Romance Morphology. = Comparative Romance Grammar, vol. III.* 1984.
31. GUILLAUME, Gustave: *Foundations for a Science of Language.*
32. COPELAND, James E. (ed.): *New Directions in Linguistics and Semiotics.* Co-edition with Rice University Press who hold exclusive rights for US and Canada. 1984.
33. VERSTEEGH, Kees: *Pidginization and Creolization. The Case of Arabic.* 1984.
34. FISIAK, Jacek (ed.): *Papers from the VIth International Conference on Historical Linguistics, Poznan, 22-26 August. 1983.* 1985.
35. COLLINGE, N.E.: *The Laws of Indo-European.* 1985.
36. KING, Larry D. & Catherine A. MALEY (eds): *Selected papers from the XIIIth Linguistic Symposium on Romance Languages, Chapel Hill, N.C., 24-26 March 1983.* 1985.
37. GRIFFEN, T.D.: *Aspects of Dynamic Phonology.* 1985.
38. BROGYANYI, Bela & Thomas KRÖMMELBEIN (eds): *Germanic Dialects:Linguistic and Philological Investigations.* 1986.
39. BENSON, James D., Michael J. CUMMINGS, & William S. GREAVES (eds): *Linguistics in a Systemic Perspective.* 1988.
40. FRIES, Peter Howard (ed.) in collaboration with Nancy M. Fries: *Toward an Understanding of Language: Charles C. Fries in Perspective.* 1985.
41. EATON, Roger, et al. (eds): *Papers from the 4th International Conference on English Historical Linguistics, April 10-13, 1985.* 1985.
42. MAKKAI, Adam & Alan K. MELBY (eds): *Linguistics and Philosophy. Festschrift for Rulon S. Wells.* 1985 (publ. 1986).
43. AKAMATSU, Tsutomu: *The Theory of Neutralization and the Archiphoneme in Functional Phonology.* 1988.
44. JUNGRAITHMAYR, Herrmann & Walter W. MUELLER (eds): *Proceedings of the Fourth International Hamito-Semitic Congress.* 1987.
45. KOOPMAN, W.F., F.C. Van der LEEK , O. FISCHER & R. EATON (eds): *Explanation and Linguistic Change.* 1986
46. PRIDEAUX, Gary D. & William J. BAKER: *Strategies and Structures: The processing of relative clauses.* 1987.
47. LEHMANN, Winfred P. (ed.): *Language Typology 1985. Papers from the Linguistic Typology Symposium, Moscow, 9-13 Dec. 1985.* 1986.
48. RAMAT, Anna G., Onofrio CARRUBA and Giuliano BERNINI (eds): *Papers from the 7th International Conference on Historical Linguistics.* 1987.
49. WAUGH, Linda R. and Stephen RUDY (eds): *New Vistas in Grammar: Invariance and Variation. Proceedings of the Second International Roman Jakobson Conference, New York University, Nov.5-8, 1985.* 1991.
50. RUDZKA-OSTYN, Brygida (ed.): *Topics in Cognitive Linguistics.* 1988.

51. CHATTERJEE, Ranjit: *Aspect and Meaning in Slavic and Indic. With a foreword by Paul Friedrich.* 1989.
52. FASOLD, Ralph W. & Deborah SCHIFFRIN (eds): *Language Change and Variation.* 1989.
53. SANKOFF, David: *Diversity and Diachrony.* 1986.
54. WEIDERT, Alfons: *Tibeto-Burman Tonology. A comparative analysis.* 1987
55. HALL, Robert A. Jr.: *Linguistics and Pseudo-Linguistics.* 1987.
56. HOCKETT, Charles F.: *Refurbishing our Foundations. Elementary linguistics from an advanced point of view.* 1987.
57. BUBENIK, Vít: *Hellenistic and Roman Greece as a Sociolinguistic Area.* 1989.
58. ARBEITMAN, Yoël. L. (ed.): *Fucus: A Semitic/Afrasian Gathering in Remembrance of Albert Ehrman.* 1988.
59. VAN VOORST, Jan: *Event Structure.* 1988.
60. KIRSCHNER, Carl & Janet DECESARIS (eds): *Studies in Romance Linguistics. Selected Proceedings from the XVII Linguistic Symposium on Romance Languages.* 1989.
61. CORRIGAN, Roberta L., Fred ECKMAN & Michael NOONAN (eds): *Linguistic Categorization. Proceedings of an International Symposium in Milwaukee, Wisconsin, April 10-11, 1987.* 1989.
62. FRAJZYNGIER, Zygmunt (ed.): *Current Progress in Chadic Linguistics. Proceedings of the International Symposium on Chadic Linguistics, Boulder, Colorado, 1-2 May 1987.* 1989.
63. EID, Mushira (ed.): *Perspectives on Arabic Linguistics I. Papers from the First Annual Symposium on Arabic Linguistics.* 1990.
64. BROGYANYI, Bela (ed.): *Prehistory, History and Historiography of Language, Speech, and Linguistic Theory. Papers in honor of Oswald Szemérenyi I.* 1992.
65. ADAMSON, Sylvia, Vivien A. LAW, Nigel VINCENT and Susan WRIGHT (eds): *Papers from the 5th International Conference on English Historical Linguistics.* 1990.
66. ANDERSEN, Henning and Konrad KOERNER (eds): *Historical Linguistics 1987.Papers from the 8th International Conference on Historical Linguistics,Lille, August 30-Sept., 1987.* 1990.
67. LEHMANN, Winfred P. (ed.): *Language Typology 1987. Systematic Balance in Language. Papers from the Linguistic Typology Symposium, Berkeley, 1-3 Dec 1987.* 1990.
68. BALL, Martin, James FIFE, Erich POPPE &Jenny ROWLAND (eds): *Celtic Linguistics/ Ieithyddiaeth Geltaidd. Readings in the Brythonic Languages. Festschrift for T. Arwyn Watkins.* 1990.
69. WANNER, Dieter and Douglas A. KIBBEE (eds): *New Analyses in Romance Linguistics. Selected papers from the Linguistic Symposium on Romance Languages XVIIII, Urbana-Champaign, April 7-9, 1988.* 1991.
70. JENSEN, John T.: *Morphology. Word structure in generative grammar.* 1990.
71. O'GRADY, William: *Categories and Case. The sentence structure of Korean.* 1991.
72. EID, Mushira and John MCCARTHY (eds): *Perspectives on Arabic Linguistics II. Papers from the Second Annual Symposium on Arabic Linguistics.* 1990.
73. STAMENOV, Maxim (ed.): *Current Advances in Semantic Theory.* 1991.
74. LAEUFER, Christiane and Terrell A. MORGAN (eds): *Theoretical Analyses in Romance Linguistics.* 1991.
75. DROSTE, Flip G. and John E. JOSEPH (eds): *Linguistic Theory and Grammatical Description. Nine Current Approaches.* 1991.
76. WICKENS, Mark A.: *Grammatical Number in English Nouns. An empirical and theoretical account.* 1992.
77. BOLTZ, William G. and Michael C. SHAPIRO (eds): *Studies in the Historical Phonology of Asian Languages.* 1991.
78. KAC, Michael: *Grammars and Grammaticality.* 1992.

79. ANTONSEN, Elmer H. and Hans Henrich HOCK (eds): *STAEF-CRAEFT: Studies in Germanic Linguistics. Select papers from the First and Second Symposium on Germanic Linguistics, University of Chicago, 24 April 1985, and Univ. of Illinois at Urbana-Champaign, 3-4 Oct. 1986.* 1991.

80. COMRIE, Bernard and Mushira EID (eds): *Perspectives on Arabic Linguistics III. Papers from the Third Annual Symposium on Arabic Linguistics.* 1991.

81. LEHMANN, Winfred P. and H.J. HEWITT (eds): *Language Typology 1988. Typological Models in the Service of Reconstruction.* 1991.

82. VAN VALIN, Robert D. (ed.): *Advances in Role and Reference Grammar.* 1992.

83. FIFE, James and Erich POPPE (eds): *Studies in Brythonic Word Order.* 1991.

84. DAVIS, Garry W. and Gregory K. IVERSON (eds): *Explanation in Historical Linguistics.* 1992.

85. BROSELOW, Ellen, Mushira EID and John McCARTHY (eds): *Perspectives on Arabic Linguistics IV. Papers from the Annual Symposium on Arabic Linguistics.* 1992.

86. KESS, Joseph F.: *Psycholinguistics. Psychology, linguistics, and the study of natural language.* 1992.

87. BROGYANYI, Bela and Reiner LIPP (eds): *Historical Philology: Greek, Latin, and Romance. Papers in honor of Oswald Szemerényi II.* 1992.

88. SHIELDS, Kenneth: *A History of Indo-European Verb Morphology.* 1992.

89. BURRIDGE, Kate: *Syntactic Change in Germanic. A study of some aspects of language change in Germanic with particular reference to Middle Dutch.* 1992.

90. KING, Larry D.: *The Semantic Structure of Spanish. Meaning and grammatical form.* 1992.

91. HIRSCHBÜHLER, Paul and Konrad KOERNER (eds): *Romance Languages and Modern Linguistic Theory. Selected papers from the XX Linguistic Symposium on Romance Languages, University of Ottawa, April 10-14, 1990.* 1992.

92. POYATOS, Fernando: *Paralanguage: A linguistic and interdisciplinary approach to inter-active speech and sounds.* 1992.

93. LIPPI-GREEN, Rosina (ed.): *Recent Developments in Germanic Linguistics.* 1992.

94. HAGÈGE, Claude: *The Language Builder. An essay on the human signature in linguistic morphogenesis.* 1992.

95. MILLER, D. Gary: *Complex Verb Formation.* 1992.

96. LIEB, Hans-Heinrich (ed.): *Prospects for a New Structuralism.* 1992.

97. BROGYANYI, Bela & Reiner LIPP (eds): *Comparative-Historical Linguistics: Indo-European and Finno-Ugric. Papers in honor of Oswald Szemerényi III.* 1992.

98. EID, Mushira & Gregory K. IVERSON: *Principles and Prediction: The analysis of natural language.* 1993.

99. JENSEN, John T.: *English Phonology.* 1993.

100. MUFWENE, Salikoko S. and Lioba MOSHI (eds): *Topics in African Linguistics. Papers from the XXI Annual Conference on African Linguistics, University of Georgia, April 1990.* 1993.

101. EID, Mushira & Clive HOLES (eds): *Perspectives on Arabic Linguistics V. Papers from the Fifth Annual Symposium on Arabic Linguistics.* 1993.

102. DAVIS, Philip W. (ed.): *Alternative Linguistics. Descriptive and theoretical Modes.* 1995.

103. ASHBY, William J., Marianne MITHUN, Giorgio PERISSINOTTO and Eduardo RAPOSO: *Linguistic Perspectives on Romance Languages. Selected papers from the XXI Linguistic Symposium on Romance Languages, Santa Barbara, February 21-24, 1991.* 1993.

104. KURZOVÁ, Helena: *From Indo-European to Latin. The evolution of a morphosyntactic type.* 1993.

105. HUALDE, José Ignacio and Jon ORTIZ DE URBANA (eds): *Generative Studies in Basque Linguistics.* 1993.

106. AERTSEN, Henk and Robert J. JEFFERS (eds): *Historical Linguistics 1989. Papers from the 9th International Conference on Historical Linguistics, New Brunswick, 14-18 August 1989.* 1993.

107. MARLE, Jaap van (ed.): *Historical Linguistics 1991. Papers from the 10th International Conference on Historical Linguistics, Amsterdam, August 12-16, 1991.* 1993.

108. LIEB, Hans-Heinrich: *Linguistic Variables. Towards a unified theory of linguistic variation.* 1993.

109. PAGLIUCA, William (ed.): *Perspectives on Grammaticalization.* 1994.

110. SIMONE, Raffaele (ed.): *Iconicity in Language.* 1995.

111. TOBIN, Yishai: *Invariance, Markedness and Distinctive Feature Analysis. A contrastive study of sign systems in English and Hebrew.* 1994.

112. CULIOLI, Antoine: *Cognition and Representation in Linguistic Theory. Translated, edited and introduced by Michel Liddle.* 1995.

113. FERNÁNDEZ, Francisco, Miguel FUSTER and Juan Jose CALVO (eds): *English Historical Linguistics 1992. Papers from the 7th International Conference on English Historical Linguistics, Valencia, 22-26 September 1992.*1994.

114. EGLI, U., P. PAUSE, Chr. SCHWARZE, A. von STECHOW, G. WIENOLD (eds): *Lexical Knowledge in the Organisation of Language.* 1995.

115. EID, Mushira, Vincente CANTARINO and Keith WALTERS (eds): *Perspectives on Arabic Linguistics. Vol. VI. Papers from the Sixth Annual Symposium on Arabic Linguistics.* 1994.

116. MILLER, D. Gary: *Ancient Scripts and Phonological Knowledge.* 1994.

117. PHILIPPAKI-WARBURTON, I., K. NICOLAIDIS and M. SIFIANOU (eds): *Themes in Greek Linguistics. Papers from the first International Conference on Greek Linguistics, Reading, September 1993.* 1994.

118. HASAN, Ruqaiya and Peter H. FRIES (eds): *On Subject and Theme. A discourse functional perspective.* 1995.

119. LIPPI-GREEN, Rosina: *Language Ideology and Language Change in Early Modern German. A sociolinguistic study of the consonantal system of Nuremberg.* 1994.

120. STONHAM, John T. : *Combinatorial Morphology.* 1994.

121. HASAN, Ruqaiya, Carmel CLORAN and David BUTT (eds): *Functional Descriptions. Theorie in practice.* 1996.

122. SMITH, John Charles and Martin MAIDEN (eds): *Linguistic Theory and the Romance Languages.* 1995.

123. AMASTAE, Jon, Grant GOODALL, Mario MONTALBETTI and Marianne PHINNEY: *Contemporary Research in Romance Linguistics. Papers from the XXII Linguistic Symposium on Romance Languages, El Paso//Juárez, February 22-24, 1994.* 1995.

124. ANDERSEN, Henning: *Historical Linguistics 1993. Selected papers from the 11th International Conference on Historical Linguistics, Los Angeles, 16-20 August 1993.* 1995.

125. SINGH, Rajendra (ed.): *Towards a Critical Sociolinguistics.* 1996.

126. MATRAS, Yaron (ed.): *Romani in Contact. The history, structure and sociology of a language.* 1995.

127. GUY, Gregory R., Crawford FEAGIN, Deborah SCHIFFRIN and John BAUGH (eds): *Towards a Social Science of Language. Papers in honor of William Labov. Volume 1: Variation and change in language and society.* 1996.

128. GUY, Gregory R., Crawford FEAGIN, Deborah SCHIFFRIN and John BAUGH (eds): *Towards a Social Science of Language. Papers in honor of William Labov. Volume 2: Social interaction and discourse structures.* 1997.

129. LEVIN, Saul: *Semitic and Indo-European: The Principal Etymologies. With observations on Afro-Asiatic.* 1995.

130. EID, Mushira (ed.) *Perspectives on Arabic Linguistics. Vol. VII. Papers from the Seventh Annual Symposium on Arabic Linguistics.* 1995.

131. HUALDE, Jose Ignacio, Joseba A. LAKARRA and R.L. Trask (eds): *Towards a History of the Basque Language.* 1995.

132. HERSCHENSOHN, Julia: *Case Suspension and Binary Complement Structure in French.* 1996.

133. ZAGONA, Karen (ed.): *Grammatical Theory and Romance Languages. Selected papers from the 25th Linguistic Symposium on Romance Languages (LSRL XXV) Seattle, 2-4 March 1995.* 1996.
134. EID, Mushira (ed.): *Perspectives on Arabic Linguistics Vol. VIII. Papers from the Eighth Annual Symposium on Arabic Linguistics.* 1996.
135. BRITTON Derek (ed.): *Papers from the 8th International Conference on English Historical Linguistics.* 1996.
136. MITKOV, Ruslan and Nicolas NICOLOV (eds): *Recent Advances in Natural Language Processing.* 1997.
137. LIPPI-GREEN, Rosina and Joseph C. SALMONS (eds): *Germanic Linguistics. Syntactic and diachronic.* 1996.
138. SACKMANN, Robin (ed.): *Theoretical Linguistics and Grammatical Description.* 1996.
139. BLACK, James R. and Virginia MOTAPANYANE (eds): *Microparametric Syntax and Dialect Variation.* 1996.
140. BLACK, James R. and Virginia MOTAPANYANE (eds): *Clitics, Pronouns and Movement.* 1997.
141. EID, Mushira and Dilworth PARKINSON (eds): *Perspectives on Arabic Linguistics Vol. IX. Papers from the Ninth Annual Symposium on Arabic Linguistics, Georgetown University, Washington D.C., 1995.* 1996.
142. JOSEPH, Brian D. and Joseph C. SALMONS (eds): *Nostratic. Sifting the evidence.* 1998.
143. ATHANASIADOU, Angeliki and René DIRVEN (eds): *On Conditionals Again.* 1997.
144. SINGH, Rajendra (ed): *Trubetzkoy's Orphan. Proceedings of the Montréal Roundtable "Morphophonology: contemporary responses (Montréal, October 1994).* 1996.
145. HEWSON, John and Vit BUBENIK: *Tense and Aspect in Indo-European Languages. Theory, typology, diachrony.* 1997.
146. HINSKENS, Frans, Roeland VAN HOUT and W. Leo WETZELS (eds): *Variation, Change, and Phonological Theory.* 1997.
147. HEWSON, John: *The Cognitive System of the French Verb.* 1997.
148. WOLF, George and Nigel LOVE (eds): *Linguistics Inside Out. Roy Harris and his critics.* 1997.
149. HALL, T. Alan: *The Phonology of Coronals.* 1997.
150. VERSPOOR, Marjolijn, Kee Dong LEE and Eve SWEETSER (eds): *Lexical and Syntactical Constructions and the Construction of Meaning. Proceedings of the Bi-annual ICLA meeting in Albuquerque, July 1995.* 1997.
151. LIEBERT, Wolf-Andreas, Gisela REDEKER and Linda WAUGH (eds): *Discourse and Perspectives in Cognitive Linguistics.* 1997.
152. HIRAGA, Masako, Chris SINHA and Sherman WILCOX (eds): *Cultural, Psychological and Typological Issues in Cognitive Linguistics.* 1999.
153. EID, Mushira and Robert R. RATCLIFFE (eds): *Perspectives on Arabic Linguistics Vol. X. Papers from the Tenth Annual Symposium on Arabic Linguistics, Salt Lake City, 1996.* 1997.
154. SIMON-VANDENBERGEN, Anne-Marie, Kristin DAVIDSE and Dirk NOËL (eds): *Reconnecting Language. Morphology and Syntax in Functional Perspectives.* 1997.
155. FORGET, Danielle, Paul HIRSCHBÜHLER, France MARTINEAU and María-Luisa RIVERO (eds): *Negation and Polarity. Syntax and semantics. Selected papers from the Colloquium Negation: Syntax and Semantics. Ottawa, 11-13 May 1995.* 1997.
156. MATRAS, Yaron, Peter BAKKER and Hristo KYUCHUKOV (eds): *The Typology and Dialectology of Romani.* 1997.
157. LEMA, José and Esthela TREVIÑO (eds): *Theoretical Analyses on Romance Languages. Selected papers from the 26th Linguistic Symposium on Romance Languages (LSRL XXVI), Mexico City, 28-30 March, 1996.* 1998.

158. SÁNCHEZ MACARRO, Antonia and Ronald CARTER (eds): *Linguistic Choice across Genres. Variation in spoken and written English.* 1998.

159. JOSEPH, Brian D., Geoffrey C. HORROCKS and Irene PHILIPPAKI-WARBURTON (eds): *Themes in Greek Linguistics II.* 1998.

160. SCHWEGLER, Armin, Bernard TRANEL and Myriam URIBE-ETXEBARRIA (eds): *Romance Linguistics: Theoretical Perspectives. Selected papers from the 27th Linguistic Symposium on Romance Languages (LSRL XXVII), Irvine, 20-22 February, 1997.* 1998.

161. SMITH, John Charles and Delia BENTLEY (eds): *Historical Linguistics 1995. Volume 1: Romance and general linguistics.* n.y.p.

162. HOGG, Richard M. and Linda van BERGEN (eds): *Historical Linguistics 1995. Volume 2: Germanic linguistics.Selected papers from the 12th International Conference on Historical Linguistics, Manchester, August 1995.* 1998.

163. LOCKWOOD, David G., Peter H. FRIES and James E. COPELAND (eds): *Functional Approaches to Language, Culture and Cognition.* n.y.p.

164. SCHMID, Monika, Jennifer R. AUSTIN and Dieter STEIN (eds): *Historical Linguistics 1997. Selected papers from the 13th International Conference on Historical Linguistics, Düsseldorf, 10-17 August 1997.* 1998.

165. BUBENÍK, Vit: *A Historical Syntax of Late Middle Indo-Aryan (Apabhraṃśa).* 1998.

166. LEMMENS, Maarten: *Lexical Perspectives on Transitivity and Ergativity. Causative constructions in English.* 1998.

167. BENMAMOUN, Elabbas, Mushira EID and Niloofar HAERI (eds): *Perspectives on Arabic Linguistics Vol. XI. Papers from the Eleventh Annual Symposium on Arabic Linguistics, Atlanta, 1997.* 1998.

168. RATCLIFFE, Robert R.: *The "Broken" Plural Problem in Arabic and Comparative Semitic. Allomorphy and analogy in non-concatenative morphology.* 1998.

169. GHADESSY, Mohsen (ed.): *Text and Context in Functional Linguistics.* 1999.

170. LAMB, Sydney M.: *Pathways of the Brain. The neurocognitive basis of language.* 1999.

171. WEIGAND, Edda (ed.): *Contrastive Lexical Semantics.* 1998.

172. DIMITROVA-VULCHANOVA, Mila and Lars HELLAN (eds): *Topics in South Slavic Syntax and Semantics.* 1999.

173. TREVIÑO, Esthela and José LEMA (eds): *Semantic Issues in Romance Syntax.* 1999.

174. HALL, T. Alan and Ursula KLEINHENZ (eds.): *Studies on the Phonological Word.* 1999.

175. GIBBS, Ray W. and Gerard J. STEEN (eds.): *Metaphor in Cognitive Linguistics. Selected papers from the 5th International Cognitive Linguistics Conference, Amsterdam, 1997.* 1999.

176. VAN HOEK, Karen, Andrej KIBRIK and Leo NOORDMAN (eds.): *Discourse in Cognitive Linguistics. Selected papers from the International Cognitive Linguistics Conference, Amsterdam, July 1997.* 1999.

177. CUYCKENS, Hubert and Britta ZAWADA (eds.): *Polysemy in Cognitive Linguistics. Selected papers from the International Cognitive Linguistics Conference, Amsterdam, 1997.* n.y.p.

178. FOOLEN, Ad and Frederike van der LEEK (eds.): *Constructions in Cognitive Linguistics. Selected papers from the International Cognitive Linguistic Conference, Amsterdam, 1997.* n.y.p.

179. RINI, Joel: *Exploring the Role of Morphology in the Evolution of Spanish.* 1999.

180. MEREU, Lunella (ed.): *Boundaries of Morphology and Syntax.* 1999.

181. MOHAMMAD, Mohammad A.: *Word Order, Agreement and Pronominalization in Standard and Palestinian Arabic.* n.y.p.

182. KENESEI, Istvan (ed.): *Theoretical Issues in Eastern European Languages. Selected papers from the Conference on Linguistic Theory in Eastern European Languages (CLITE), Szeged, April 1998.* n.y.p.

183. CONTINI-MORAVA, Ellen and Yishai TOBIN (eds.): *Between Grammar and Lexicon.* n.y.p.
184. SAGART, Laurent: *The Roots of Old Chinese.* 1999.
185. AUTHIER, J.-Marc, Barbara E. BULLOCK, Lisa A. REED (eds.): *Formal Perspectives on Romance Linguistics. Selected papers from the 28th Linguistic Symposium on Romance Languages (LSRL XXVIII), University Park, 16-19 April 1998.* 1999.
186. MIŠESKA TOMIĆ, Olga and Milorad RADOVANOVIĆ (eds.): *History and Perspectives of Language Study.* n.y.p.
187. FRANCO, Jon, Alazne LANDA and Juan MARTÍN (eds.): *Grammatical Analyses in Basque and Romance Linguistics.* 1999.
188. VanNESS SIMMONS, Richard: *Chinese Dialect Classification. A comparative approach to Harngjou, Old Jintrn, and Common Northern Wu.* n.y.p.
189. NICHOLOV, Nicolas and Ruslan MITKOV (eds.): *Recent Advances in Natural Language Processing II. Selected papers from RANLP '97.* n.y.p.
190. ALEXANDROVA, Galia, Olga ARNAUDOVA and Michele FOLEY (eds.): *The Minimalist Parameter. Selected papers from the Open Linguistics Forum, Ottawa, 21-23 March 1997.* n.y.p.
191. BENMAMOUN, Elabbas (ed.): *Perspectives on Arabic Linguistics Vol. XII. Papers from the Twelfth Annual Symposium on Arabic Linguistics.* n.y.p.
192. SIHLER, Andrew L.: *Language Change. A brief introduction for students of ancient languages and language history.* n.y.p.